RACISM, CULTURE, MARKETS

D0223097

Racism, Culture, Markets explores the connections between cultural repre-sentations of 'race' and their historical, institutional and global forms of expression and impact.

John Gabriel examines the current fixation with market-place philosophies in terms of the crisis in anti-racist politics and concern over questions of cultural identity. He explores issues such as the continuing relevance of terms like 'black' as a basis for self-definition, the need to think about identities in more fluid and complex ways, and the need to develop a much more explicit discussion of the construction of whiteness and white identities.

Racism, Culture, Markets brings together a range of historical and contem-porary case studies including the Rushdie affair, the Gulf War, debates around fostering, adoption and domestic violence, separate schooling, the service economy and its employment practices, tourism in the Third World, the Bhopal chemical disaster, and racism in the new Europe. His case studies also consider the role played by contemporary media and popular culture in these debates, including film, television, music and the press.

John Gabriel is Senior Lecturer in Cultural Studies at the University of Birmingham. He has published widely on racism and politics in Britain and is co-author of *The Local Politics of Race* (1986).

RACISM, CULTURE, MARKETS

John Gabriel

London and New York

First published 1994
by Routledge
11 New Fetter Lane, London EC4P 4EE

Simultaneously published in the USA and Canada
by Routledge
29 West 35th Street, New York, NY 10001

Typeset in Monotype Times New Roman
by the EPPP Group at Routledge
Printed and bound in Great Britain
by Mackays of Chatham plc, Chatham, Kent

British Library Cataloguing in Publication Data
A catalogue record for this book is available from the British Library.

Library of Congress Cataloging in Publication Data
A catalog record for this book has been requested.

ISBN   0–415–09491–7 (hbk)
       0–415–09492–5 (pbk)

CONTENTS

ACKNOWLEDGEMENTS

I am indebted to many people who have helped me to write this book. My first thanks go to Birmingham University: to the School of Social Science for financially supporting my research in the United States; to Yvonne Jacobs for her work on the bibliography; to Yvonne (again!) and Marie Walsh for their help with the preparation of the manuscript, and to staff and student members in the Department of Cultural Studies, who have encouraged me in a variety of ways (and by a variety of means!) to think again! I would also like to thank employees and staff of McDonald's in the UK and US for their time and encouragement; the staff, parents and former pupils of Small Heath School, Birmingham; the staff at the libraries of Birmingham University, the Bobst Library, New York University, and the staff at the Schomburg Centre for Research in Black Culture, Harlem, for their advice and help. Thanks are also due to Rebecca Barden at Routledge and to the readers for their helpful comments on the manuscript. I would also like to acknowledge the inspiration, encouragement and support given to me, over the years, by my parents, Pauline and Geoffrey. Finally, I would like to thank Stephanie Linkogle for reading the manuscript and for all her detailed comments and suggestions.

Part I

HISTORIES AND CONTEXTS

1

INTRODUCTION

BACKGROUND CONCERNS

A number of issues and questions have emerged from both my research and teaching which have influenced the themes and issues around which this book has been written. Questions which are important in any writing context; for example, what is the point of the book, who is it for, and who has the expertise to write it, all take on a particular significance in the context of writing about 'race'. In my own case, I have regularly been asked to justify my own role both as an academic and teacher. What kinds of knowledge make up, or should make up, the academic study of 'race'? What role should a teacher, in my case a white teacher, play in courses on 'race' and ethnicity? What should be the focus of such courses? Should she/he be primarily concerned with racism and racial inequality (however these terms are defined) or something else? How far should courses expect students to think about themselves, as black, Jewish, British Asian, or in non-racial/ethnic terms? What role should 'non-white' student experience play in the course?

The above questions have been a constant source of dialogue and debate for many with whom I have been involved in both a research and teaching context. Moreover, my own answers to these questions and to some extent the questions themselves have changed over time. In both my research and teaching and hence the focus of this book, my aim has been to analyse cultural processes within institutions, including the production of racist knowledges, whilst at the same time relating these institutional contexts to media forms, including the press, television and film. Whilst I have wanted to retain a British institutional focus, I have also aimed to explore the historically and globally varied forms of racism. Whilst there remains a strong focus on inequality, I have also wanted to acknowledge the importance of incorporating potentially diverse cultural and ethnic forms of expression, which can be assessed in terms of their oppositional effects.

The concern of cultural studies with questions of identity has encouraged me, albeit with some apprehension, to reflect on my political history in terms

3

of my own white ethnicity, as well as my gender and age. As Stuart Hall has rightly observed, it is very difficult to convince the English that they are just another ethnic group. White ethnicity always manages to hide behind its negative constructions of otherness (Hall, 1991a: 21; see also Balibar, 1991: 60). This idea has encouraged me to confront a real danger in teaching and institutional politics: that of imposing or projecting both a history and a political outlook onto others whose experiences and perspectives are very different from my own. In planning this book, I have thus tried to accommodate student interests and experiences, while at the same time giving prominence to the writings of those whose experiences, political perspectives and theoretical positions have emerged in different circumstances to my own.

The importance Hall attaches to white ethnicity serves to emphasise that the subject of 'race' is not just about 'black' people. It is as much about 'white' as it is about 'black' culture. Moreover, the term 'black', however inclusively it is defined, cannot accommodate the diversity of ethnicities of potential importance in the field of 'race'. Hence, an important aim of the book is to analyse dominant white institutions and the means by which white knowledges have been constructed historically. A book on 'race' which makes 'black' people the exclusive object of study and, moreover, relies on 'black' experience alone, is not only unfair in terms of the burden it places on those who would be expected to 'resource' such knowledge, it is also ill-founded in terms of the need for a much broader, analytical focus of the kind suggested above.

It follows, therefore, that the examination of historical and global forms of racism and the analysis of the construction of racist knowledges take the book beyond the experience of any one person or group. Moreover, the more we explore the intellectual and political contributions of a variety of writers as well as the experiences of a diverse student group, the clearer it becomes that there is no one single, authentic perspective that goes with being black or, for that matter, with being a woman or lesbian or gay, or indeed being white. Such an assumption not only does a disservice to the complexity of perspectives around each of these identities. Taken to its extreme, the idea of a single, authentic, perspective born out of being black or a woman would also make both writing and reading and teaching and learning redundant, since those who already possessed the necessary experiential credentials would have nothing more to learn while the rest would be precluded from writing and learning simply by dint of who they were.

The term 'race' has been a focus of academic and political debate and controversy since it was first used in the seventeenth century. Does it stand for biological groups or groups that are (wrongly) assumed to possess biological differences? If it is the latter then, how are they distinguished? By skin colour or other physical characteristics? Or is 'race' more of a political term, used to mobilise groups around issues and demands? If 'race' is used in this political sense, then we still might ask which groups does it mobilise and why do/should they share a common political agenda? Or is 'race' a term which

4

has been used as a way of maintaining economic relations of production? All these alternative ways of thinking about 'race' imply the existence of a recognisable and definable group. Alternatively 'race' could refer to an idea, or belief in the existence of groups which do not exist. Robert Miles (1993) has consistently argued that to use the term 'race' in any other sense than this is to legitimise racist classifications, since it confers a reality on groups which are known, other than in racist discourse, not to exist.

In what follows 'race' stands for an idea, not a fixed, biological type. However, it also stands implicitly for those groups who experience racial discrimination, unequal treatment and exclusion. The question then remains, who are the object of racist ideas or who define themselves in terms of their racial identity? I do not think it is possible to answer this absolutely. Context, both in terms of when and where, is all-important. The analysis of how and why groups define themselves and others in religious, national, ethnic terms, the circumstances under which 'race' has varyingly come to be associated with these social categories (some authors refer to this process as racialisation) and with what consequences, are all of central concern in what follows. Given the controversy surrounding the term 'race', and because its meaning does not correspond to its biological definition, I have enclosed it in inverted commas.

My use of the term 'black' also calls for some discussion. In general I use it in accordance with how groups, organisations and communities have identified themselves. Sometimes this means it is used in an inclusive sense which links all groups who claim to have been the object of racism. In such cases, therefore, it could potentially include members of physically 'white' groups (e.g. Irish, Jewish). On the other hand where groups identify themselves in other ways, for example in terms of ethnicity or national identity, I shall use the latter terms instead. Finally, there are contexts in which black refers to a particular ethnicity or national identity, for example African-Americans in the United States. In those cases I will use the term black and qualify with reference to the particular group in question. I shall return to a discussion of the shifts in the use of these forms of identification in subsequent chapters.

There are enormous difficulties in the use of all of the above terms. First there is always the danger of making assumptions on behalf of groups and of assuming a consensus when none exists. Moreover, insofar as the state (including the academy) accepts such different ways of defining groups ('black' is the most recent example) there is always a sense in which it appropriates those terms and detaches them from their original context and meaning. This in turn creates the impetus on the part of groups themselves to discover new cultural definitions. Second, the very use of one term may also be taken to imply the rejection of another. To discuss a group in terms of one category potentially draws a fixed or exclusive boundary around it which is at odds with how individuals and groups mobilise around different identities at different times. Finally, there is the relationship between how groups define themselves and how they might be understood analytically. The latter might establish connections between groups in terms of shared social and economic conditions, common cultural processes and forms of political mobilisation and resistance. My aim is to address these problems throughout the book without offering any guarantee that they will, or for that matter can, be resolved.

Beyond these conceptual issues, the wider political climate has also played an important role in shaping the organisation of and rationale for this book. The late 1980s witnessed a significant backlash against local authority anti-racist initiatives. The latter were seen by their critics on the right and, in particular, the tabloid press, as part of what became dubbed the 'loony left'. The mud stuck and subsequently helped to secure a third Conservative general election victory in 1987. Consequently, many Labour authorities, with the exception of the GLC, which had itself been abolished, began to dismantle their race relations units, cut back on community projects, and backpedal on equal opportunity policy initiatives (see Gabriel, 1989b and Gordon, 1990). Political expedience (that is, the prospect of a further erosion of electoral support) and a lack of political commitment to anti-racism were both important factors in promoting what was very politely called the 'new realism'.

Criticisms of local authority anti-racism, however, were not confined to the political right. For example, black intellectuals like Paul Gilroy attacked it for its failure to win over popular support (in the way, to use his example, movements like Rock against Racism had in the 1970s). Moreover, according to Gilroy, it alienated those it claimed to be benefiting by developing both a bureaucratic language and institutional structures far removed from their experience. Finally, through its emphasis on inequality and racism, the discourse of anti-racism effectively cast 'black' people in the role of passive victims and, relatedly, categorised people according to some seemingly fixed racial/ethnic identity (Gilroy, 1990).

A renewed sense of pessimism emerged on the Labour left as a direct consequence of this effective backlash against municipal socialism and particularly against anti-racist policies and initiatives. The idea that Labour-held councils could become islands of socialism in a very deep blue sea seemed increasingly untenable by the end of the decade. Moreover, events in the Soviet Union and Central and Eastern Europe confirmed this sense of crisis and compounded a collective sense of uncertainty. This created a sense of beleaguerment and battle-weary scepticism with regard to the efficacy of local politics and, relatedly, a growing disillusionment with the Labour Party. The book in part, thus grew out of a personal sense of political frustration and uncertainty and the need to rethink the assumptions and parameters of the study and politics of race and racism.

The broad political conditions associated with Thatcherism also had profound implications for higher education. During the 1980s, the rolling back of the public sector was experienced in the form of chronic under-funding. The displacement of public sector values by market-place philosophies manifested itself in a number of ways: the buying in of temporary, short-term contract

6

employment; the reduction in real terms of student grants and the introduction of loans; unprecedented levels of student hardship and poverty; an increase in student numbers with no corresponding increase in library provision, teaching resources or administrative/pastoral support, and new top-down management styles together precipitated a decline in morale and a deterioration of working conditions in higher education which were without historical precedent.

Part of the context in which this book has been written must therefore be understood in relation to the above changes and uncertainties. The combined effects of the crisis of anti-racist politics, the deteriorating environment in higher education and an increase in the overall numbers and diversity (in terms of degree background) of students have all left their mark on what follows.[1] These concerns are reflected in the organisation of the chapters which adopt an indicative case study rather than a comprehensive textbook approach, leaving space for more case studies and the opportunity to pose new questions as well as address those debates as yet unresolved. The adopted style is intentionally open-ended and interdisciplinary. My aim is to problematise issues and ideas rather than offering 'right' answers. Whilst there are numerous lines of argument and recurrent themes, my aim is not to present them as either exhaustive or complete.

SOME PRELIMINARY QUESTIONS

The case study approach is advantageous in another sense. It has allowed me to pose a variety of questions, which utilise the concepts and theories normally associated with distinct academic specialisms. The first is concerned with representations, meaning literally how aspects of the world are 're-presented', in newspapers, film, television, on the radio and in everyday conversation. Cultural studies has made the analysis of representations, the processes and conditions under which they are produced and the different ways the same forms of representation are interpreted or read, a key focus of study.

A useful illustration of some of the ideas involved here is the amateur video of the incident involving the police beating of Rodney King in Los Angeles in 1991. The assumption that the video provided irrefutable evidence of police guilt was made by seemingly everyone except the jury, who subsequently found the officers not guilty. The case revealed the ways in which the 'reality' of police violence against African-Americans could be 're-presented' to a jury in such a way that the beating appeared justified. Where the court case was held, the composition of jury, the way in which the video was shown and interpreted by the defence council, provided the basis for a contradictory interpretation of events seemingly unambiguously captured on film. The fact that a different jury watching the same video subsequently found some of the police officers guilty of violating Rodney King's civil rights only serves to underline the potential for contradictory interpretations. The variety of ways of representing 'race' and ethnicity, how and why representations are differently interpreted and understood, and how these relate to questions of identity, together constitute an important focus of this book.

The Rodney King case begs a second set of questions: how institutions, including the police, operate in ways which serve to sanction, condone or just ignore such cases of flagrant abuse of position and power. By institutions, I mean bodies with their own relatively discrete cultures (including regimes of representation) and policy-making processes, but which are also shaped (economically, politically and culturally) by their relationship to other institutions. For example, an understanding of the circumstances surrounding the Rodney King beating would be incomplete without an analysis of the Los Angeles Police Department. The latter might include an ethnographic study of everyday life in the police department, integral to which would be an understanding of institutional power. As Foucault suggests, the latter can and should be explored at a micro level: how discourses legitimise power, how control over knowledge is an important precondition of power, its objectifying effects and the tactics, strategies and techniques of power which make it part of a dynamic set of processes and relations, not the fixed property of an individual or office (Foucault, 1980). Such a study could also look at policing policies, rules and procedures (including those regarding arrest) and the relationship between the police department and the wider legal framework, demographic and economic characteristics of the city and state, and federal policies insofar as the latter impact on police/community relations.

The analysis of institutions in these terms also makes possible an analysis of forms of opposition, contestation and resistance, as well as alternative cultural forms. These can be explored at the representational level (music, film, etc.), but equally importantly we might ask how such alternatives emerge through institutional struggle. Institutions thus provide sites of struggle (the relational, dynamic aspect of power) which we can probe in terms of regimes of representation, forms of identity as well as other more material outcomes. In other words, the analysis of institutional struggles forms an important part of any discussion of questions of identity as well as inequality. To take the Rodney King case once again, it would be important to assess the impact of the street uprisings, including the subsequent decision to press federal charges against the officers. Opposition can be conscious, as it was in the Rodney King case, or may be visible only in terms of its effects, i.e. through its nonconformity to mainstream culture.

Examples in this book, which are covered in varying degrees of depth, include organised struggles (Women Against Fundamentalism, the 500 Years of Resistance Campaign), policy initiatives (drawing on discourses of equal opportunities and affirmative action), alternative cultural forms (film and music) and, finally, those which emerge almost spontaneously and almost accidentally but which have a potentially profound impact on traditional forms of ethnic identity. The innovative fusing of traditionally distinct languages (for example Punjabi and Creole) in the school playground is one example of this. All of these interventions can be assessed in terms of their emergence, development and effects.

A final set of questions relates 'race' and ethnicity to a wider set of global processes. There are a number of ways of looking at these: the international migrations and transfers of labour and capital; the rapid expansion of communication networks; western representations of 'the Third World'; the relationship of 'local' to 'global'; the emergence of new transnational identities, and cultural, including media, flows across national boundaries. The above factors have provoked an important crisis of old nation-state identities and new articulations of racism, transcending its former links with nationalism. The incorporation of global perspectives is all the more urgent, given these changes. In drawing on the discourses of political economy and cultural theory, they also serve to complement the micro-institutional analysis described above.

At this point I do not wish to theorise the relationship between these questions and perspectives. My aim is to use them in the context of particular examples in order to establish the more specific relationships between them. For the moment, they represent something of a rag-bag of a framework which aims to relate representations of 'race' and ethnicity to an analysis of institutions, sites of resistance and opposition (as well as the emergence of alternative institutions and forms of cultural expression), all within the context of a wider set of global processes. This framework seeks to reconcile ideas and perspectives from sociology, social policy and cultural studies, an aim which presumably puts what follows at the margins of all three! In its favour, on the other hand, the eclecticism proposed here could be thought of as an antidote to the tendency towards institutionalisation and/or professionalism, characteristic of all three areas of study. The dangers of such tendencies have been summed up by bell hooks when she wrote:

> Unless we're wary, cultural studies and other discursive practices can be appropriated by existing systems of domination, cultural studies cannot and will not serve as a critical intervention disrupting the status quo.
>
> (1991: 132)[2]

The organisation of the book reflects these concerns: Part I (this chapter and the one that follows) attempts to locate the concerns of the book in a historical context. Chapter 2 explores cultural representations of race and begins to assess those attempts to theorise their production. The aim of this theory section is to introduce ideas and raise questions to be taken up throughout the book and to illustrate the importance of linking any assessment or 'reading' of representations of race in the press, on TV and in film to an understanding of historical and institutional context.

In Part II, the focus switches to institutional contexts; to the family (Chapter 3), education (Chapter 4) and work (Chapter 5), and looks at the way in which cultural representations, articulated in a variety of discourses (political and academic as well as mass media), are institutionally expressed and how these are implicated in life-shaping conditions. How we live domestically and with whom, how we are educated and where and how we earn a living are about as life shaping as you can get. Within this broad framework a diverse range of examples is used to illustrate these connections, including fostering and adoption, domestic violence, separate Islamic schools, opting out and McDonald's hamburgers.

The last of these examples suggests the need to look at global influences and relations, which is the focus of Part III. Once again the possibilities are numerous and extend well beyond the scope of what is undertaken here. In Chapter 6, the focus is on both representations of and relationships with the Third World whilst Chapter 7 explores developments in Europe and assesses one left political response to recent changes. In conclusion, I shall return to the broad theoretical context of the book as well as pulling out some emergent themes from the case studies. The first concerns the pivotal role of the market as an organising mechanism for thinking about and living with ideas of 'race'. The second highlights the numerous ways in which 'racial' differences have been naturalised across a range of discursive contexts, including politics, policy arenas and popular culture. A discussion of what these ideas imply in terms of intervention will conclude the book.

2

HISTORY AS PRESENT: PRESENT AS HISTORY

A visitor to Manchester Art Gallery during the spring of 1990 might have entered one of the rooms, under the impression that it contained just another collection of portraits and parlour room scenes so common in eighteenth- and nineteenth-century west European art. However, what all the paintings had in common, apart from their western codes of perspective, was their inclusion of one or more black (African) figures. As Sander Gilman has observed, artistic representations consist almost exclusively of icons which 'serve to focus the viewer's attention on the relationship between the portrayed individual and the general qualities of the class' (1992: 171). So what were the black figures in the paintings supposed to tell us about black people in general, and their relationship to whites? Well, most were positioned on the periphery of the painting, usually somewhere near the frame. Even when they were not, what was striking was the consistency of the portrayal of their roles: subordinate and servile, with facial expressions (fearful and awe-struck) to match. 'The figure of the black servant in European art is ubiquitous' (ibid.: 174) and this collection was no exception.

As houseboys for instance, their positioning was used to highlight the focal point of the painting: their white mistress. They were invariably to be found kneeling, with heads tilted upwards, gazing at a dominant white, female, figure, thus encouraging the spectator to do the same. Their lowly status, reflected in posture and look, was used to reinforce the superiority and importance of the central figure. Their black skins, juxtaposed with the whiteness of the central figures, played on commonsense associations of whiteness with superiority and purity, and blackness with a 'natural' servile status. The presence of both white (female) and black (male) bodies also played on ideas of deviant sexuality, a dominant iconographic theme of eighteenth-century art (ibid.: 175). Moreover, the common juxtaposition of white mistress and black slave/servant in parlour scenes of the period could be seen to symbolise and hence reinforce a wider relationship: between mother country and child colony (Dabydeen, 1987: 32).

The point of the exhibition was, in fact, to challenge dominant artistic

11

representations of black people during this time.[1] It achieved this, most effectively, I believe, in a number of ways. The very fact of bringing these paintings together in the same room encouraged visitors to see the 'racial' connections between them. In case they did not, each painting was accompanied by a written commentary. The exhibition also included an audio cassette of black verse. It turned what could have been an uncritical acceptance of those representations (thus adding to our stock of historical understandings, or rather misunderstandings) into a provoking and questioning experience.[2]

Manchester's 'Fear and Fantasy' exhibition may be used to illustrate a number of themes I wish to develop in this chapter. It serves to remind us how past representations live on in our art museums and galleries, without comment or question. Our passive, uncritical acceptance of these historical images of subordination suggests that notions of hierarchy run deep in our collective consciousness. Although 'classical' English painting offers a rather esoteric example in this respect, this chapter will draw on a wider range of examples to illustrate cultural (with a small and a capital C) forms of English racism.

Second, the exhibition illustrated how the same images can either reinforce or contest dominant representations of racial otherness. Context, here, is all-important. In the Manchester exhibition, the immediate context was provided by the commentaries and the audio cassette of black verse referred to above. More widely, the exhibition can be considered in the context of the history of anti-racism, a term which is itself of recent origin, even if the struggles of which it speaks have a much longer history. Other examples will be used in this chapter to illustrate the limitations of exploring representations and the meanings attached to them without taking account of context.

The exhibition begs the general question of how ideas of race, or racial 'otherness', is constructed via cultural institutions and discourses. The second section will begin to outline some theoretical strands here, although I will be developing these ideas throughout the book with reference to other writers. Bearing in mind Raymond Williams' view of culture as the living present and not just some classical tradition (1961), the third section will move from historical cultural forms with a present to contemporary cultural forms with a past. The first of these is the controversy surrounding Salman Rushdie's novel *Satanic Verses*, which may be described as cultural, both in terms of the text itself (with a capital C?) and in terms of its impact on ways of life or lived experience: what Gramsci called the difference between public and private forms of cultural production.

This example will be followed by a brief assessment of another example of lived culture, that is for those fortunate enough to have survived it: the Gulf War. The work of Edward Said, which will be discussed in the second section, provides a fitting backdrop to this recent global military encounter. International conditions in the 1980s; the collapse of East European communism; OPEC oil pricing and supply, and domestic political circumstances in the US all contributed to the conflict. However, what helped 'necessitate' the war, or made it seem both inevitable and desirable in the hearts and minds of the western 'allies', was the capacity of the pre-war media machine to draw on the cultural pool of ideas and imagery of the Arab and Islamic Middle East. Said calls this cultural pool Orientalism.

None of the cultural texts mentioned so far in this chapter could be described as popular in a mass sense, although the impact of the last two examples was clearly widely felt. In the final section I shall try to rectify this with an examination of one of the most popular contemporary cultural forms, television. I shall explore representations of 'racial' otherness in the wider context of television's historical role and television's relationship to other cultural forms discussed in this chapter. These seemingly disparate case studies illustrate the range of cultural forms within which 'race' appears, from 'high' to 'low' to lived culture, as well as showing the significance of cultural context as a site for reworking and rethinking the past.

PRODUCING RACIST KNOWLEDGES

What follows is certainly neither a chronological nor an exhaustive history of racist thought. Others have written more thorough and extensive histories of racism and black struggle; Michael Banton (1967, 1977), Jaques Barzun (1965), Christine Bolt (1971), Angela Davis (1981), Peter Fryer (1984), Thomas Gossett (1963) and Paul Rich (1986), to name a few. For all this scholarship, there remain enormous gaps in our knowledge and understanding. For example, we need a history of racism which charts its 'sharp changes of direction, its subterranean phases and its explosions' (Balibar, 1991: 40). My examples are drawn from what seems to me to be an inexhaustible pool of possibilities. The point of the case studies in this chapter is rather to highlight the ways in which historical representations of race both draw on the past and at the same time are reworked in the present, according to new historical circumstances: 'what, to borrow a term from Nietzsche, we might call the contemporary transvaluations of racism' (ibid.: 44). In turn, these circumstances provide us with the means to look back at history through new lenses. In both past and present, 'racial' otherness is not merely constructed but contested, so that the meanings attached to the term reflect the shifting, sometimes contradictory outcomes of these cultural (in all senses of the word) struggles.

My aim here is not to provide an exhaustive account of attempts to theorise the production of racism. I am not even aiming to map out the key theoretical traditions. Others have attempted this, for instance John Rex and David Mason (1986) and Fiona Williams (1989). My purpose here is to develop an analysis, incorporating some key concepts, that might be used to shed light on processes surrounding the construction of 'race' and racism. The intention then would be to modify and develop it in subsequent chapters. I shall begin with a discussion of what have been for me some influential contributions to my understanding of how, and under what conditions, racism is produced.

Cultural processes and the origins of Eurocentric thought: Martin Bernal's *Black Athena* and Edward Said's *Orientalism*

Voted book of the year by the *Observer* newspaper and the *New Statesman* when it was published in 1987, *Black Athena* aroused enormous lay and academic interest all over the world, not least in Greece where the government established a commission with the aim of discrediting Bernal's arguments (Bernal,1991). Bernal approaches the question of the origins of racism via two related questions which, for him, lie at the heart of the project of *Black Athena:* what are the origins of western civilisation and how do we come to believe in one explanation (of its origins) over another? The widely held belief is that western civilisation has been built on the foundations laid by the ancient Greeks. But where, Bernal asks, did Greek culture come from? At least two conflicting sets of views or models have been proposed to answer this question. The first, the ancient model, which was dominant right up until the nineteenth century, was built on the assumption that the origins of Greek culture were largely Egyptian, that is African. However, from the nineteenth century onwards, a new explanation emerged, based on the idea that the origins of Greek culture could be traced to Indo-European culture. Volumes I and II of *Black Athena* examine the ancient model's fall from grace in the nineteenth century. To prove the black (African) origins of western civilisation, Bernal cites an impressive array of evidence drawn from the following fields: etymology, used to demonstrate the extent to which Greek language is derived from Egyptian; mathematics, in order to show the influences and connections between the 'great men' of Greek mathematics and Egypt (for example Pythagoras, who was trained in Egypt); astronomy, where European scientists of a much later period, like Newton and Copernicus, openly acknowledged their debt to Egyptian science; religion, where he traces the source of numerous biblical references back to Egypt; and archaeology, finds from which have confirmed contact with, and the influence of, Egypt.

Why, then, despite the evident links between Egypt and Greece, did the ancient model fall into disrepute in the nineteenth century? What Bernal does is to answer this question by posing another, this time rhetorical, question. How could Britain justify its political, economic and cultural subordination of whole populations and vast land masses on the grounds that these peoples were inherently inferior when, according to well-established and accepted knowledge, it was the same peoples who inspired the development of western civilisation? The answer was that both contradictory sets of beliefs could not be sustained and so the ancient model gave way to the Aryan model, which attributed western civilisation to Indo-European origins and not black African. Western historiography thus set about rewriting history, eliminating and/or 'whitening' Egyptian culture (what colour was Cleopatra?) and playing up European influences.

14

One very important inference to be drawn from Bernal's analysis is that we cannot understand cultural racism without understanding a wider set of economic and political factors, although he himself does not go into detail as to what those factors were exactly. Bernal merely acknowledges that ideas associating black people with moral and intellectual inferiority infiltrated popular, elite and scientific culture, *systematically*, at a time when Britain was engaged in military conquest, colonial annexation and the expansion of its empire in the eighteenth and nineteenth centuries.

One of the most important contributions of *Black Athena* was to show how deeply politicised the classical disciplines really are, however 'value free' they may seem or however much their scholars may wish them to be. I shall return to Bernal's argument later but his view that academic knowledges are shot through with politics is shared by another cultural analyst of the construction of racist knowledges, Edward Said, in his work on Orientalism. Said is a Palestinian living and working in the United States. Dubbed 'The Professor of Terror' in the magazine *Commentary*, he describes his experience in the following way:

> The life of an Arab Palestinian in the West, particularly in America, is disheartening. There exists here an almost unanimous consensus that politically he does not exist.. The web of racism, cultural stereotypes, political imperialism, dehumanising ideology holding in the Arab or the Muslim is very strong indeed, and it is this web which every Palestinian has come to feel as his uniquely punishing destiny.
>
> (1978: 27)

I want to link Said's analysis of Orientalism with Bernal's arguments and consider their combined contribution to our understanding of the historical production of racist knowledge. Before I do so I shall attempt to summarise what I have taken to be the main points of Said's arguments. The first is a definition. In broad terms, Orientalism refers to a 'mode of discourse with supporting institutions, vocabulary, scholarship, imagery, doctrines, even colonial bureaucracies and colonial styles' (ibid.: 2). The 'Orient' was thus constructed and represented through western ideologies and institutions.

Second, and relatedly, Orientalism is based on the premiss of a fundamental division of the world into the Orient and the Occident. Poets and novelists, as well as political commentators, have taken this distinction as their starting point. Of particular importance here was the collective notion of the Occidental 'us' which became integrally bound up with the idea of European superiority and various forms of Eurocentric racism (ibid.: 8).

Third, the forms of Orientalism have changed with changing historical circumstances. Three major periods, taken from Said's account, will serve to illustrate these shifts. The first can be illustrated with reference to Dante's *Divine Comedy,* written at the beginning of the fourteenth century. There, in his imaginary vision of hell, the inferno, not so far from Satan's pit, was

15

Muhammed, Prophet of Islam, damned for his heresy. During this period, Orientalist constructions invariably focused on religion. Cultural assaults on Islam and on Muhammed (including the idea of Muhammed as impostor) coincided with the expansion of the Islamic Empire deep into south-west Europe.

The second broad period identified by Said fell between the enlightenment in the latter half of the eighteenth century and 1945, during which constructions of the Orient were adapted to the emerging secular world view and notions of 'progress' and rationality. In this context, Islam was regarded as medievally backward. Different discourses varyingly articulated this. In the 'science' of anthropology, Arabs were held to be inferior, whilst in political discourse texts were woven around the paternalistic idea that colonial subjugation would not only benefit the West (notably Britain and France) but also the Orient itself. Said cites Balfour's defence of Britain's continuing imperial role in Egypt as an example (ibid.: 31ff.).

In the period after World War II, the United States has become the dominant post-imperial empire. During this period, according to Said, constructions of the Orient have been couched more in policy jargon, in terms of stability and, linked to this, the maintenance of economic interests, particularly oil. However, underpinning this policy discourse, and sometimes running through it, is the principle of superiority. Here, Said quotes from Kissinger's 'Domestic Structure and Foreign Policy' essay, in which he distinguishes cultures that have benefited from the Newtonian revolution from those that have not. This distinction is used to justify the imposition of 'international order' by the United States on those parts of the world not guided by such principles (ibid.: 46–7).

Any summary of Said's Orientalism would be incomplete without reference to his notions of power and ideology. Power, he argues, is crucial to our understanding of how the 'Orient' was Orientalised. At the heart of Orientalism was a project aimed at dominating (and possessing) the Orient (ibid.: 3). However, the power of Orientalism can only be understood with reference to ideology. In this sense Orientalism is seen as a knitted together discourse, both convincing and coherent. It is not just made up of myths or lies that would go away if the truth were told. Such is the authority of Orientalism, Said claims, that it establishes canons of taste and value. In this sense, Orientalist knowledge can never be objective.

What Said provides, and what I have attempted to summarise, is a framework for analysing cultural processes of constructing 'otherness'. In Said's case 'others' are loosely Middle Eastern Arabs, Palestinians and Muslims. Otherness is a status defined in the negative; designed to subordinate and possess. Its flip side is the 'us' or 'we' whose collective national, European, 'western' identity rests, in part, on these kinds of exclusion. In Stuart Hall's words, 'Identity is always, in that sense, a structured representation which only achieves its positive through the narrow eye of the negative' (1991a: 21). In a similar vein, in the context of an essay on the relationship between racism and nationalism, Balibar writes, 'the racial-cultural identity of "true nationals" remains invisible, but can be inferred (and is ensured) *a contrario* by the alleged, quasi-hallucinatory visibility of the "false nationals": the Jews, "wogs", immigrants, "Pakis", natives, Blacks' (1991: 60).

Numerous examples of these negative constructions are provided by Said, but they also appear in a Palestinian Solidarity campaign pamphlet, *Anti-Arab Racism in the Media* (GLC, 1984). So, for instance, in film, Arabs are varyingly presented as: lustful, for example the character of Valentino in *The Sheikh;* violent, in *Lost Patrol, Beau Geste, Black Sunday* and *Exodus*, and corrupt, for example in *Casablanca*. Said summarises the depiction of Arabs in films and TV thus: 'The Arab is associated either with lechery or bloodthirsty dishonesty. He appears as an oversexed degenerate, capable. . . of cleverly devious intrigues, but essentially sadistic, treacherous, low' (1978: 286–7). In popular literature, Erica Jong's *Fear of Flying* (1973) has a chapter on 'Arabs and other animals', whilst news coverage of the Arab–Israeli conflict has marginalised the Palestinian perspective in numerous ways, including the under-reporting of Palestinian deaths.

Two further stereotypes, playing on assumptions of wealth and greed, have gained prominence since 1974 and the OPEC oil crisis. Once again, it is important to see how specific characteristics gain prominence according to changing economic and political circumstances. The fact that a number of OPEC member countries are non-Arab has not prevented the following popular connections from being made: Opec = Arab = greed = holding the world to ransom. Said's comments with regard to the nature and force of ideologies is well illustrated here. No amount of direct refutation, on its own, would undermine this 'well knitted together' discourse. It has a whole history and a multitude of related discourses to draw on and from which to gain sustenance.

Juxtaposing Bernal and Said in this way throws up some interesting points of contrast as well as similarity. Both are concerned with examining cultural processes which produce racist knowledges and the political and economic conditions with which they historically coincide. Both are interested in the changing forms of racism. Placed alongside one another, they serve to illustrate how racism shifts its target group, in this case from black African to Middle Eastern.[3]

Despite their similarities and strengths, both Bernal and Said can be said to have made some important omissions. For example, Bernal's central argument rests on the rejection of the role of Indo-European in favour of African culture in the development of Greek and hence western civilisation. In other words his argument rests on the omission, exclusion and suppression of the signific- ance of Indian civilisation, which as far as racial politics in post-war Britain is concerned, is another 'black' culture. I shall return to this argument in Chapter 6. Similarly, the restriction of Orientalism to the Near East has in effect ignored the very significant 'other' Orient, extending to China and the Far East. There are many examples here of constructing 'Chineseness' which could be accommodated within Said's analysis of constructing the Orient (see for example, Merch, 1974: ch. 2). In both Bernal and Said's account there is little, if any, discussion of the importance of gender specific forms of representing racial otherness and the patriarchal cultural processes underpinning these forms. I shall return to the many implications and issues relating to this omission later in this chapter and elsewhere in the book with reference to the work of black (in its inclusive sense – see above p. 5) feminists.

Psychoanalysis and racism

Neither Bernal nor Said draws explicitly on psychic processes in the works cited above, although Homi Bhabha has made effective use of *Orientalism* to draw out a psychoanalytic dimension in Said's work (Bhabha, 1990). The work of Bhabha and the revival of interest in the work of Frantz Fanon are testimony to the growing concern to theorise race in psychoanalytic terms. In a provoking article on the role of mimicry, Bhabha has argued that colonial powers employed different strategies to maintain their dominance. Mimicry was one. Through mimicry, the colonisers sought to impose their culture, while making sure that subordinate culture was still different enough to confirm their sense of superiority: the 'same but not quite'. The motives for this were both political and psychic. Nevertheless, while colonial powers fed their own narcissistic desire to define themselves in terms of otherness, the need to maintain difference sowed the seeds of a potential threat or menace in which marginal cultures sought to liberate themselves and for the first time, observe the observer (Bhabha, 1986b: 201).

The 'primary strategic function' of colonial discourse is the creation of a space for 'subject peoples' through the production of knowledges in which 'surveillance is exercised and a complex form of pleasure/unpleasure is incited' (Bhabha, 1990: 75). The knowledges produced are stereotypical, although Bhabha introduces a novel interpretation of this term:

> I argue for the reading of the stereotype in terms of fetishism. The myth of historical origination – racial purity, cultural priority – production in relationship to the colonial stereotype functions to 'normalise' the multiple beliefs and split subjects that constitute colonial discourse as a consequence of its process of disavowal. The scene of fetishism functions similarly as at once, a reactivation of the material of original fantasy – the anxiety of castration and sexual difference – as well as a normalisation of that difference and disturbance in terms of the fetish object as the substitute for the mother's penis.
>
> (ibid.: 79)

The impact of these processes of disavowal/desire on the colonised mind was a major theme of Frantz Fanon's *Black Skin, White Masks.* The internalisation

18

of oppression ('I was battered down by. . . intellectual deficiency. . . racial defects') was coupled with the desire to take the settler's place, in Fanon's case the French colonial settler. Beyond this, however, was a rejection of colonial culture encapsulated in the negritude or black consciousness movement. This coincides with Bhabha's own account. Ultimately, mimicry destroys colonial authority through the continual slippage of desire and difference. Further-more, the legitimacy of colonial representations is undermined. Colonial discourse is thus split between that which takes reality into consideration and that which replaces it by a product of desire and rearticulates reality as mimicry. This leads to narcissism and paranoia on the part of the colonial power (Fanon, 1986: 205).

The relationship between coloniser and colonised is thus one of extreme psychic ambivalence. On the one hand, there is a narcissistic demand for domination. There is a splitting process here which is crucial to the formation of identity: the splitting of who one is from that which is the other: 'this is the Other that one can only know from the place from which one stands. This is the self as it is inscribed in the gaze of the other' (Hall, 1991b: 48). On the other hand, there is a desire to be the other. Stuart Hall talks about this in the context of the West's current obsession with cultural difference, whether this takes the form of international travel, cuisine, or the wonders of the ancient world (see Chapter 6). In this way the over-corporate, over-integrated form of western economic power 'teases itself with the pleasures of the transgressive other'. The desire to be different is at odds with the desire to control and all that entails.

White middle-class male identities were thus formed in a colonial context, in part through the splitting off of that part of themselves deemed unaccept-able. What followed was a psychic process of *denial* (an emotional defence) which included repression of aggression and ruthlessness, and then *projecting* those unacceptable characteristics (dependency, uncontrolled sexuality, etc.) onto colonial subjects (Pajaczkowska and Young, 1992: 202–3).

> These projections leave White, middle class, male identity as one of safety, power, control, independence and contentment, perhaps smug or self-righteous. Yet this is an illusory identity because it is actually highly dependent on its others to shore up its sense of security, to reflect back the disowned parts of itself as inferior, contemptible, dependent, frightened or threatening, perhaps excremental.
>
> (ibid.: 204)

This last point relates to the idea of 'subjectification', 'a process whereby people become subjected and regulated through the kinds of identities as-sumed in discourse' (Wetherell and Potter, 1992: 79). An important feature of Margaret Wetherell and Jonathan Potter's analysis of Pakeha (i.e. white settler) racist discourse is their premiss that the psychological field is constituted through the social domain of discourse (ibid.: 75) and their attempt to draw on the tools of a Marxist/psychoanalytic tradition. Potter and Wetherell's idea that discourses, and in particular what they call interpretive repertoires, provide the basis for 'manufacturing versions of actions, self and social structure in talk' (ibid.: 90) constitutes an important mechanism linking discourse, identity and action. I shall return to these questions and in particular to that of identity in Parts II and III.

Marxist theory and racism

My intention here is to pull out some key ideas from Marxist contributions to the analysis of racism, rather than to undertake a comprehensive or detailed evaluation of the field. This has been undertaken elsewhere (Gabriel and Ben-Tovim, 1978; Miles, 1993; Anthias, 1990; Solomos, 1986). The two most important aspects of these contributions have been to define racism as an ideology and to link its origins and forms to global economic developments and the nation state. Exactly how these are linked has been the object of an as yet unresolved and at times heated debate. One consequence of this debate has been the fragmentation of the study of race and ethnicity, with those more concerned with cultural forms and processes working almost in isolation from those concerned with an analysis rooted in political economy. The latter, in particular, is either implicit in, or peripheral to explanations reviewed so far. Indeed, political economy is a field which has remained largely unploughed by cultural theorists. One aim of this book is to bring these two important traditions (bearing in mind that each tradition has its own internal debates and differences) closer, not for the sake of some convenient compromise but because each on its own begs questions which can only be addressed with reference to the other.

For my purposes now I have chosen to focus, briefly, on the work of Robert Miles, whose rigorous analysis of racism and use of Marxist theories of ideology and political economy have made an important contribution to our understanding of racism. I shall return, in subsequent chapters, to the broad tradition which Miles, for our present purposes, represents. For example, in Chapters 6 and 7 I will draw on the work of A. Sivanandan, particularly his analysis of imperialism and the global movements of labour and capital. For now, I shall summarise what are for me some of the main points of Miles' analysis of racism.

The first is his definition of racism, which is the starting point of his analysis. 'All racisms are instances of ideological marginalisation, within a social formation, of a supposedly distinct social collectivity. . . which has been signified as naturally different, usually (but not exclusively) by reference to real or alleged biological characteristics' (Miles, 1993: 101). Moreover, as ideologies (in Miles' sense of the term) racisms are discourses representing human beings in distorted and misleading ways (1989: 42). Racism's specific representational characteristics include reference to (usually, though not always) biological differences; nature; negative characteristics; definitions of 'self' through the

20

construction of 'otherness' (racialisation refers to the processes of inclusion and exclusion entailed here), and the more or less coherent assembly of stereotypes, images, attributions and explanations present in lived culture (ibid.: 79). Finally, Miles argues that within its own terms, racist ideologies offer plausible practical solutions to their alleged problems.

The second point is that whilst these broad elements of racism remain constant, their forms vary enormously. Miles himself, in his writing, discusses differences between colonial and non-colonial contexts, including Kenya and Australia under British colonial rule and the situation in post-war Britain and, within Britain between Scotland and England and Jews in Europe. Variations, therefore, have to take account of political and economic context as well as the variety of 'assemblies' of stereotypes, depending on the group in question. Jews, Aboriginals, Africans, Chinese and, as we saw in the case of Orientalism, Middle Eastern Arabs and Muslims. This list is by no means complete, of course, but it gives some indication of the scope of racialised discourses. This argument also implies, in contrast to Bernal's, that historically, racism is not necessarily tied to colonialism, but can emerge within colonial contexts, for example anti-Semitism in Europe.

The third point is that institutionalised racism must be seen to result from racist ideologies. It is not enough to argue that any inequalities between black and white must be the result of institutional racism. It must rely on a racialised discourse. Miles gives the example of recruitment practices which result in under-representation of black staff. He argues that this is not institutional racism, because such word-of-mouth practices could equally limit women. Attempts to link institutional racism to consequences rather than to ideologies (Miles describes this as inflating the concept) detract from the precision of the term and makes it impossible to isolate racism's role from other contributory factors, for example class and gender. I shall return to this argument in Chapter 3.

Finally, the ideology of racism and the process of racialisation were used to structure and maintain capitalist class relations in the colonial period, although as Miles has argued it should not be assumed that racism is intrinsically tied to this period. Miles argues that processes of signification, including racism but also sexism and nationalism, are harnessed to economic and political ends. This does not mean that racial and class divisions always coincide or that the state conspires to manufacture racism. It just means that any examination of processes of racialisation and racist systems of signification cannot be understood outside of these very important structuring mechanisms.

Miles rightly reminds us of the need for conceptual clarification and precision and that the tools of political economy should be integrated into an analysis of cultural forms and processes. It is also important, however, to relate these points to questions of political strategy, when the factor of conceptual precision might end up playing a secondary role. This raises an important difference between Bernal and Miles on the one hand and Said on the other:

21

the extent to which their accounts imply the possibility of objective knowledge. For Miles, the idea that racism is a 'distortion' implies some objective reality in which those ideological relationships might be stripped down to their bare (class?) essentials. In contrast Wetherell and Potter in their analysis of Pakeha racism are less concerned to disentangle false (ideological) from true (class) relations than to establish how 'facts' attain their 'factual' status, and the consequences of these constructions (1992: 67). Bernal, like Miles, also commits himself to an authentic version of history, embodied in the ancient model (although this is maintained with only partial consistency, see Gabriel, 1989a), whereas Said is a much more consistent relativist. The 'Orient' is a western construction, or succession of western constructions, not to be compared with some real world view, but at most, just constituting a series of alternative forms of representation.

In all the above accounts, ideas of 'race' are reworked in different sets of historical circumstances and with different groups as their primary focus. Both Bernal and Said lay bare the cultural means by which such domination is secured. At the same time, Bernal acknowledges the counter-influence of oppositional knowledges and foresees the re-emergence of the ancient model in the latter part of the twentieth century. The danger of historical sweeps of this magnitude is that they obscure blips and reversals. It is not that easy, for example, to detect evidence of what Bernal refers to as the 'inexorable progress of anti-racism' in Britain and Western Europe (witness the Fascist revival in the latter part of the 1980s) or the United States in the latter quarter of the twentieth century. A more specific account of circumstance is necessary, one that takes account of time, place and the peculiarities of context. Attempts to theorise the production of racist knowledges using psychoanalysis make an important contribution to an underdeveloped level of our understanding but cannot on their own explain in what social and political circumstances stereotypical knowledges become more significant. Nor do such attempts clearly establish the mechanisms linking the psychic and social realms. The work of Robert Miles amongst others complements this level of analysis by focusing on historical examples within a Marxist analysis.

ORIENTALISING THE PRESENT

Salman Rushdie's *Satanic Verses*

I now want to examine two recent political crises: the controversy surrounding the publication of Salman Rushdie's *Satanic Verses* and the Gulf War, with the help of some of the key ideas discussed so far. In particular, I want to look at the ways in which the construction of public debates around these events served to fuel a racist backlash against Muslims and other religious minorities in Britain. Religious differences were thus racialised and debates polarised along racial/religious/class lines. My intention is not to take sides in the debates, as such, but to analyse the origin of different positions (e.g. the 'freedom' of expression argument in white, western, liberal discourse), and the extent to which some positions were widely aired, whilst others, including, to a large extent, discourses articulating the effects of these debates on lived culture within south Asian communities, were silenced.

Most people will be familiar with the chronicle of events surrounding Salman Rushdie's book, *The Satanic Verses*. It was published in the UK on 26 September 1988 and banned in India in November, just three days before it won the British Whitbread prize for literature. It became the object of protests in Bradford, in January 1989, where it was ceremonially burnt, and in Islamabad in February, where six people were killed in demonstrations over its publication. Two days later, on 14 February, the Ayatollah Khomeni issued a fatwa (death sentence), calling for the execution of the author, who immediately went into hiding (under armed guard), where he has remained, public appearances apart, ever since. Although Rushdie subsequently expressed his profound regret that the book had distressed Muslims, Iran renewed its call on every Muslim to send the author to hell. In December 1990, much to the shock of many of his supporters, Rushdie announced his allegiance to Islam, only to renounce it again in December 1991, when he simultaneously called for the publication of the paperback edition of the book. His somewhat inconsistent attempts at compromise with Islam have so far failed to lift the fatwa. Despite British government attempts to have it lifted, the fatwa has been consistently reaffirmed by the Iranian government, most recently in September 1993.

This only provides the briefest account of some of the events, or moments, in what has become known as the 'Rushdie affair'. Surrounding these events is a wider and more significant set of issues. The reaction to the novel, in this sense, is as important as the substance of the novel itself. However, before considering the nature of this response it may be helpful to say a little about the book itself, although even 'summaries' are reactions and my own understanding of the book is quite different now to what it was soon after publication. What follows is inevitably framed by subsequent events and readings.

In one sense, *The Satanic Verses* is a novel about migration and how that experience works on people's sense of identity. Religion is central to the novel and is expressed in a clash of opposites: good and evil, personified in the two central characters, Saladin and Gibreel. The discontinuities and continuities surrounding their lives and their resulting sense of themselves is a central concern of the book. Its seemingly incongruous juxtapositions, the absence of linear narrative and its surrealistic sequences, alternating fantasy and reality, have encouraged critics to describe *Satanic Verses* as an important piece of postmodernist, magic realist fiction (which Rushdie is said to have introduced to English literature in a previous novel, *Midnight's Children*, 1981). In *Satanic*

Verses the reader is one minute on a beach in England with two passengers who have been thrown from an aircraft, and the next on a mountain with Mahound (another word for devil, and intended to be confused with the prophet Muhammed) who was in receipt of verses for the Koran, which turn out to have come from the devil. (The book's defenders have argued that Gibreel only *dreams* he has intervened in altering verses of the Koran.) By any standards the book is, at the very least, highly irreverent, but its irreverence, it has to be said, is not confined to Islam. Its targets include the British state which it accuses of racism, as the following quote illustrates.

> The three immigration officers were in particularly high spirits, and it was one of these. . . who had 'debagged' Saladin with a merry cry of, 'Opening time, Packy; lets see what you're made of!' Red-and-white stripes were dragged off the protesting Chamcha, who was reclining on the floor of the van with two stout policemen holding each arm and a fifth constable's boot placed firmly upon his chest, and whose protests went unheard in the general mirthful din.
>
> (Rushdie, 1988:157)

There were two initial western responses, not so much to the novel itself, but to the wave of protests that its publication had provoked amongst Muslim communities, both in Britain and internationally.[4] The first can be described as the dominant liberal response, which in essence was to defend the novel as part of a wider principle of the freedom to publish. In a television programme, *Blasphemers' Banquet*, written and narrated by Tony Harrison, the poet defiantly drank an alcoholic toast to Rushdie at the Omar Khayyam restaurant in Bradford, in the company of four other blasphemers, Voltaire, Molière, Byron and Omar Khayyam. The clear point of the programme was to relate Rushdie's situation to other struggles around censorship and the freedom to publish. This was underlined in a poem by Harrison, aptly called 'The Satanic Verses', published in the *Observer*. It is worth noting Harrison's use of a famous English nationalist anthem, William Blake's 'Jerusalem' to defend Rushdie and attack censorship. In the concluding lines the poet throws down the following challenge:

> I shall not cease from mental strife
> nor shall my pen sleep in my hand
> til Rushdie has a right to life
> and books aren't burnt or banned

In a similar vein, Michael Ignatieff defended the book on the grounds that the principle of the individual right to publish could not be curtailed by religious doctrine. According to Ignatieff, the question boiled down to the difference between tolerance and intolerance (*Observer*, 2 April 1989). Elsewhere, members of the liberal arts establishment rallied around Rushdie in the following terms: 'Where we waver in our resolve to defend the crucial freedoms involved in this matter we are ourselves joining the mob' (Harold Pinter, *New Statesman and Society*, 31 March 1989: 25); 'The most hideous sight is that of a burning book' (Alan Plater, ibid.: 28); 'Without free speech there can be no reason' (Peter Hall, ibid.: 29).

Although, seemingly, at political odds with each other, the liberal response complements a second reaction to the affair, best summed up in a speech given at the Birmingham mosque by the then Home Secretary, Douglas Hurd. In it he exhorted Muslims to 'have a clear understanding of the history and institutions of Britain, of its democratic processes – at both national and local level. . . [otherwise] they will not make the best of their lives and their opportunities as British citizens' (cited in Qureshi and Khan, 1989: 6). The Rushdie affair brought closet assimilationists, like the Home Secretary, un-happy with notions of cultural pluralism and anti-racist initiatives, out into the open. The affair coincided with the 1980s backlash against anti-racism and the revival of assimilationism (the idea that Muslims, in this case, should conform to (dominant) British cultural values). These views were expressed in the wake of the Rushdie affair by one-time Labour MP, ex-Liverpool University politics tutor, Robert Kilroy-Silk, in an article in the *Times*:

> It is of course, one of the hallmarks of British culture that it is prepared to tolerate other points of view. . . . But accepting and tolerating other religions and cultures within our own does not mean that we have to defer to them. Why should we? If Muslim immigrants cannot and will not accept British values and laws then there is no reason at all why the British should feel any need, still less compulsion, to accommodate theirs. We are not supplicants in our own country.
>
> (17 February 1989)

In a fascinating dialogue on the Rushdie affair, Homi Bhabha and Bhikhu Parekh (1989) discuss the strengthening of fundamentalist values in the context of a society, like Britain, where there appears little scope for adapta-tion, at least so long as the views of Douglas Hurd and Kilroy-Silk hold sway. However, both agree that underpinning the West's response has been the assumption that the post-enlightenment value of 'freedom' is absolute. This notion of 'freedom', espoused by both liberal writers and politicians of the right and centre, is integrally bound up in a version of national identity: one that relies on constructing western secular values as somehow more advanced, more civilised and less oppressed than those of Islamic fundamentalism.

I would argue, although I am not sure that Edward Said would agree, that Said's analysis of Orientalism provides an extremely valuable basis for making sense of western reactions to the Rushdie affair. At the heart of western thinking about Rushdie and Islamic reactions to the publication is the western assumption that 'our present is your future'. The idea of the backwardness of Islam, its pre-secular 'fanaticism' and its dubious religious credentials (a point reinforced by Rushdie himself in his character of Mahound) all resonate with older Orientalist discourses. John Tomlinson makes a point in a different context which is of relevance here when he writes, 'the fact that these very values have a particular cultural provenance (*western* liberalism) is a complication which is rarely probed' (Tomlinson,1991: 6).

To this sense of superiority, embedded in liberal discourse, was added a conservative sense of outrage at the idea that those Muslims who lived in Britain but whose national credentials were still in doubt were making demands on indigenous white society.[5] The Rushdie affair thus fed on and, it should be argued, fed into, a public articulation of assimilationism, which had already re-established itself in attacks on the anti-racist initiatives of the GLC and other Labour authorities in the latter part of the 1980s.

The unexpected alliances and divisions thrown up by the affair were heightened by the emergence of an anti-liberal faction within conservative opinion. The latter can be seen in the following intervention by Christopher Monkton in the *Evening Standard*. In this article the author departs from the consensus viewpoint to support the principle of censorship against Rushdie and his liberal supporters:

> The outstanding characteristic of the 'liberal' establishment is their flagrant illiberality. They demand tolerance, yet they are themselves wickedly intolerant. Rushdie and the chattering coterie of Antonia Fraser look-alikes and boudoir Bolsheviks from the literary *demi-monde* who support him have insisted on his 'freedom to publish', though they have in the past been shrill in their demands that others who write racialist works should be silenced.

> (24 February 1989)

Monkton went on to support the censorship of blasphemous writing, whatever the religion under attack. It is hard to know whether the author was more concerned to censor Rushdie's fictional exposure of British racism or genuinely affronted by Rushdie's satirical attack on Islam. In any event, he resorted to a defence of traditional values, in this case religion, in order to attack the 'freedom' of the author. As such, his intervention marked an interesting point of conflict between liberal and conservative factions of the establishment and stood in opposition to an alliance of liberals across the political spectrum. This alliance included Said himself who, arguably, took up a position within Orientalist discourse to defend Rushdie's right to publish (see for example *Index*, 1989: 17).

In fact, very few have stepped outside Orientalist discourse to challenge these arguments, at least not within the mainstream media. Those who did are worth looking at precisely because they were marginalised, since the processes which secured their marginal status and the dominance of the liberal/assimilationist (Orientalist) alliance are central to an understanding of cultures of racism. Many issues and questions were obscured by or hidden beneath the consensus spectrum of opinion. Very few writers, for example, questioned the so-called 'freedom' to write or any contradictions or qualifications attached to this so-called 'freedom' principle. Very few discussed the impact of the reaction to the controversy surrounding the book on racial tension and harassment in places like Bradford whose working-class Muslim community was not able to benefit from police protection or a close literary circle of friends, not to mention the support (albeit grudging at times) of the political establishment. Although to entertain such thoughts seemed tantamount to national betrayal, a few dissenting voices did rise up above the din of the liberal political and literary establishments. My aim here is not only to question the underlying assumptions, coherence and social consequences of the establishment's response to the affair. It is also to highlight a body of opinion which was more or less silenced throughout the affair, for reasons, I have suggested, that have to do with the dominance of western liberal, 'Orientalist' thought.

In a lecture delivered at Cornell University, Ali Mazrui made a powerful case against hypocrisy in the West's reaction to the fatwa and calls for censorship against Rushdie. Mazrui contrasted the treason laws in the West with the blasphemy laws in the East. How does the West deal with those who betray the state – Peter Wright in Britain or the Rosenbergs in the United States – or how do we explain, for example, state reprisals like the bombing of Libya in 1986? In a cynical rhetorical retort Mazrui writes that in all cases it is 'murder by remote control'. The difference lies in 'a style of doing it'. The fatwa 'is not more immoral', it is 'the way it was done, it was just bad taste'. The Ayatollah 'announces it on the radio instead of sending his spy to do it for him' (cited in Appignanesi and Maitland, 1989: 225).

The *Observer*, too, ran a piece pointing out the inconsistency of British governments' reaction to publications concerned with Islam and India going back over sixty years. For example, A. C. Osborn's *Must Britain Lose India?* was banned in the 1930s by the India Office because it was strongly critical of British rule. Osborn was criticised by the Under-Secretary of State as 'one of those disgusting birds who like to foul their own nests' (*Observer*, 2 April 1989). On the other hand, G. K. Chesterton was asked by the India Office to remove offensive references to Muslims in his *Short History of England*, a request to which he unhesitatingly agreed (ibid.). In all, according to Rukhsana Ahmed, the British banned over 5,000 books during their rule in India (*Daily Jang*, 16 March 1989).

The freedom of speech principle was questioned from a somewhat different angle by John Berger in a piece in the *Guardian*. In it, he compared the curtailment of the rights and freedoms of the artist with the rights of the Muslim community to be free from harassment (25 February 1989). Max Madden drew attention to the limits of the principle of free speech in a letter to the same paper:

> In a multi-racial, multi-cultural, multi-faith Britain we must realize that the
> freedom of speech is pretty meaningless in a society where substantial

ethnic minorities and religious minorities feel their views are not adequately understood or represented

(23 January 1989)

Furthermore, the debate surrounding the book effectively diverted attention from the lived consequences of the whole affair for Muslims in Britain. The escalation of attacks on the Asian community, post-*Satanic Verses*, received limited coverage in the mainstream media. In a Radio 4 programme, *Children of the Book*, young Muslims spoke of the deterioration in their social relationships with the white community and the 'polarisation of the racial scene'. Western responses to the book, the verbal and printed attacks on Muslims, the calls to assimilate and the idea of Muslims threatening British 'freedoms', all contributed to a climate in which overt racial hostility and abuse towards Muslims could be understood and accepted. The credence given to attacking Islamic fundamentalism from all sectors of opinion fused with attacks on Muslims and Asians in general, which of course were not new, but were lent latent support and sympathy through the framing of the debate (Qureshi and Khan, 1989: 33). A new vocabulary of racist terms, including 'Muslim', 'Rushdie', 'Ayatollah', 'Mullah', all of which were now used pejoratively, emerged directly out of this climate. In a very sharp critique of Rushdie and his establishment support, Nicholas Ashford wrote:

My second regret is that the Rushdie issue has now fuelled the fires of anti-Muslim sentiment in the country and elsewhere in the West. Such feelings are never far below the surface. Popular newspapers trot out stereotypes. . . Islam is presented as a primitive narrow-minded religion still anchored in the Middle Ages. . . I have long suspected that the West's arrogant disdain of Islam is based in part on the realisation that the growth and increased assertiveness of the Islamic faith (of which fundamentalism is undoubtedly a part) is taking place at a time when Christianity is in decline.

(cited ibid.: 32)

Elsewhere, Floya Anthias and Nira Yuval-Davis argue:

Since the 'Rushdie affair', the exclusion of minority religions from the national collectivity has started a process of racialisation that especially relates to Muslims. People who used to be known for the place of origin, or even as 'people of colour' have become identified by their assumed religion. The racist stereotype of the 'Paki' has become the racist stereotype of the 'Muslim fundamentalist'.

(1992: 55)

Similarly, in an article in the *Guardian*, young Muslims described living in Bradford, 'post-Rushdie'. 'We've always got along together here. . . since this Rushdie thing, white lads have come down looking for trouble' (11 July 1989).

One of the victims, Goharremah Ali, aged thirteen, was 'knocked to the ground and repeatedly kicked' (ibid.).

The press, albeit unwittingly and indirectly, helped legitimise such attacks by their sponsorship of views, expressed by Kilroy-Silk and others, condemning the Muslim community's response to *Satanic Verses*. A local Birmingham newspaper's reporting of the murder of Pharbin Malik by her father illustrates this. Under the heading 'Sacrificed for Allah', it reports that Pharbin's father slit her throat rather than accept her conversion from Islam to Christianity. The coverage given to the murder fed anti-Islamic feeling at the height of the Rushdie affair. Juxtaposed, as it was, with reports of militant anti-Rushdie protests, the article could only have served to harden stereotypes of the Islamic community in a city with a significant Muslim population (*Birmingham Daily News*, 6 July 1989).

According to Martin Amis, the effects of novels can never be calculated. They always happen by accident (*New Statesman and Society*, 31 March 1989). If this is true, then it gives authors absolute freedom from responsibility for what they write. On the other hand, it could be argued that Rushdie's conscious preoccupation with postmodern literary developments, his sense of himself as a lone artist, born partly out of his academic background and the literary circles in which he moved, placed him outside the collective concerns and experiences of many working-class Muslims. To say that these factors are not known in advance and cannot be calculated to any degree seems almost too convenient an excuse for the liberal literary establishment. If the real intention were to attack Islamic fundamentalism, then, arguably, an attack from within Islam itself was always more likely to secure moderate support and prove less offensive to those whose lives remained so intimately bound up with their religion. The irony is that Rushdie's attack on racism in the context of an attack on Islam actually fuelled a racist backlash and polarised Islamic and non-Islamic communities. It left little or no space for the debate he wished to provoke.

The class divide between Rushdie and many Muslims in Britain partly helps to explain the course of events prior to and after the publication of *Satanic Verses*. Rushdie's privileged position allowed him to site his protest in literature, with a pen or an Amstrad as his weapon, while Muslims had to resort to public street protest and to book burning to highlight their grievances. Within the terms of liberal democracy, Rushdie and his supporters appeared reasonable and responsible, whilst their opponents were regarded as fanatical and backward.

> The *Satanic Verses* affair revealed another serious problem of the Muslim Community in Britain: its political powerlessness. . . both the younger generation who have been born here and the old timers who have settled here for decades felt frustration at not being able to make their voice heard.
>
> (Qureshi and Khan, 1989: 21)

The Gulf War

The capacity of racist knowledges to adapt and surface at opportune historical moments was also in evidence during the Gulf crisis and War of 1990–1. Said's analysis once again is particularly instructive here, in making sense of western reactions to Iraq's intervention in Kuwait and of the West's subsequent decision to support Kuwait militarily by declaring war on Iraq. A number of factors had shifted western attention towards the Middle East, not least of which was the Rushdie affair. Other factors included the Iranian revolution and the revival of Islamic fundamentalism from the late 1970s onwards; the hostage situation in Lebanon; the alleged threat posed by Gadaffi in Libya; the struggle for a Palestinian state, and last but by no means least, domestic economic crises in the West, particularly in the United States. These circumstances were foregrounded in the run-up to the Gulf War as a result of sweeping political changes in Eastern and Central Europe and the removal of the threat of war from the other side of the iron curtain.

At one level it is possible to see the Gulf War as another Falklands War, born of domestic crises in both the United States and Britain; acting both to divert and enhance the standing of the Bush Administration and the Thatcher Government. Media coverage of the ensuing conflict also resembled that of the Falklands, with its adventure stories and tales of romance, heroism and patriotism in the making. In the case of the Gulf crisis, since its escalation coincided with Christmas, the tabloids, in particular, were able to inject some festive sentiment into their coverage. Strategic use was made of a highly resonant expression of national cultural identity through stories of shipments of Christmas puddings to 'our lads' juxtaposed with references to the non-celebration of Christmas in Islam.

There was another more important difference between the wars in terms of media coverage. The myth of General Galtieri's Argentinian forces (the 'Argies') had to be created *during* the Malvinas dispute. In the Gulf War, the western media already had a well-established repertoire of stereotypical images and characteristics to make sense of the crisis: hence the portrayal of Saddam as a volatile, violent and merciless tyrant (*Sun*, 3 August 1990); the threat of a new Islamic empire (*Daily Mirror*, 3 August 1990), and Iraqis as sexually threatening (*Sun*, 15 December 1990). Alongside this, the press, including the glossy Sunday supplements, took the opportunity to promote more enticing, exoticised versions of 'eastern' female sexuality. These racialised constructions played off and into well-established symbolic, mythical and metaphorical discourses which I have argued elsewhere can be understood with reference to Said's Orientalism and Bhabha *et al.'s* analysis of the conflicting, ambivalent motives on the part of the post-colonial power to define, possess and control post-colonial 'other' via desire and disavowal.

Orientalism provided a whole set of discourses through which the Gulf crisis/War could be read. The previously rehearsed stereotypes of violence, immorality, promiscuity, fanaticism and greed were brought into play to support political and economic interests, in this case those of the British and American governments, and the interests of the sectors of the economy most reliant on cheap oil. However, the outcome of struggles around those expressed interests was by no means certain. Neither the war nor the reworking of Orientalist themes was inevitable. In fact, at one point in the course of the crisis (it subsequently became known) a section of the US political establishment would have been happy to see oil prices pushed up by Saddam, thereby maintaining the prices of, and safeguarding, the domestic oil industry. Moreover, it was alleged by some commentators that, prior to the war, the United States had agreed, through one of its diplomats, to turn a blind eye to Iraq's 'domestic' boundary dispute with Kuwait.

The Gulf War offers some interesting parallels with the Rushdie affair, particularly in terms of its impact on domestic racism and including the way 'Saddam' replaced 'Rushdie' as a term of abuse in the school playgrounds and on the streets. Once again the public (media) and private (lived) forms of cultural production intersect. Levels of violence and harassment of Muslims, and south Asian communities generally, became a feature of the war and its aftermath. It also provoked a debate within the Muslim community itself, some advocating British military withdrawal and support for Iraq, others making explicit their religious and sectional differences with Saddam. The media response helped to unite Muslims and south Asians of different political and ethnic backgrounds. An article in the *Independent* was one example of a more refined response, not unlike liberal defences of *The Satanic Verses*. Whilst the tone appeared sympathetic to Muslim culture, the article nevertheless argued that Muslims must abide by British laws and values. The choice is a version of Norman Tebbit's cricket test which challenged those who lived and were settled in England to support the English cricket team. If they could not, and supported India, Pakistan or the West Indies instead, then they should ask themselves whether they might be better off living in the country to which they had greater loyalty. In other words the choice for black people in Britain was assimilation or repatriation/emigration.

Opposition to the war, like opposition in the Rushdie affair, rarely found an outlet in the mainstream media. With support for the war coming from all three major political parties in Britain, advocates of the maintenance of sanctions (which the CIA had admitted were working just prior to the declaration of war) and a diplomatic solution found themselves isolated and cast in the role of traitors. Occasional articles in the liberal press bravely stepped outside this consensus, notably those by John Pilger (see *New Statesman and Society*, 25 January 1991), only to be submerged beneath dominant images of news-hungry journalists in battledress behind 'allied lines' or moving toy soldiers and tanks around what looked like a papier mâché model of the Gulf region in a late-night newsroom studio. The capacity of western governments to win support for the war and, by implication, a Kuwaiti regime notorious for its human rights abuses and autocratic leadership, was largely made possible by the media's exploitation of Orientalist myths, on the one hand, and the effective use of narratives of adventure and romance into which war coverage so readily fitted, on the other.

One source of opposition, as yet unmentioned in this discussion, was the collective political response of black women, to both the Rushdie affair and the Gulf War. This represents an extremely important, if complicating, dimension to the above debates. As I suggested earlier, there is little evidence in either Bernal or Said's accounts that women populate the world. In Said's account, for example, we are given little sense of how patriarchal discourses were integrally bound up with Orientalism. Moreover, whilst the latter was made up entirely of representations and western mythical constructions, feminists have sought to challenge not just western myths but real oppression within their own communities.

The risk of using public forums, for example the Rushdie affair and the Gulf War, to challenge patriarchal forms relates to what bell hooks warns of when she talks about feeding the white racist imagination. This danger was well illustrated in the Rushdie affair, with commentators like Kilroy-Silk in his *Times* article attacking Islam for its treatment of women, which he then contrasted with the freedoms of western women. His disingenuous attack on female oppression under Islam was part of a wider racist attack on Islamic culture and the call on Muslims to assimilate. The article had the further advantage of constructing an image of the West as free of patriarchy and other forms of social division.

Likewise, during the Gulf War the press highlighted the oppressions suffered by Muslim women (not just in the Arab states but in Pakistan) as part of the generalised construction of the backwardness of the Orient *vis-à-vis* the progressiveness of the West. Once again the war provided an opportunity for Muslim women with a limited opportunity to exploit media attention to highlight their oppression. In their view, the risks of their arguments feeding racist imaginations were outweighed by the need to express their opposition to fundamentalism and the absence of an alternative political space in which to do so. This raises a very important point with regard to relationships between gender and racial oppression: rather than attempt to resolve them in any absolute or abstract sense, it is more useful to assess such relations and priorities in terms of particular sets of conditions and, relatedly, questions of political strategy (Connolly,1991).

The Gulf War provides a useful case study for the exploration of some of the themes taken up earlier in the chapter. The period 1990–1 was the global setting for a reworking of Orientalist themes in both public and private forms of cultural production. The body bags, the civilian deaths in Iraq, the heightened racial tension in Britain were all part of this production, but were not the inevitable acting out of Orientalist ideology or the economic or political interests of the US and other western governments. An analysis of the crisis provides a much more fluid picture, in which there was no obvious or pre-given consensus of western interests. These had to calculated, constructed and contested. The media, and the tabloid press in particular, played its part in drawing the cultural battle lines in ways which made the war seem not only necessary and inevitable, but one in which in 'the national interest' was at stake.

FROM DANTE TO *DALLAS*: TV CULTURE

The examples discussed so far bear witness to the important role played by institutions in producing and legitimising cultures of race. However, political, academic and media institutions have all been referred to without making explicit reference to, arguably, the most important mass medium of the last half of this century: television. The latter, it has been argued, has become *the* prime medium of entertainment, instruction and information, with the written word coming a poor second. Some measure of television's significance was confirmed in the Bullock Report, *Language for Life*, in which it was reported that British children aged between five and fourteen spent more time watching TV than they did at school – approximately 25 hours a week (cited in Masterman, 1980: 197).

Furthermore, whilst whole disciplines have been devoted to the significance of literature and drama, television's codes and regimes of representation have been taken very much for granted. The idea that TV is a window on the world has only recently been challenged and it is now acknowledged, by media researchers at least, that television plays an important part in helping to shape and define our perceptions and understandings of the world and our sense of reality. The processes of producing and consuming television have thus become an important focus of cultural study. Here I am particularly concerned with television's role in defining race, how representations have shifted over time (television has a history too, now, as a visit to the London's Museum of the Moving Image confirms, although by no means exhausts) and how television has become an increasingly important site for contesting and reworking dominant forms of representing race. Race has tended to be restricted, in British research, to African-Caribbean and south Asian ethnicities. The association of race with these particular ethnicities to the virtual exclusion of others, and the assumption that individuals and groups can or wish to be defined exclusively in these terms is an important question. Overall there is very little research as yet to draw on here, especially in the area of contestation. At best, this section aims to map out existing debates and to provide a framework, for exploring these shifts, whilst recognising the potential richness of what remains a relatively uncultivated research field.

One extremely fruitful line of research would be to think about differences between US and home-produced television. A tradition which dates back to when cultural critics like Matthew Arnold and the Leavises attacked the US for its industrial barbarism, materialism, rootlessness and cultural vacuity. Amongst the more recent intellectual avant-garde of postmodernism there is a strong anti-American current, too, illustrated in the writings of Jean Baudrillard (see e.g. Baudrillard, 1988) who described America as a giant hologram. This tradition provided important fodder for television's cultural critics, particularly in its early days as an object of mass consumption.

Against these critics emerged an alternative perspective within cultural studies, which has been more willing to recognise the significantly subversive aspects of US culture. Dick Hebdige, for example, has explored different ways in which North American culture has served to radicalise British culture (Hebdige, 1988). His work explores how representations of teenagers in the cinema and television of the 1950s, evoked lastingly in the screen characters played by James Dean, the novels of Jack Kerouac and the beat poetry of Allen Ginsberg, together provided an array of subversive forms for Britain's emerging post-war youth sub-cultures (cited in Webster, 1988: 182ff.).

Duncan Webster (ibid.) develops this idea with reference to the crime genre in TV, films and novels. What American popular culture did, he argues, was to take murder out of the parlour, the library or the living room and onto the street, thus bringing it within reach of working-class readers and audiences. American culture, in this sense, was a threat in class terms. The crime fiction of British writers like Dorothy Sayers and Agatha Christie reflected their familiarity with middle-class lifestyles. Although class was not the overt issue on which British taste was being judged by its custodians, such as the Leavises and the BBC, it was not far beneath the surface (ibid.: 190). Audience-based research with a specific focus on representations of race and ethnicity (including white ethnicities) would undoubtedly enrich our understanding of these differences.

Without considering the significance of North American TV culture *per se* but nevertheless looking at televisual representations of black African-Caribbean and African-American cultures and identities in general, Angela Barry (1988) noted some important changes. Prior to the 1970s, three myths dominated the screen, although it should be stressed that the myths themselves had been around in other popular cultural forms (advertisements, magazines, posters, etc.) long before television technology, in some cases pre-dating their first television screen appearance by at least half a century and sometimes a lot longer (see e.g. Pieterse, 1992).

First, black people appeared on television primarily as 'entertainers', thus reinforcing a myth dating back to renaissance drama (Fryer, 1984). Barry notes that the first TV programme ever broadcast in the UK, in 1936, was *Buck and Bubbles*. Both characters were black and described as 'versatile comedians who dance, play the piano, sing and cross chat'. Since then there have been numerous black performers, including Nat King Cole, Harry Belafonte and Cy Grant. Later programmes like *Jazz 625*, *Top of the Pops*, *Ready Steady Go* included black artists. Barry's use of the term 'myth' here is not meant to imply that black people did not entertain but that the preponderance of black entertainers served to define and hence to restrict black culture, that is to limit its capacity to those prescribed roles. Black sportspeople are entertainers of a different kind, but entertainment in all its forms fits easily into centuries-old biological arguments, in which black identity was associated with physical prowess and other 'natural' physical abilities, leaving white cultures to monopolise mental achievements.

The second set of representations revolved around constructions of 'The Third World' and the role of dependency cultivated through what has been described as the 'coup, war, famine syndrome' of reporting. Images of starving children have appeared regularly on British television since the Nigerian civil war in the mid-1960s. The dependent child visually and symbolically reinforces the idea of Africa as childlike and dependent on the mother country. I shall return to these particular forms of representation in Chapter 6.

Finally, the myth of the black as troublemaker was born, in television terms, in the street conflicts of Nottingham and Notting Hill in 1958 and continued through into the 1970s with the moral panic about mugging. Stuart Hall *et al.* (1978) have explored how the state, notably government, the police and the media, reinforced one another's constructions of the problem of law and order. The latter became synonymous with black street crime, mugging in particular. Mugging, a populist and evocative term borrowed from the United States, had no status in criminal law. Although some research has been carried out on the press, little attention has been paid to the role television played in sensationalising the so-called street 'riots' of the 1980s and how this coverage helped to consolidate the myth of the black law-breaker. I shall come back to Barry's argument shortly but here I want to devote some space to one of the most important figures of post-war race relations, whose views took centre stage in the late 1960s and 1970s in television coverage of immigration: Enoch Powell.

Of all his well-documented and reported interventions on race, Enoch Powell's most significant, a landmark in terms of media history in British race relations, was his Birmingham speech of 1968. In it, he attacked the race relations bill which sought to tighten up anti-discrimination laws. He argued that the only way to tackle discrimination was to stop immigration and warned of the impact of the presence of black immigrants in his constituency in Wolverhampton. (When Powell referred to immigrants, he, and the majority of others, including legislators, meant black immigrants. It is worth noting that his speech coincided with talk of further immigration from Kenya.) He spoke of the inevitability of conflict if immigration continued and put forward a vision of the future with funeral pyres and rivers flowing with blood. To support his predictions, he threw in a few unsubstantiated anecdotes of constituents who claimed to have had excreta pushed through their letterboxes by black immigrants.

Such was the media's take-up of Powell's speech that 96 per cent of the UK's adult population was aware of its contents within a matter of days of its reporting (cited in Cashmore and Troyna, 1983: 212). The speech was significant for three reasons. First it challenged the unwritten liberal consensus that the media would not debate race in such sensationalist and inflammatory terms. Powell's speech broke that consensus. In doing so, it did something else: it set the agenda for future discussions about race around what Stuart Hall has called a racist chain of meaning. This chain began with immigration and the numbers of black immigrants, and then moved on to the problems created as a result of black immigration – overcrowding, unemployment, moral decline and so on – and finally arrived at solutions, aimed at reducing the numbers, through tighter immigration control and repatriation. This racist line of reasoning, or racist logic as Hall describes it, helped set the national agenda on race in Britain for over two decades. A series of clips taken from BBC Television's *Question of Immigration* and used, subsequently, in BBC2's *It Ain't Half Racist Mum* (Open Door series, 1979), clearly showed how the debate was framed almost entirely around Powell's arguments and how participants were invited, cajoled and in some cases harassed into responding in the terms set by Powell and the chairperson, Robin Day (see also Hall, 1981a).

The myths of entertainer, dependant and troublemaker around which Barry organises her discussion can be witnessed in a variety of television genres apart from those already mentioned. Comedy is one example. The common response of professionals to allegations of racial bias in comedy is that it's just good fun. If anything, they have argued, drawing attention to stereotypes in a light-hearted way can bring different communities closer together (reported in BBC's *The Black and White Media Show*, 1988). Alf Garnett, perhaps the most famous racist role in comedy (BBC's *Till Death Us Do Part*, first broadcast in 1966), has been defended by his creator Johnny Speight on the grounds that we, the television audience, are invited to laugh *at* the bigot and his racism, not *with* him. There are some important questions here. How are audiences invited to relate to the comedy, in terms of both the comic characters and their jokes? Are they laughing at the racists or the racist jokes? Are they laughing at themselves or at the object of the racist jokes? Is it just innocent and/or do we risk trivialising the whole case against racism by focusing on comedy? Or, again, is it that its apparent innocence provides a more subtle source of racist legitimations? Stuart Hall has argued convincingly that television entertainment is not just important on its own but in the way that it conditions what we see in factual programmes.

One group who would clearly disagree with the view that humour is neutral are TV's advertisers. They have seen how the clipped mini-narrative form of the advert lends itself to the use of stereotypical humour. Adverts are highly condensed, compressed narratives that often employ mystificatory and mythologising representations of 'other' from Germans to Japanese to flat-capped Yorkshireman, to Sikh Elvis look-alikes. Their potential lies in their ability to communicate a variety of messages in a short period of time. Judith Williamson's study of advertisements aimed to unpack what appears on the screen, that is signifiers, to reveal their hidden meaning, the signified. To date, little work has been done to apply this process of decoding to unpack the hidden racial structures and messages behind television advertising. It is easy to underestimate or overlook the importance of these brief, seemingly innocuous and harmless interludes in TV viewing (Williamson, 1978).

To emphasise this last point I shall take an example of an advertisement, for Southern Comfort, which was shown at cinemas and on television in 1990–1 and again in 1993. It is another mini-narrative, set in the deep south of the United States with echoes of a bygone age (of plantations and paddle steamers). It follows a night in the life of a young white male from 'the country' who, having put the final touches to his appearance, gets driven into town to 'the city', where he meets his 'date' (a black woman). After spending the evening drinking (Southern Comfort, of course) and dancing, they end up on the riverside with a passing steamship in the background, with his arm around her shoulder and the accompanying caption, 'Who are you mixing it with?' At one level, the advert could appear quite challenging. The 'mixing', which the advert promotes, appears to transgress traditional barriers against interracial relationships as well as urban/rural divisions. The mixing of black and white urban and rural appeals, superficially at least, to an apparent universalism, beyond the particularities of race and class.

There are other messages, however, concealed in the advert's narrative form. Its white, male character, for example, dominates both the action and the other characters from beginning to end. In narrative terms the advert is all about his night. His smooth, groomed white appearance (as he is driven into town on the back of an open truck) sets him apart from the black onlookers who eye him with envy and suspicion. At the bar, he inhabits a white male fantasy world: meeting up with an attractive black woman, drinking Southern Comfort, dancing and, at the end of the evening, on the riverside, looking nostalgically across at the passing steamship with his arm protectively and romantically around his partner.

The 'you' being hailed in the caption 'Who are *you* mixing it with?' is clearly white and male. The dominance and centrality of the white male character in the action virtually secures that the caption will be read this way. No one else has an active role to play. The black female character is only 'mixing it' in response to his initiative, hence her limited capacity to hail. The ambiguity of the term 'mixing' in the caption connects the ordering of the drink with the idea of white masculine control and possession of both his partner and, more broadly, the black community. It is the white male, after all, who has transport, clothes and style. It costs money to mix it. Mixing means drinks and it means sex. It means men doing 'it' to women. Mixing also implies difference. The differences/contrasts on which the advert plays ultimately serve to undermine any initial appeal to universalism. In the context of the deep south, with its historical connotations, the advert plays on themes of desire, taboo and possession; on the sexuality of white male slave-owners and their black female slaves.

While Barry recognises that many of the above myths have not been eliminated altogether from television,[6] she does want to acknowledge the emergence of important and conscious attempts to challenge these assemblies of stereotypes. For instance, *Love Thy Neighbour*, a situation comedy first screened in the 1970s, showed black people who were not singing, starving or thieving. Both *The Fosters* (a situation comedy) and *Empire Road* (a drama series) attempted to promote non-stereotypical, apolitical roles using an all-black cast. The same can be said of the more recent US *Cosby Show* and *Desmond's*. Against the accusations of blandness and tokenism (Daniels, 1992), these programmes, particularly the early examples, not only challenged stereotypical representations but began to promote a new class of black (African-Caribbean) actors and writers.

Thanks to pressure from anti-racist organisations and groups, the uprisings in the 1980s, institutional pressure from the Commission for Racial Equality and the legal framework laid down by the 1976 Race Relations Act, the period from the 1970s onwards has seen a growing number of programmes aimed specifically at the black community: *Eastern Eye, Ebony* and *Black on Black.* There has been an increasing number of programmes dealing with racism and racial discrimination in a variety of institutional settings, for example on council estates, in schools and in the criminal justice system. Documentary histories have been made about migrations and emigrations, protest movements, black lesbian and gay sexuality and masculinity, the role of black women in political movements and their involvement in community groups. However, these oppositional forms should be examined more closely before any conclusive assessment is reached. The fact that they are growing in number and high in quality should not hide the fact that these programmes account for a small part of the total amount of broadcasting time. Scheduling is another important factor here. Many of them have been shown late at night, and/or on channels which normally attract lower ratings, that is Channel 4 and BBC2.

The issue of minority programming has continued to be an object of controversy and debate. On the one hand, such programmes have been accused of being over-ambitious as well as ghettoising and of being divisive in their effects. On the other they have been seen to provide a route into the mainstream for black producers as well as an opportunity to document black struggles. They were at least, it was argued, a foot in the door. Subsequently, the policy of commissioning independent productions, initially by Channel 4 from 1982 and, later, by the BBC, helped to promote the work of black writers, including Hanif Kureishi and Caryl Phillips and production companies out of which have emerged highly acclaimed series like *Birthrights* (see Pines, 1992). Ironically, in the case of Kureishi, although his work was promoted out of an attempt to target black writers and production companies, his own work is critical of such boundaries. In both *My Beautiful Laundrette* (1984) and *The Buddha of Suburbia* (1990; televised 1993) Kureishi consciously sets out to transgress traditional racial/ethnic divisions and to create multi-dimensional characters whose gender, sexuality and class play an equally important part in their sense of themselves and their relationships to others.

Television soaps vary in the ways in which they address issues of 'race', both in terms of plot and characterisation. *EastEnders*, for example, consciously uses story lines to educate its audience (about 18 million in 1993) in issues of concern to black people (again almost exclusively of African-Caribbean and south Asian background), as well as to challenge stereotypical assumptions. This contrasts with other soap dramas, in which the cast is all white, for example the Australian soap *Neighbours*, or the American *Dallas*.[7] In Australia it would not seem out of place to meet people of Aboriginal, South East Asian origin. It would in Ramsay Street. Like people with disabilities, they are notable for their absence or the brevity of their appearances in *Neighbours*. Other soaps rely on de-racialising their characters, by ignoring issues of difference. *Brookside* at one time fell into this category but in the early 1990s has included cases of racial and sexual harassment within its plot lines, although not, arguably, to the point where the audience was expected to think about the black characters, in an exclusive or essentialist way, as 'carriers of race'.

There are arguments for and against racialised forms of representation. On the one hand, it is important to represent black people not just as carriers of sickle cell or bound by an arranged marriage: there is more to being black and living in Britain than this. On the other hand, to ignore the significance of being black and/or British, female and so on is almost worse. When this happens, potentially rich and complex forms of characterisation built around different identities (sub-cultural, gendered, as well as black British) give way to assimilated, non-problematic roles. One obvious solution is to include much larger black casts playing a diversity of roles, expressing positive forms of identity as well as acknowledging the continuing significance of racially imposed identities and corresponding forms of resistance. *EastEnders*, which is the most cited example, is a long way from this. Its black African-Caribbean and south Asian families and characters have always been marginal to mainline plots, have rarely stayed long enough to establish themselves as central and authoritative, and have often been used disproportionately to develop 'racial' issues and story lines built around their social problems (Daniels and Gerson, 1989). On the other hand, if it were not for the map of London's East End at the beginning of each programme, it could easily be forgotten that Albert Square is situated in an area where racial attacks are a daily routine and where the British National Party won its first seat, on Tower Hamlets Council.

The foregoing discussion is premised on the assumption that television does affect its viewers in some way. There are two ways of thinking about effects. One is the idea referred to above that television is innocent, that it merely reports events in the world at large or, when it is entertaining, entertaining is all that it is doing. In his writing on the media, Stuart Hall has argued that TV plays an important role in the formation and orchestration of public opinion. In the Open Door programme, *It Ain't Half Racist Mum*, which was shown, late at night, on BBC2, Stuart Hall and Maggie Steed demonstrated the importance selection and context played in inviting potentially quite conflicting responses in viewers. Who is chosen to be interviewed, how the questions are framed, the tone and manner of the interviewer, the views to which the interviewer or chairperson defers or takes as the 'middle ground', all make a difference. The following were used to illustrate these processes at work: an interview with a member of the Ku-Klux-Klan,[8] who was given a chance to give a message to the people of Britain; an interview with Martin Webster, a leading figure in far right politics and finally, the pivotal role given to Enoch Powell in the studio debate on immigration referred to above. The views of these and other people were made respectable by the way in which the programme was presented, by whom and in what context. As an audience, we are nudged towards this interpretation or that, depending on how we are addressed and how the facts are presented.

The idea that programmes let the facts speak for themselves, and that intelligent viewers make up their own minds, avoids the thorny reality that television cannot but take a stance and that this bias is evident from the highest to the lowest levels of decision-making within broadcasting institutions. Decisions not to intervene are as, if not more, significant as decisions actively to take a position. The refusal to comment on racist chanting at football matches to a television audience, many of whom will share those prejudices, is tantamount to saying that such behaviour does not really matter. Notions of 'balance' or equivalence assume that the sides were even to begin with, and/or that the choice we are being invited to make is a fair one and that such choices can be made without reference to the kinds of historical contexts of racism discussed earlier in this chapter.

In addition to this more qualitative research, survey-based findings support these arguments. In the early 1970s Hartmann and Husband found that media-derived ideas about minority groups in the UK were more conducive to the development of hostility towards them than to acceptance (Hartmann and Husband, 1974). Another piece of research carried out by Kemelfield evaluated the positive effects of TV schools programmes concerned with children from other cultures. The impact of these programmes was measured on a group of 9–12-year-olds. The author concluded that the programmes did indeed make a difference, helping to reduce stereotypes, but more so in predominantly white areas (cited ibid.). This finding raises important questions about television audiences; their backgrounds, how they watch television and with whom. All these factors, which have become of increasing interest in cultural studies of the media, have a potential bearing on our understanding of the ways in which racisms and ethnicities are constructed, confirmed and challenged through television.

The above discussion confirms that, despite its significance, television is an undeveloped area of research in terms of racial representations, institutional access and audience studies. Attempts to look more closely at particular periods in TV history and relate these to wider discourses on race are in their early stages (Daniels, 1993). Studies of black issues on TV have tended to focus almost exclusively, in the British context, on African-Caribbeans and south Asians. While in one sense this is understandable, it has meant that other ethnicities have consistently been overlooked. Moreover, whilst the issue of under-representation of black and ethnic minorities in front of and behind the cameras remains and research is beginning to bear fruit, the displacement of traditional ethnic/racial forms of representation, for example in the work of Hanif Kureishi, makes talking about under-representation (under-representation of whom and representations of what?) highly problematic.

CONCLUSIONS

A number of important themes have emerged from this chapter and I will attempt to summarise them here. The chapter had several aims, the first of which was to examine representations of 'race' and the meanings attached to them, in terms of various features of their context. The 'Fear and Fantasy' exhibition offered a good example of how racist texts, seemingly only capable of communicating racist forms of representation, could, in a different setting, with accompanying commentary and black voices, be used to challenge their own racism. The same texts can elicit dominant and oppositional meanings, confirming that ideas of 'race' are always contingent and relative, shifting and shiftable, capable of working this way and being reworked in that.

Context also helps to explain responses to the publication of Salman Rushdie's *Satanic Verses*. The attack on fundamentalism, the revival of assimilationism in the late 1980s and the defence of liberal freedoms not only provoked an escalation of racial violence but helped to construct unities within the Muslim community where there were clearly differences, for instance between generations and religious groups and around gender. Women Against Fundamentalism acknowledged these differences and took the opportunities provided by the affair and, subsequently, the Gulf War, to publicly attack patriarchal forms within the Muslim community.

Class also played a significant part in the unfolding of events surrounding the publication of *The Satanic Verses*. In some ways what was being defended were the class privileges of the bourgeois intellectual, irrespective of ethnic background. The liberal defence of the novel, Rushdie's own view of his rights as an author over the collective rights of Muslims, cannot be understood fully without reference to class. In this respect, Robert Miles' concern to provide space to consider the articulations of race with class is well illustrated in the Rushdie affair. Each of these terms on its own offers a partial explanation, at best, of the reactions to, and effects of, the book's publication.

Contexts often have a global dimension, and the Gulf War provided an important example of how existing Orientalist discourses were reworked in a

41

context provoked by a set of international political and economic conditions and the 'interests' (for example relating to oil prices and political survival) constructed and fought over. Discourses of 'otherness' thus lie semi-dormant only to be revived at opportune historical moments. Bernal's analysis of the wider historical conditions which gave rise to the Aryan model is extremely relevant here. The media played a crucial role in the reworking of these old themes. Articles on the 'Arab mind' appeared replete with all the old stereo-types. Saddam himself both personified these traits and at the same time was widely regarded as a demonic version of the Arab personality. Sudden concern for Arab women became the focus of a number of articles attacking patriarchal oppression, which sometimes indulged in the exoticised myths of 'Oriental' sexuality or otherwise concentrated on the repressions of purdah, child brides and the harem culture.

Opposition was effectively marginalised in both the Rushdie affair and the Gulf War. Said's work provides an excellent backcloth and framework against which to make sense of both events and the forms of representation associated with them. Racist discourses played an important role here, and their articula-tion with nationalist themes undermined opposition still further. In the case of *The Satanic Verses*, a consensus (based very much on Orientalist themes) was established virtually across the political spectrum. Against a background of defending hallowed western freedoms and calls on Muslims to assimilate or repatriate, opposition to this consensus appeared almost treacherous. Likewise, opposition to the war in the Gulf, including attempts to identify the West's real motives for military aggression, or concerns expressed about defending Kuwait, with its record on human rights abuses, met with charges of treachery. Support for the war was secured through intense media pressure that highlighted Iraqi iniquities (once again in Orientalist terms) as much as it hid alternative versions of events.

'Race' has saturated culture in every sense in which the latter has been defined. This chapter began with eighteenth-century art and Renaissance drama and ended with contemporary television soap drama. Culture has also been used to refer to lived experience and the workings of institutions in addition to texts. Shifts in televisual representations have been detected over the last fifteen or so years, ironically at a time when nationalist and racist discourses have dominated much contemporary debate. Once again context is important here, and broadcasting institutions have their own histories of 'race', in urgent need of investigation. At the same time, it is important to acknowledge some powerful continuities, reworkings of old racist themes in new televisual forms, not least of which is the continuing near exclusion of non-whites at all levels of cultural production in broadcasting. In Part II I shall look more closely at institutions: not those most commonly associated with producing culture, for example the press or television, but institutions never-theless still very bound up with producing cultures of race.

Part II

INSTITUTIONAL SITES

3

'THERE'S NO PLACE LIKE HOMEPLACE': RACISM, ETHNICITY AND THE FAMILY

The aim of this part of the book is to examine some key social institutions, both as sites of contested interpretations of race and ethnicity and, relatedly, as mechanisms for structuring very real and, between groups, widely divergent, lived experiences. The three social institutions of the family, education and work shape our lives in significant ways in terms of identity, cultural allegiances and material conditions. I shall look at the ways in which all three have become the focus of political struggle. There are definite cultural processes involved in defining the norms of these institutions. How these are established, contested, defined and redefined, by whom and with what consequences, are the core questions to be addressed over the next three chapters.

The first section of this chapter will examine dominant white constructions of the black family in terms of what Patricia Hill Collins calls 'controlling images'. These effectively pathologise all cultural deviations from what is assumed to be the (white Eurocentric) norm. These 'pathologies', however, differ for specific ethnicities and it is important to acknowledge the different racisms at work here. Moreover, these public, pathologised versions and even the dominant 'norm' of the white nuclear family bear little resemblance to family relations as they are lived out. In other words, the variety of family forms exists independently of those dominant racist forms of representation. I will use evidence primarily from African-American, African-Caribbean and south Asian families in this chapter. This largely reflects the state of research to date, although the bias should not be understood to preclude other ethnicities. On the contrary, in the British case there is a lot of work to be done on less 'visible' ethnic groups, for example the Chinese and Irish communities. I shall use the term 'black' to refer to those who have been both the object of racist constructions of the family and the subject of alternative cultural forms, but I will also refer to specific ethnicities, including white ethnicity, as the particular context demands.

The reliance on the work of African-American feminists reflects the importance of their contribution to our understanding of racism and its relationship to the family. Whilst there are some connections between the US and the UK, both in terms of the African diaspora and, at another level, through the sharing of knowledge of research and policy initiatives on the family, it is important to recognise the problem of extrapolating from one to the other, given the specificities of their respective histories. In other words, we cannot assume that cultural representations of the black family in the US will necessarily be institutionally inscribed in British social policy. I have thus attempted to draw on work from the US, not so much at an empirical level, but to provide an apparatus of concepts and ideas which can be used to organise and make sense of the British context.

In Chapter 2 I looked at a variety of cultural processes underpinning the construction of 'white' racist thought. Within the latter, a particularly decisive cultural strategy in dominant constructions of family forms, and one which will recur in subsequent chapters, is that of *naturalisation*. Most notable in this respect is the yardstick of a nuclear family, that is a white heterosexual couple with children, against which all other family arrangements are measured. The imposition of this benchmark, even in the face of changing demographic family patterns (Worsley, 1987: 155), serves to culturally disconnect and undermine any alternative to the so-called norm. The nuclear family, with all its heterosexual, marital, reproductive trappings, becomes a 'natural' way to live. Any other way, including lone parent families, lesbian or gay relationships, non-marital partnerships, childless couples, extended families under one roof and singles, appears somehow deviant, backward and destructive: in a word, unnatural (Barrett and McIntosh, 1982: 34ff.).

Of course, the attribution of these characteristics to black families has not gone uncontested. The negative associations have been directly challenged and alternative family forms have been defended as positive, legitimate and a source of community strength rather than a pathological source of societal breakdown. Although cultural assaults on the black family have implicated both black men and women, it has mainly fallen to women to counter these and find alternative ways of making sense of gender relations and family culture within the black community. Hence much of the work in this chapter draws on what may be described, broadly, as black feminist thinking, with the proviso that this body of work contains many diverse and sometimes conflicting strands. Whilst it is true, in principle, that families are about men as much as they are about women, historically women have taken greater responsibilities in the sphere of domestic work, including child care, and have been at the forefront of struggles against forms of domestic oppression. This point applies equally to the case studies developed later in this chapter. So although both fostering/adoption and domestic violence have obvious male dimensions to them, there remains a strong case for drawing on the work of feminists and looking, particularly, at the role of women in this chapter.

The second and third sections move beyond the realm of conflicting representations, since these battles should not be isolated from their institutional context. One of my main aims here is to show how cultures of race are inscribed in, and contested on, institutional terrains. The effects of these inscriptions and struggles are profound and immediate. They affect all manner of family arrangements. In this chapter I will illustrate these effects with reference to the debates surrounding the fostering and adoption of black children and the issue of domestic violence. I will highlight the significant role played by the state, through its institutions, especially those of local government, which have helped to shape lived culture in very marked ways by providing an important terrain of struggle on which issues of child care and domestic violence have been contested and experienced. The tendering of state services to the private sector, on an ever-increasing scale, has provided an important backdrop to the more specific developments described below. The Croydon adoption case will show the media's role in 'naturalising' certain relationships over others and of constructing a common sense which is used to simplify and polarise interpretations of such issues, in this case around 'love' on the one hand and 'race' on the other.

My choice of fostering and adoption and then domestic violence may appear more arbitrary than it is, although a recurrent argument in this book is the possibility, actually the necessity, of extending the examples and issues explored here. I have decided to focus on fostering and adoption for three reasons: its policy focus; the centrality of the question of cultural identity; and Paul Gilroy's important contribution to the debate (1987: ch. 2) which enables the discussion to be related to broader themes in the book as a whole. The issue of domestic violence was chosen not only because it provides an excellent example of state racism but also, thanks to the work of Amina Mama (1989a, 1989b), because it illustrates the way in which women have mobilised around this issue on the basis of their gender, ethnicity and, at other times, in terms of their black identities. Running through this chapter is the central question of identity. The examples confirm the need to think about identity in complex, shifting and contextual terms, rather than in abstract, absolutist formulations.

CONTROLLING IMAGES, CONTESTATIONS

In this section I am concerned with dominant forms of representing black families with particular reference to the role of black women. In some cases these representations have been resisted and contested. In others, the alleged pathologies of alternative forms of family life and gender have been, on the contrary, defended and celebrated. I shall begin by looking at various features of the wider political and historical context in which dominant culture has defined itself through constructions of otherness, in this case with reference to other family and gendered forms. I shall then look at the ways in which black feminists have challenged these dominant representations, including struggles aimed at dominant patriarchal forms within their own communities. The risk entailed here, of prioritising gender over anti-racist struggles, has become an important focus of political debate and will be discussed with reference to the writings of African-American feminists and the organisation Women Against Fundamentalism (WAF), already referred to in Chapter 2. White feminist traditions have also developed their own representations and interpretations of patriarchy and the role of the family, some of which have been challenged by black feminists who have sought to establish the ethnic and/or racial specificity of their experience. I shall consider these before looking, finally, at attempts by black lesbians and gays to contest racially specific forms of homophobia, create alternative family forms and to develop strategies around their racial, gendered and sexual identities.

Not for the first time, in July 1993 Conservative politicians brought the family into the media spotlight with an attack on lone parents, or more specifically single mothers, whose numbers were allegedly increasing at great cost to the state. In a two-page spread, the *Daily Mail* asked, 'Who is to blame?' Each of the columnists offered their own explanations which included feminism, the welfare state, the mothers themselves and the fathers (6 July 1993). The assumption running through the debate, of course, was that whatever the explanation, lone parenthood was the problem. This was the latest in a series of public statements from the1970s onwards associated with the political culture of the new right. The promotion of the family, or at least a particular version of it, fitted extremely well into the new right's peculiar mix of neo-liberal economic policies and traditional conservatism. According to Ferdinand Mount:

> The family as we know it – small, two generation, nuclear, based on choice and affection. . . is neither a novelty nor the product of unique historical forces. The way most people live today is the way most people have always preferred to live when they have had the chance.
>
> (1982: 153)

What was being propagated here was the idea of the nuclear family as some kind of universal absolute, or intrinsic cultural form. Anything else, according to Mount, had either been a figment of historians' or social scientists' imaginations or imposed against people's implied natural instincts. Moreover, developments in new reproductive technologies and debates surrounding parental rights over their children's sex education and access to contraception each provided further opportunities to strengthen the position of the nuclear family.[1] Meanwhile, 'alternative' families were materially penalised as well as culturally ostracised in the 1980s as a result of Conservative policies relating to tax credits, unemployment and child benefits (David, 1986).

Against a historical background which goes back much further than the 1980s, black families have come to symbolise and epitomise the threat to the nuclear family norm. Alleged differences in family size, variations on the traditional gendered parenting roles and religious differences as they affected family practices, have all fed into and off a well-established reservoir of racist discourses which held black families responsible for a variety of social ills including educational failure, civil disturbance (in the 1980s) and, in the case of the south Asian families, child brides, runaway brides and suicides. Whilst the arguments relied on implied and explicit notions of cultural inferiority, alleged biological differences (for example in sexuality and intelligence) have never been far from the surface of debate. In the late 1960s, a psychometrician in the United States, Arthur Jensen, dismissed the idea of compensatory education on the grounds that social engineering could not redress biological inequalities between black and white (Jensen, 1969). His views were subsequently echoed by a British psychologist, Hans Eysenck, who supported the notion of innate racial inferiority.

Just as support for the nuclear family was bound up with a critique of attempts to transcend traditional gender roles, so attempts to blame black families (using biological or cultural arguments), have gone hand in hand with pathologising black women. Patricia Hill Collins (1990) uses the idea of 'controlling images' of black womanhood to indicate the powerful effects of these dominant constructions. She identifies four such images of black women: the mammy, the welfare mother, the matriarch and the Jezebel. The images are both contradictory and, at the same time, mutually reinforcing. For instance, the image of the mammy, that is the black woman as paid domestic servant, conflicts with the welfare mother who can afford not to work, thanks to state benefits. These images were not only contradictory but misrepresentative of women's roles. Although 'uncle Tom and Sambo have always found faithful companions in Aunt Jemima and the Black Mammy' (Davis,1981: 5), the mammy stereotype bore little resemblance to the outdoor plantation work undertaken by most black women under slavery.

These ideas are well illustrated in a fascinating account of the 1991 case of Anita Hill, a black law professor in the United States, who brought charges of sexual harassment against Clarence Thomas, a black nominee to the Supreme Court. According to Wahneema Lubiano (1992), Hill's failure to win the case can be understood in terms of the mobilisation of two narratives (read 'controlling images'), of the 'welfare queen' and the 'black lady' (corresponding to Collins' 'welfare mother' and 'matriarch'). On the one hand there was Emma Mae Martin, Thomas' sister (the 'welfare queen') whom he had publicly mocked for 'getting mad when the mailman was late with her welfare check' (Marable,1992: 65),[2] and Hill herself, embodying the 'black lady' overachiever, whose success, with that of other black women, brought about collapse of black patriarchy and the breakdown of the black family. Between these two narratives stood Thomas himself, the embodiment of a self-made man; the walking antithesis of welfarism and dependency culture. Small wonder, given the possibility of mobilising such tropes on his behalf, that opinion inside and outside the hearings swung in Thomas' favour.

A central theme of the influential Moynihan Report, published in the US in 1965,[3] was the idea that black women were forced into paid work because of the absence of the male breadwinner and then failed to provide adequate maternal care for their children.[4] Once again, according to Angela Davis, this had little to do with historical fact. In practice, the black family adapted in extremely subtle and sophisticated ways to the coercive and repressive slave system. To prove this point, Angela Davis cites Herbert Gutman's study, *The Black Family under Slavery and Freedom* (1976): 'It was not the infamous matriarchal family he discovered, but rather one involving wife, husband, children and frequently other relatives, as well as adoptive kin' (Davis, 1981: 14). Slavery also provided an important historical context for the emergence of the Jezebel image. This image, associated with promiscuity and sexual aggressiveness, gave white slave-owners a rationale for sexual violence against black slave women (Collins, 1990: 77). In common with the other 'controlling images' the objectification of black women under slavery was thus integrally tied to the need for a highly disciplined, repressed and reproductive slave work-force.

The image of the matriarch has played a particularly important role, not only in the way that it was used by Moynihan as evidence of social breakdown within the black community, but also in its effects on black gender relations from the 1960s onwards. In her analysis of the black liberation struggles of the 1960s, Michele Wallace talks about an implicit agreement that black women would not challenge black patriarchal forms in order to prioritise their shared struggle against racism. However, Wallace maintains that:

> the black man has not really kept his part of the bargain they made when she agreed to keep her mouth shut in the sixties. When she stood by silently as he became a 'man' she assumed that he would subsequently grant her her long overdue 'womanhood'. . . . But he did not.
>
> (1979:14)

She goes on to attribute the failure of the black movement in the 1960s to the failure by black men to wage struggle with the full involvement of black women (ibid.: 81). Black women like Alice Walker, Michele Wallace and Patricia Hill Collins have broken the silence and begun to challenge forms of black masculinity dominant in the 1960s and endorsed by black leaders like Malcolm X, Eldridge Cleaver and Stokely Carmichael. In her novel *The Color Purple* (1982), Alice Walker was one of the first black writers to confront sexual abuse within the black community through her portrayal of Mister's relationship with Celie.

Michele Wallace and other feminists' criticisms of gender relations and representations of women in the films of Spike Lee form another example of 'going public' on patriarchy. On the one hand Wallace acknowledges the potential dangers of focusing on gender questions in Lee's films, given their ground-breaking achievements in other respects. Nevertheless, she argues that it is not only desirable to look at gender but inevitable, given the inseparability of gender and race. You cannot deal with one without the other. According to Wallace:

Films like *Do the Right Thing* about racism entirely miss their mark, they re-inscribe the very thing they aim to dislocate, when they trivialise or deny the importance of women's oppression in general and the problems of black women in particular. Moreover, to do so makes no sense in terms of the material reality of representations of 'race' in American culture, which has always been profoundly entangled with issues of gender, sexuality and the female body.

(ibid.:109)

The idea that black women have subordinated struggles against patriarchal forms within their own communities to the struggle against racism, is not peculiar to African-American or African-Caribbean women. I have already looked at this issue in the context of the Rushdie affair, when the whole south Asian, not just Muslim, community, felt under attack, as a result of which it became harder for feminists to challenge religious fundamentalism within their own community. 'Women are expected to submerge their own interests to uphold the. . . anti-racist tradition' (Sahgal and Yuval-Davis, 1990: 35). Nevertheless, Women Against Fundamentalism (WAF) did use the affair to highlight their oppression under Islam. In Chapter 2 I referred to questions of calculation and strategy involved here. A related issue which serves to illustrate the complexity of these relationships and strategic priorities has been that of separate Muslim schools. In opposing such schools, black women have targeted and prioritised patriarchal oppression within the Islamic community.[5] However, such were the complex political configurations of the debate that their opponents on this issue included not only Islamic as well as Powellite separatists, but also supporters of multiculturalism and cultural diversity, including the Commission for Racial Equality (1990). On the other hand, they were joined in their opposition to such schools by those who advocated cultural assimilation and who denied the significance of racism. The paradoxes, here, can only be understood with reference to the articulation of the politics of gender with well established battle lines in the politics of race.

So the political context in which allegiances to gender and/or race are forged is all important here. Bell hooks takes a different view to some of those authors referred to above when she talks about the potential dangers of creating negative images of black men without taking account of how these images relate to context, form, audience and experience. As hooks explains:

While I do not share the assumption that contemporary Black women writers maliciously create negative images of Black masculinity, it is true that whenever these images appear in their work they risk appropriation by the popular racist white imagination.

(hooks, 1991: 71)

Angela Davis develops a similar point in 'The Myth of the Black Rapist' (in Davis, 1981), which I shall refer to later in this chapter. For black organisations like WAF, those risks have been calculated, and the dangers are outweighed by the potential gains in terms of gender relations.

In contrast to these dominant constructions of black families and black women in particular, there exist many alternative forms of black femininity. The very existence of organisations like WAF is indicative of alternative political cultures as well as potential differences within and between south Asian women. However, these alternatives often remain suppressed under the weight of all-pervasive stereotypes. Nevertheless, powerful images of women marching, protesting, publicly speaking out against fundamentalism have served to demystify prevalent representations of south Asian women as passive, exotic and accepting of their repressed and subordinate roles. The assumption that south Asian women are prevented from leaving the home is challenged by the significant role Asian women play in the work-force, although variations depend on religious differences as well as the economic and demographic character of an area, which also helps to structure job opportunities and affects both the degree of participation and the kinds of jobs available. The most striking examples, so to speak, of an active Asian female work-force have been illustrated in work-place struggles, at Grunwick, Chics and other factories (see Ramdin, 1987 and Fryer,1984). More recently, in 1992, there began a struggle by south Asian women to unionise at Burnsalls, a West Midlands factory in Smethwick, in order to resist low pay, forced overtime and flagrant violations of health and safety regulations. The dispute, still unresolved a year later, came to symbolise a wider struggle against sweatshop conditions.

Beyond the work-place, in popular culture, unidimensional representations of south Asian women have been contested and displaced in Gurinder Chadha's film, *Bhaji on the Beach* (1993). Age, friendship networks, political outlook and country of birth all helped to define a complex and varied range of British south Asian identities. A day trip to Blackpool (a pointedly, English, working-class custom) organised by the Asian Women's Centre in Birmingham, provided the setting for the story lines to develop as well as expressing a range of outlooks and experiences (some shared, others conflicting) represented by the different characters: a lone parent, two teenage women, a pregnant student, a visitor from India and the feminist organiser of the trip. The film did not attempt to offer easy solutions to the issues (including abortion, domestic violence and arranged marriage, racist violence, intergenerational differences) it raised. On the contrary, the strategies pursued reflected the complexity of the situations they confronted. These were partly dictated by family expectations, personal ambitions and emotional ties as well as a wider sense of attachment (or otherwise) to Britain.

Despite these realities, the 'white racist imagination' has seized on aspects of south Asian culture and, in so doing, has emphasised its backwardness (and by implication the 'forwardness' of the West), with particular reference to the subordinate role of women. Arranged marriages, bride prices, child brides, suttee, have all received media attention in ways which feed into the general ethnocentrism of the media's predominantly white audiences. Deploring 'otherness' helps to define 'us' as superior. For example, the idea of an arranged marriage, the forms of which vary widely, where partners are selected and negotiated over by families and sometimes go-betweens, and where the young people themselves are given varying degrees of say, is compared unfavourably (explicitly or by implication) with the assumed freedom of choice governing 'western marriages'. In practice, arranged marriages constitute an alternative to western forms of mate selection. According to Parmar, they not only vary in the form and degrees of 'arrangement' but, more importantly, are an accepted and preferred alternative for many Asian women (Centre for Contemporary Cultural Studies,1982). Many, if not all, of these subtleties and preferences are lost on western commentators, who invoke the term 'culture conflict' to describe the experience of young Asian women growing up in Britain: conflict, that is to say, between 'western' 'freedoms' and 'eastern' oppression. These forms of representing and constructing differences are compatible in form, if not in content, with Edward Said's analysis of Orientalist discourse discussed in Chapter 2.

There have been some important challenges to these western-influenced notions of 'freedom'. Earlier I referred to some in the context of debates provoked by the publication of *Satanic Verses*. Hazel Carby has also challenged western notions of freedom, with reference to female adolescence. She cites an Asian schoolgirl who asks, 'where is the freedom in going to a disco, frightened in case no boy fancies you, no one asks you to dance or your friends are walked home with boys and you have to walk home in the dark alone' (1982: 216). This quote challenges a number of 'freedoms' that are commonly taken for granted in the West, but which are themselves circumscribed by considerations such as the availability of places to meet, the threat of sexual abuse and harassment, as well as culturally loaded notions of physical attractiveness. At each stage here, the roles women play are heavily reliant on the dominant roles played by men. The more the West has preoccupied itself with the lack of freedoms associated with other cultures, the more oblivious it has been to the limits of its own.

Attacks on gender relations and family relationships in non-western cultures invariably use a nuclear family with heterosexual, monogamous marriage partners and their biological children as their yardstick. So the assumption that black African-Caribbean families are invariably broken, that is, headed by single parents, implies some alternative idyllic state of an unbroken marital relationship. The suggestion that black women head these households and do so by combining paid work outside the home with domestic and child-rearing responsibilities inside, relates to a further stereotypical assumption, again expressed in the Moynihan Report referred to above, that working women make poor mothers. While these attitudes prevail for white women too, in the case of black women they take on a particular

significance which relates to the racially specific nature of dominant controlling images of black women and the pathology of the black family. (For a
further critique of these myths see Parmar, 1982.)

Differences between white and African-Caribbean families in Britain un-
questionably exist, but more important are the interpretations of such
differences, and the inconsistencies in institutional response and support. Of
particular significance here are the ways some family practices are regarded
as the hallmark of success, and hence institutionally supported, while others
are socially frowned on as well as under-resourced and undermined in a
myriad of ways. Cultural and institutional reactions to women in paid work
and lone parents are obvious examples. Twice as many African-Caribbean
women are in paid work as white women and 31per cent of African-Caribbean
families are single parents compared to 10 per cent of whites (Phoenix,1988).
Black women not only suffer disproportionately from general inadequacies in
child care provision and support for lone working parents. The specificity of
the threat to them is compounded by the inscription of racially specific
controlling images into institutional practices.

So far in this section I have examined various dominant constructions of
the black woman and the black family alongside a range of black feminist
responses and alternatives. The question of conflicting identities or allegiances
around gender and race has been an important feature of this discussion. In
one final arena of debate, in which racial allegiance has been prioritised over
gender, a number of black feminists have defended the family, in opposition
to white feminist critiques of the nuclear family. Hazel Carby and Pratibha
Parmar in Britain, and bell hooks and Angela Davis in the United States, have
challenged traditional feminist arguments on three counts.

First they have questioned the commonly held view amongst feminists that
the family is, by definition, a site of oppression for women. This argument has
been widely supported within feminism (see for example Barrett and
McIntosh, 1982). In contrast to these arguments, which view families as sites
of abuse, oppression and psychiatric disturbance for both women and children, many black women view the family as an institution which provides an
important source of collective support against the daily experience of racism.
Bell hooks talks about the black family as providing private space 'where we
do not directly encounter white racist aggression' (1991: 47). She also recalls
how her own family, or the 'homeplace', as she refers to it, played a crucial
part in her development: 'I would not be writing this essay if my mother, Rosa
Bell, daughter to Sarah Oldham, grandmother to bell hooks, had not created
the homeplace in this liberatory way' (ibid.: 45–6). Patricia Hill Collins, whose
analysis is by no means identical to that of hooks, agrees with her on this point.
Although she openly recognises the contradictory aspects of the institution of
black motherhood, she also acknowledges its potentially empowering role for
black women. In their roles as mothers and 'community other mothers' (taking
on a motherhood role for black children in general), black women have

provided an important haven and alternative institutional source of support for their family (1990:115ff.).

Second, black feminists have argued that reproductive rights, especially forms of birth control, have distinct meanings for black women. For white western feminists, these issues are part of a wider agenda enabling women to control their own lives. Decisions about child bearing in the context of a society with inadequate child care facilities and continuing pressure for women to take responsibility for child rearing has made reproduction a key site for feminist struggles. However, for black women, the testing of contraceptives like Depo Provera as well as the sterilisation programmes on Third World women carried out by multinational drug companies in collusion with governments and right-wing pressure groups, have made these same issues objects of oppression rather than liberation. The failure of western feminism to acknowledge this is seen by black feminism as a feature of its Eurocentricity. As Angela Davis points out, the histories of birth control and abortion rights were different for black and white women. For black women, birth control is associated more with involuntary sterilisation. In the US, in the years up to the decriminalisation of abortion in 1973, 80 per cent of abortion-related deaths were of African and Puerto Rican women (Davis, 1981: 203ff.). I shall return to this issue in Chapter 6.

Finally, there are the specificities that have arisen in the politics of black sexuality which have broadened the concerns of feminism and gender politics. In contesting heterosexist norms of the nuclear family, black lesbians and gays experience a further form of oppression, homophobia, both within and outside the black community. According to some black writers, heterosexism is more of a problem in the black community than it is in the white community. For example, Barbara Smith argues that the specific problem of homophobia within the black community results from the need to defend the only 'privilege', i.e. 'straightness', open to black people (cited in Collins, op cit: 194). Another idea, suggested by June Jordan, is that for many black men, lesbianism is part of the wider threat of feminism and the two are seen as linked (cited ibid.: 195). Whatever truth there is in the view that black culture is more homophobic than white, it is important to acknowledge the role played by Eurocentric thought in propagating nuclear family norms across the empire and the West's role in the destruction of indigenous lesbian cultural forms. Pratibha Parmar's film *Kush* powerfully illustrates this point with reference to Indian culture.

Lesbian and gay families and networks have provided an important source of confidence and support for those for whom homophobia is a daily experience. (Smith cited ibid.: 193). So, too, has the writing of black American authors, like Toni Morrison and Alice Walker (Carmen *et al.*, 1987: 241). Struggles around sexuality have called for autonomous groups but they have also benefited from alliances between different groups. The existence of racism within the gay and feminist communities and heterosexism in the black community has called for multiple levels of struggle, on the one hand focused autonomously on sexuality, race and gender, whilst on the other providing a shared political base where relationships between forms of oppression have been discussed and common strategies have been developed. The following is a description of one such group of black lesbian and gay union activists. It underlines the view expressed by one of the participants that 'autonomy is fundamental but so is unity'. They go on:

It was the [Union] Equal Opportunities Group which cut through all the contradictions. The comradeship, energy, and commitment of the core of the Working Party, comprising as it did a lot of very different people, was an example of the possibilities of uniting diverse interests and oppressions to the mutual advantage of all concerned, including man-agement.

(Arhens *et al.*, 1988: 140)

A similar point is made by Tamara:

For some of us, our sexuality doesn't mean that we have the luxury of organising as lesbian separatists, nor do I believe in doing so. So while my sexuality is a part of me, it's not the only thing. My race and class are equally important and this has an implication for the way I organise, or want to organise politically.

(Carmen *et al.*, 1987: 224)

The black family has thus proved both a site for patriarchal oppression and a crucial site for organising, subverting and resisting (hooks, 1991: 48). Moreover, it has to be understood in terms of its relationships with other institutional sites of struggle. A whole mythology has built up around African-American, African-Caribbean and south Asian families and the roles of women in particular. These myths have been challenged by black women in a variety of ways: questioning patriarchal forms within black communities, taking a leading role in industrial action, re-interpreting and defending the black family against attacks by some white feminists, working within autonomous groups organised around gender, race and sexuality, as well as forging alliances when the time seems strategically right to do so. What appear conflicting loyalties, allegiances and identities are much more explicable when put in the context of particular debates and struggles.

SOCIAL POLICY AND THE DEBATE SURROUNDING 'RACIAL MATCHING'

Family myths do not exist in an institutional vacuum. State institutions, through the law, policy initiatives, and the role played by agencies (the DSS, for example), provide a crucial framework which helps to define what a family is, and the relationships, obligations and rights of its members in ways which

can fundamentally alter the course of their lives. I shall illustrate these relationships with reference to the issue of fostering and adoption and the debate
surrounding the placement of black children with black parents. The use of
the term 'black' to describe these placements will become clearer in the course
of the discussion. The practice has also been termed 'racial matching' or 'same
race placements'.

In the summer of 1989, a story hit the headlines of the national press
concerning the case of a seventeen-month-old boy, of mixed race, who had
been brought up by a white foster mother. When she applied to adopt the
child, Croydon Council rejected her application and decided, instead, to place
the child with black foster parents. The white mother appealed but the court
upheld the Council's decision. This case illustrates some of the complexities
surrounding the issue of 'racial matching' in fostering and adoption, as well as
the role of the press in highlighting such issues, selecting the terms of debate
and nudging readers towards particular viewpoints. In the next section I shall
look at domestic violence, with particular reference to the work of Amina
Mama.

Overall, both of these examples, which can be thought about in terms of
social policy, highlight the connections between controlling images of black
women and black families, on the one hand, and institutional racism on the
other. The discussion of 'controlling images' above drew mainly on evidence
from the United States and the African-American family. Whilst the British
context offers somewhat different dominant images, for example in the case
of families of south Asian origin, there are also some important continuities.
The images of mammy, welfare mother, matriarch and Jezebel have found
their way into British discourse via popular film, education debates (surrounding under-achievement) and applied social science. Both popular
representations of the family, and institutional debates on fostering and
adoption and the policy terrains on which they are lived out, offer important
sites for resistance and contestation.

There are many important lines of discussion not pursued here: the assumptions underpinning and practices associated with the adoption of 'Third World'
babies, for example, including the regular advertising campaigns which provide scope for western families to 'adopt' an African child for a nominal sum.
Elsewhere, press reports from El Salvador and Guatemala in Central America
have confirmed the sale of babies for adoption into western families as well
as for pornography and prostitution and, in some cases, as part of a growing
trade in human organs (*Observer*, 26 September 1993). Likewise the campaign
to encourage western families to adopt Romanian babies in the wake of the
collapse of the communist regime is also worth exploring. In both cases the
idea of adoption enables white western capitalism to reaffirm its sense of
global superiority and benevolence over other (by implication) backward
parts of the world.

However, the focus of this discussion is the debate surrounding the adoption and fostering of children of ethnic minority background within the UK, primarily those of African-Caribbean and south Asian origin. The origins of the debate go back to the 1960s when the number of black children placed in care was increasing for a number of reasons, partly because local authorities had difficulties placing them in foster or adoptive homes. Black children were not alone in this respect. Other 'hard to place children' included children with physical and mental handicaps and sibling groups, thus forging an important common-sense link between race and disability in this context. Initially, the response to the problem of non-placement of disproportionate numbers of black children in care was to actively seek out white parents to foster or adopt. One organisation, the Independent Adoption Service, played a major role in recruiting parents for black and other 'hard to place' children. In seeking white parents for black children, statutory and non-statutory agencies held the prevalent assumption that the sooner that young black people were assimi- lated into mainstream British life, the better (not unlike the assumptions underpinning the adoption of East European and Third World babies). Mean- while, the problem of the disproportionate numbers of black children in care was commonly explained, with the help of reports like Moynihan, in terms of deficiencies specific to the black family, drawing on themes of matriarchy and black sexuality.

These assumptions were contested from the outset and counter-demands were made to increase the numbers of black adoptive parents and thus the opportunities for black children to be placed with black parents. Pressure came from the black community including, but not only, black social workers; research evidence, which highlighted problems associated with transracial adoption and, finally, initiatives like the dubiously titled 'Soul Kids' Campaign in London in the early 1970s. The latter aimed to educate black families about the needs of black children in care and to recruit substitute black parents (Arnold and James, 1989: 417).

The research evidence used to support racial matching (and hence to challenge transracial adoption/fostering) can be summarised briefly with reference to two main arguments. The first is based on the idea that black children need black parents in order to grow up with a positive sense of themselves. Studies concluded that young children, both black and white, internalise notions of black inferiority at a very early age. One pioneering test, which has been repeated many times, was carried out in the late 1940s by two black psychologists in the US, Kenneth and Mamie Clark. In it, a group of black children were given black and white dolls and then asked to choose, first, which doll they preferred and, second, which doll looked most like them. Results showed that half preferred the white doll, whilst a third also thought that the white doll looked most like them. One conclusion drawn from the test was that black children needed black role models/parents in order to develop a clear and positive sense of their own identity. The placing of black children with white foster and adoptive parents, it was argued, only interfered with the construction of positive black identity and, on the contrary, could well lead to a negative self-image and self-denial (cited in Tizard and Phoenix, 1989: 429).

Some of these arguments have been illustrated in autobiographical accounts of women of 'mixed race' background. Gail Lewis (1985), for example, writes about growing up in London in the 1950s: her mother's side of the family was white, her father's black. One of the most enduring impressions made by her account is of the importance of her black family to her, not just in terms of music, food, hair care and other features of black culture, but equally the support she received from her father's family as she encountered racism and sexual abuse, not just from outsiders, but also from within her mother's immediate family. Another young woman, Yvon Guest, was brought up by white foster parents until the age of fourteen. Like Gail Lewis, her biological father was black, her mother white. She grew up in a family environment in which racist jokes were common and racial discrimination not unknown. She was actively discouraged from thinking about herself as black and from associating with other black children on the grounds that she was better than them. The racism underpinning this sort of pressure encouraged her to see only one escape, to become as closely attached to white culture as possible (*Guardian,* 28 August 1989).

Research drawing on a larger sample has confirmed that white adoptive parents usually do not discuss issues of race with black children and also hold stereotypical views themselves. In a study carried out by Barbara Tizard (who is not herself an advocate of racial matching), the white mother of a mixed race adopted child told the interviewer:

> there are just certain traits in his character which are definitely the traits of a coloured person. There's his lack of concentration. Also, he'll suddenly switch off if he thinks you're going to tell him off. . . this is a thing the coloured races do – one notices these little things.
>
> (cited in Bagley and Young, 1981: 89)

The second set of arguments for 'racial matching' have to be put in the context of an under-representation of black foster and adoptive parents and the over-representation of black children in statutory care. Behind these disparities lies the philosophy of assimilation which dominated the overall response to post-war black immigration, including policies concerned with the family. The idea was that black children with white parents, or transracial adoption/fostering, would create a melting pot of races, as long, that is, as the white indigenous British culture remained dominant. In practice, assimilation really meant the subordination, if not elimination, of minority cultures, since no attempt was made to acknowledge, or make provision in response to, cultural differences between majority and minority groups.

Assimilation thus meant that that little effort was made to recruit black adoptive or foster parents. Consequently, the predominance of white parents was secured through the maintenance of existing policies and procedures without any explicit reference to 'race'. Racist ideas surrounding the black family undoubtedly underpinned and strengthened the case for assimilation, but from an institutional point of view these could be well hidden. Whilst cultural racisms underpin institutional practices, they may not be that visible in the day-to-day running of social work departments. Instead, the maintenance of discriminatory practices (discriminatory in terms of their consequences, in this case fewer black foster parents) appears on the surface to be a function of the maintenance of existing customs and practices rather than overtly discriminatory policies and practices. What has been referred to as 'colour blindness', that is treating everyone the same irrespective of colour, is also used to justify the maintenance of policies and practices which are anything but equal in terms of their effects. As a result, racism does not have to be formally built into official institutional policies and practices. It operates beneath the surface, manifesting itself in overt forms in the discretionary decision-making power of officials and the assumptions, insofar as they are made explicit, which continue to influence those decisions.

This last point begs a brief return to Robert Miles' arguments sketched out in Chapter 2, in which he seeks to restrict institutional racism to those instances where an explicit racial discourse is present. Institutional racism, according to Miles, should not be defined in terms of the effects or consequences of policies and practices, unless they can be linked back to an explicit system of racialised significations. The problem with this position, as the issue of fostering and adoption bears out, is more strategic than conceptual. While it seems entirely appropriate to restrict institutional racism in the way Miles suggests, it limits a potential political response in two ways. In the first place 'colour blindness', by definition, denotes the absence of a racial discourse, and yet its maintenance, in the face of continuing evidence of disadvantage and inequality, could well be sanctioned by a racial discourse which never surfaces in institutional terms. Does this mean that such features of institutional culture remain outside the parameters of the study of institutional racism?

Furthermore, the absence of positive initiatives (e.g. targeted advertising) could be partly responsible for the under-representation of black parents. Yet again the absence of an explicit racial discourse would mean that, in Miles' terms, this problem falls outside the concerns of anti-racist politics. If this were the case, then an important feature of anti-racist struggle, its concern with measurable outcomes as well as racist ideologies, would have been unjustifiably removed from its agenda, for reasons of conceptual precision and clarity. I shall attempt to show the importance of maintaining what Miles refers to as the inflated concept of institutional racism (that is, one which accommodates discriminatory effects that may or may not be tied to a racially explicit discourse) in what follows.

The argument for 'racial matching', I have suggested, has been part of a broader struggle against inequalities of condition and treatment, for both black children and would-be parents. One of the best ways to illustrate both cultural and institutional forms of racism is actually to examine attempts to challenge them. The New Black Families Project (1980–4), a campaign which sought to increase the numbers of black foster and adoptive parents, provides one such example.

The project's aim could only be achieved by calling into question and overturning the web of institutional rules and practices governing the recruitment of foster parents. This entailed, amongst other changes, redefining the (nuclear family based) criteria for selecting suitable parents. Single women and older parents with grown-up children were now considered potentially eligible for adoption and fostering, with the result that the numbers of black parents increased. Policy changes of this kind had a knock-on effect in challenging conventional cultural wisdom regarding who or what constitutes a suitable family for adoption. To return again to Miles' argument, the nuclear family may or may not be a racist construct (some would define it as Eurocentric) but it took an anti-racist strategy and project to contest its assumptions. The increase in the number of black parents also strengthened the idea that black children may benefit from having the support of black people and black culture as they grow up in a racist environment.

The project challenged the assumption that black people were just not interested in fostering and adoption. This assumption had helped to maintain existing advertising and recruitment procedures. As it turned out, changes in publicity, as well as application procedures, brought an increase in the number of black parents. In developing recruitment practices, the project made links with black churches, which became a significant resource for finding new parents (Arnold and James, 1989: 421).

Finally, the presence of black workers on the project helped to allay the misgivings and mistrust that had previously contributed to a high drop-out rate amongst black applicants. Of particular concern here had been the procedure of taking up police references. Overall, a closer, more sustained and more equal relationship between black liaison workers and parents and, whenever possible, the speeding up of the process, helped to increase the numbers of parents who successfully survived the application/vetting procedure. Overall, the effects of the project confirm the strategic benefits of working with the notion of institutional racism to tackle problems of under-representation, exclusion and discrimination, irrespective of whether these can be explicitly tied to a racialised discourse.

The case for racial matching has been part of a struggle against cultural and institutional forms of racism in social work and, beyond, in the wider cultural realm where family norms are defined and reinforced via numerous other institutional means. On the other side of the debate, the case against racial matching has produced some forceful arguments of its own and I shall come back to these in the light of the issues arising from the well-publicised adoption case in Croydon, in 1989.

Many of the ideas and debates addressed in this chapter can be explored with reference to the 1989 case (mentioned on p. 57). To recap: the white foster mother of the seventeen-month-old mixed race boy had her application to adopt him rejected and the child was eventually placed, instead, with a black family; later in the same year, the case was taken to the Court of Appeal, which found in favour of Croydon Council's decision. The ruling provoked what can best be described as a heated response in the press, both from journalists and, judging by the correspondence columns, their readers. The manner in which events and decisions were represented in both tabloid and broadsheet dailies arguably provoked a discussion and a range of opinion from a restricted and oversimplified range of options.

One of the most important themes to emerge from this above coverage was the interpretation of the Council's decision to place the child with black parents. Both the *Guardian* (25 August 1989) and the *Daily Mail* (24 and 25 August 1989), not often found sharing the same ideological bed, saw the decision as a straightforward choice between 'love' and 'race'. Framed in this way, it is hardly surprising that both papers found the local council and the court guilty of sacrificing a relationship based on love for one based on the principle of racial matching. The latter policy, which was derided as 'fashionable' by one reader, demonstrates a continuity of thinking between positions taken here and more general and widespread attacks on anti-racist initiatives during the latter part of the 1980s. 'Anti, anti-racism' grew throughout the decade as local authorities sought to challenge institutionalised racism both in their employment policies and in their delivery of services.

One common strand of this attack on anti-racism was that it allegedly interfered with people's freedom or, in this case, imposed the label 'black' on a situation in which people were acting out of love and humanity. The *Guardian* summarised the consensus amongst its readers' letters with the headline, 'Why love not colour must be the route to happiness' (28 August 1989). Presented in this way, it is hardly surprising that correspondents, in the main, opposed the Council's decision when it was presented to them as a victory for the 'unnatural' and socially engineered category of 'race' over the most 'natural' of human characteristics, love.

A second theme picked up in the coverage was the alleged separatism implied in the decision. The press were interestingly divided on this issue. Predictable, perhaps, was the charge that same-race placements helped to create black ghettos. It is easy to see how support for the white foster mother's application could form part of a wider commitment to the idea of a cultural melting pot, in which the interests of black children would best be served through integration (or rather assimilation, given the dominant role that white parents, supported by the wider culture, have always played in mixed-family relationships). This latter scenario appears much less threatening than the promotion of cultural differences through policies of racial matching.

However, not all the press, or even the tabloid press, rejected the idea of separatism. The *Sun*, in a leader headline 'The Right Choice', supported the decision on the grounds that to 'any child black, brown, white or yellow, his own cultural background is a precious legacy' (25 August 1989). This apparent deviation might be attributed to a more general tension running through political discourse on race and nationality and is reflected here in the different positions taken by the *Daily Mail* and the *Sun*. On the one hand, according to the *Daily Mail*, British identity is possible for black people, but only at a price, that of assimilation and the denial of black identity. The Conservative Party's 1983 election poster showing a young Anglicised black man with the slogan, 'Labour Says He's Black, Tories Say He's British', is a good example of this 'call to assimilate' (cited in Gilroy, 1987: 58).

On the other hand – and this is the line of argument advanced by the *Sun* on this occasion – assimilation is unworkable due to the intrinsic cultural differences between black and white. Separatism and repatriation are common themes of new right discourse; hence the support of the far right for Muslim calls for separate schools referred to above and, in this instance, separate homes for separate cultures. It is worth noting how both sides of this debate appealed to 'nature' to give legitimacy to their arguments. The 'natural' bonds of love and humanity were invoked to oppose Croydon's decision, while 'natural' differences between 'Black. . . Chinese and English' were used by the *Sun* to support it.

These two strands of thinking have been well summed up in Russell Lewis's book *Anti-Racism: a Mania Exposed* (1988), the introduction to which was written by Enoch Powell. Running through the book is Lewis's argument that assimilation (and certainly not anti-racism) is the solution to racial conflict. In contrast, in his introduction, Powell rejects assimilation as a realistic prospect and paints a much less optimistic scenario, in which he openly disagrees with the author on the future prospects for racial peace. It is worth observing that this tension is not just evident between different newspapers but surfaces within them from time to time. For example, just over a year after the Croydon case, the *Sun* ran a short article supporting the views of a black Conservative prospective parliamentary candidate, Lurline Champagnie, when she described herself as English, not black (29 October 1990). The relationship between British and black identity is at the core of the *Sun*'s problem. Should black people see themselves as black rather than British, or British rather than black? In neither case, it is worth noting, were 'black' and 'British' seen as part of the same identity.

The third point regarding the coverage of the case relates to the accuracy of the information initially released, and its impact on the subsequent framing of the dispute. In fact, on the day that *Guardian* readers were writing to the newspaper, deploring the sacrifice of love for the sake of a bigoted policy of racial matching, it was revealed (on the back page) that the decision by the Council had been taken not on grounds of race alone, but also on the suitability of the white mother as an adoptive parent. Other factors taken into consideration had been the size of her house (she already had five children), the fact that she was a single parent and that her common law husband was in prison (*Guardian*, 28 August 1989).

This belated revelation is important for two reasons. First, it shows how the *Guardian*, not generally noted for its sensationalist news coverage, encouraged an over-simplified, polarised response to the Council's decision in the way that it initially covered the story. Second, the other 'circumstances' which the Council took account of in reaching its decision confirm its attachment to a family norm from which, in this case, a white family deviated, but which, in many instances, prevents black people from becoming adoptive parents. The class bias of the Council's decision, which, incidentally, was Conservative controlled, adds a complicating twist to the case. In general, it underlines the need to view family policy in a comprehensive social context, one which includes all facets of disadvantage and potentially discriminatory practices.

It would appear from the evidence so far presented that the case against racial matching has originated within political discourses of the right, ably supported by a cross section of the British press. However, there is a body of evidence which does not rely on the kind of crude assimilationist position discussed above. For example, the idea of a 'positive black identity' has been challenged by Barbara Tizard and Ann Phoenix. All three terms, they argue, 'positive', 'black' and 'identity', imply fixed states of being which hardly match the complex, dynamic and messy reality which goes to shape how we see ourselves (1989: 433–5). Linked to this is the question of mixed race children and the category into which they should be placed. Ann Wilson (1987) suggests that they should not be seen as black or white but are a sufficiently viable group to warrant a category of their own. The very idea of a black British identity creates real problems for those seeking to base a policy of racial matching on some hard and fast distinction.

Barbara Tizard and Ann Phoenix's more recent study of young people of mixed parentage develops a number of these ideas (1993). Their findings confirmed that the young people's 'black' identity was linked to holding politicised views about racism rather than the colour of their parents, whilst a white identity was linked to friendship networks. A mixed identity was as positive as a black identity (ibid.: 174). Moreover, only half the parents gave advice on dealing with racism and encouraged young people to be proud of their black ancestry. Significantly, as many white as black parents offered such encouragement, a fact the authors also attributed to the holding of an anti-racist perspective rather than to skin colour (ibid.: 175). These findings appear to question the twin assumptions that only black identities can be positive and that only black parents can instil positive black awareness and related strategies for dealing with racism. One important conclusion to be drawn from this study is the need to analyse racial identities in terms of anti-racist perspectives rather than as a state of consciousness linked intrinsically to skin colour.

Elsewhere, there is further evidence to counter the argument that black children brought up in white environments lack self-esteem. Research carried out by Gill and Jackson (1983) suggested that although transracially adopted children's contact with black children was low, their self-esteem remained high. The problem posed by this kind of research is that of isolating all the contributory factors related to esteem, if the significance of parenthood is to be gauged. For example, self-esteem amongst young black people may well have increased since the 1950s, due to black political movements and other expressions of community identity and pride, rather than as a result of family policies on adoption and fostering.

In a debate full of ironies and twists, it is appropriate to conclude by looking at an important argument developed by Paul Gilroy (1987: 64–8). Here, too, it may surprise some to find a black radical writer attacking the principle of placing black children with black families. There are three strands in Gilroy's argument which are worth exploring. The first relates to the origins of the principle of same-race placements, which he attributes to black professional social workers. He argues that it is their contradictory position – working for the state and yet part of an oppressed minority – which is at the root of the principle, and the problem. What same-race adoption does, according to Gilroy, is to allow them to identify with the black community while at the same time serving to legitimise their professional status.

This point would require further research to confirm but it is by no means certain that the concerns expressed over issues of children in care and fostering have been the preoccupation only of black social workers. Black parents and groups, in addition to multiracial community organisations have also been involved. Moreover, those black social workers who have advocated racial matching or any other racially specific measures, far from privileging themselves, have been marginalised, ostracised, passed over for promotion, starved of resources and systematically undermined by dominant 'colour blind' or assimilationist thinking within social work departments. The idea that to advocate racial matching is either some easy solution to court favour, and/or an attempt to reconcile a seemingly contradictory position, must be questioned.

The second strand has to do with the principle of same-race placements. According to Gilroy, its advocates assume that the whole of self-image and identity is reducible to colour. This collapsing of everything, in this case to do with a child's identity, to some transcendental mystical notion of blackness, is referred to as ethnic absolutism. This is a more strident version of the criticism of 'black' identity by Tizard and Phoenix mentioned above. The critique of the idea of identity as intrinsic or fixed, in this case black identity, lies at the heart of recent poststructuralist contributions to cultural theory.

Stuart Hall (1991b: 47ff.) suggests a number of features of identity, which he particularly associates with theoretical spaces opened up in psychoanalysis and feminism. The first is that identities are always *incomplete*, that is, always in the process of formation. Furthermore, identity means a *process of identification*, constructed through splitting that which one is from that which is the other. At the same time, it is an *ambivalent* process, one compounded by feelings of love and desire. In turn, the impact of this process of defining oneself in terms of otherness acts back on the self. This is what Fanon referred to when he described his reaction to being described as black: exploded and recomposed in the gaze of the other. Third, identity is always based partly on *narrative,* that is on selective representations and stories that help constitute our sense of ourselves (always bearing in mind that these narratives are never told without reference to the other). Fourth, since identities, as a result of the above processes, are constantly slipping, shifting and sliding, *signification depends on a contingent and arbitrary stop.* This is inevitable because, as Hall says, 'you have to be positioned somewhere in order to speak' (ibid.: 51).

This last point is important because it attempts to move beyond the solipsistic versions of poststructuralism which draw on Derrida's discussion of difference and *différance.* It is also important because it ties in with the political debate at the heart of Gilroy's critique. For Gilroy, supporters of same-race adoption have defined identity as intrinsic, static and essential, that is in ways precisely opposite to those characteristics outlined by Hall. However, there is another way of understanding 'racial' matching, which is entirely compatible with Hall's use of identity. According to this view, the use of black identity to underpin the principle of racial matching was not arbitrary but strategic; contingent yes, but calculated on the basis of prevailing conditions, for example the lack of black parents and the over-representation of black children in care. The positioning in terms of black identity allowed these conditions to be recognised and acknowledged. Furthermore, insofar as they still exist, there has to be a strong case for continuing to think in terms of black identity.

To concede this is not to preclude or deny other identities and subjectivities. It is still possible to acknowledge the idea of complex, shifting and multiple identities, any of which may be invoked in differing circumstances. Gail Lewis, for example, not only saw herself in terms of her black identity, but also in terms of her gender, class and sexuality. In other words, black does not have to designate an exclusive or essential identity but can be understood, alongside other sources of identity, in contingent, complex and, above all, strategic terms.

Finally, the third strand of Gilroy's argument sees same-race placements, not only as oversimplifying and reducing complex questions of identity, but also as mirroring the right's (and the new racism's) preoccupation with difference. In other words, the mystical sense of national and racial belonging that Enoch Powell and Peregrine Worsthorne have spoken and written about and which the *Sun* endorsed in its defence of Croydon Council, echoes the arguments for same-race placements. Hence, Gilroy could point to the similarities, both analytical and political, between radical black social workers and community activists and the arguments put forward in the *Sun* to support his critique of same-race placements. The debate has indeed thrown up all kinds of strange alliances, not all of them confined to the advocates of racial matching. On the other side Gilroy himself forges some unlikely alliances. The implications of his argument would be readily accepted, for example, by those advocating assimilation and/or refusing to acknowledge racism.

A central difficulty with Gilroy's argument is that it ignores the political context in which the struggle for same-race placements has been fought. The campaign for racial matching has been shown to be part of a wider political struggle to increase the number of black adoptive parents and to increase the number of black social workers, both of whom are under-represented. It is a strategic struggle in another sense, too, in that it has forced social work agencies to look at their procedures and practices, which have led to the over-representation of black children in care and an under-representation of black parents eligible and willing to adopt. In other words, the campaign has to be seen as part of the struggle against cultural and institutional forms of racism.

To sum up then, critics of racial matching have rightly rejected absolutist notions of black identity which can and have underpinned many of the arguments for racial matching, and, importantly, they have drawn our attention to the complex processes surrounding the construction and multiple sources of cultural identity. That identity cannot be reduced to a simple, singular form was well evidenced in Gail Lewis's autobiography of her younger years in London in the 1950s. However, I have also argued that it is possible to defend racial matching without basing it on an assumption of intrinsic difference between black and white or on absolutist and fixed notions of identity. On the contrary, the principle can be analysed and understood in terms of the relative significance of black in the current political and cultural climate. It follows that once the principle is understood as part of a wider political strategy, arising out of a particular set of circumstances and context, then it is important to base any assessment of it, not on abstract terms, but on the specificities of that context.

DOMESTIC VIOLENCE

As I pointed out at the beginning of this chapter, I have chosen to focus on domestic violence because it can be used to explore the nature of the state's response to the issue, which can be seen to have a specifically racial and ethnic dimension. It also demonstrates the integral relationship between domestic violence against black women and gender relations in general, irrespective of ethnicity. There are also questions of political strategy around the issue, including institutional responses to it, that have been raised by black women. My concern once again in this section will be on cultural representations, state policies and forms of resistance.

Amina Mama's work on domestic violence provides a very powerful analysis in this respect (1989a, 1989b). The significance of her work not only lies in the way that she builds her analysis out of black women's experience of institutional practices and power, but also, through this, in her contribution to our understanding of the relationships between gender, race, class and ethnicity and their implications for political strategies relating to the family. Her analysis, therefore, provides an excellent basis on which to continue to address questions of cultural and political identity.

An important starting point in Mama's work is her acknowledgement of the significance of a wider set of political and cultural changes that have been responsible for shaping the framework of public provision within which black women have experienced the welfare state. Political shifts over the decade of the 1980s increasingly emphasised self-help at the expense of public provision. This was part of the new right's political agenda. During this period state support became increasingly marginal and residual as individuals and markets were deemed to be more efficient means of allocation as well as more effective promoters of freedom of choice. The idea of public provision as a right had always been at odds with the idea of provision as a privilege, so that in the consumer, market-oriented climate of the 1980s, rights were further undermined, nowhere more so than in the case of black people. Consequently, according to Mama, it became a matter of civic duty to keep service departments like housing and social services as empty as possible, especially of black people. Underpinning these practices has been the debate about immigration, referred to in Chapter 2, which has been framed in terms of numbers of black immigrants and reflected in immigration legislation itself, with its denial of entry to those who may seek 'recourse to public funds'.

Second, Mama uses the issue of domestic violence to illustrate the specificities of gender, race and ethnicity. In terms of gender, domestic violence has a long cultural history in Britain which has been enshrined in laws on physical chastisement as well as in folk sayings ('A woman, a spaniel and a walnut tree, the more they are beaten the better they be'; an old English saying c. 1600, cited in Mama, 1989a: 147) and customs, for example the use of the ducking stool and the whip for those women 'who did not know their place' (ibid.: 150). Present law and practice is less explicit and public but legal principles of 'toleration' and 'provocation' are still widely used to condone domestic violence and to discredit and undermine its victims.

There is an important 'race' dimension to gender inequalities. For instance, one important consequence of Thatcherism in the field of housing has been its impact on women who are homeless as a result of leaving situations of domestic violence. Disproportionate numbers of these women have been forced to live in unregulated bed and breakfast accommodation. For black women, however, the waiting lists for alternative accommodation are longer and cases have been known of black women being housed or offered housing in areas known for high levels of racial harassment. Black women thus share a legacy common to women in general, but also have experiences which are specific to them. Their suspicion, not only of housing departments but of the criminal justice system, is often founded on evidence of police indifference as well as outright harassment, not to mention discrimination in the judicial and penal system.

All these factors serve to deter black women from seeking legal solutions to problems of domestic violence (Mama, 1989a: 301). To add to this, some women face the prospect of deportation if they choose to leave a violent domestic situation (1989b: 35). The overall experience of racism across a variety of statutory agencies makes escape that much tougher for black women (ibid.: 37), with the result that some women have chosen to prioritise the struggle against racism over that of domestic violence. In the words of one black writer, 'What's the point of taking on male violence if you haven't dealt with state violence?' (Bryan *et al.*, 1985: 175). This takes us back to the questions of mobilisation and strategy around racism and/or patriarchy discussed above with reference to the family in general, and to the questions of political calculation illustrated with reference to Women Against Fundamentalism.

Some years before Mama's work on domestic violence, Angela Davis commented on the long history of black women's rightful mistrust of the legal system and the wider racist culture in her discussion of the 'myth' of the black rapist (1981: 172ff.). She argued that the myth of black rape was, from the outset, used to justify violence and terror, including lynching, against the black community. Periods in which the black community posed the greatest threat, for example following the Civil War, coincided with the propagation of the myth of the black rapist. Of more concern, but hidden beneath this myth, had been the sexual abuse of black women by white men. Indeed, sexual abuse played an integral part of the repressive regime on the slave plantations. Latterly the white rape of 'Third World' women was tolerated, if not condoned, in the Vietnam War (ibid.: 177). Davis was thus critical of those feminists who, by perpetuating the myth of the black rapist, downplayed the significance of white sexual violence against black women.

Davis's argument suggests a hierarchy of oppressions with racism dominant over patriarchy for black women. Evidence to the contrary has been provided by Gemma Tang Nain who argues that in terms of employment opportunities and work patterns, as well as relationships to domestic labour, black women are closer to white women than they are to black men (1991). Despite black feminist critiques of white feminism, she argues that there is much common ground for gender-based alliances. Some authors have claimed that oppressive domestic labour is common to both black and white women and that white feminists have also underestimated the potentially supportive role that their own families could play (Brittain and Maynard, cited ibid.: 9). In other words, black and white women share more in common than feminists on both sides have suggested. On the specific issue of rape, Nain argues that lynching and contemporary forms of physical violence against women belong to distinct historical periods. In other words, we should not use the myth of the black rapist to conceal the issue of domestic violence in the black community.

Beyond race and gender, there are also specificities based around ethnicity. Cultural stereotypes often relate to specific ethnicities of black women, and these in turn enmesh with public policy and provision in different ways. For instance, Mama argues that statutory provision has been quicker to acknowledge the 'cultural needs' of the Asian community than of African-Caribbean women. Her evidence confirms that funding for Asian refuges has been more forthcoming than for other groups of black women. Moreover, commonly held assumptions regarding south Asian and African-Caribbean communities, and women in particular, have also affected institutional responses. 'If the former are passive, exotic, quiet and inspire paternalism, then the latter are aggressive, promiscuous, violent-like-their-men and more threatening than mysteriously silent' (Mama, 1989b: 43). Furthermore, whilst she concedes that local authorities have been more willing to fund Asian refuges in response to 'cultural needs', she also notes that these refuges have invariably been run by men, both within and outside local authorities.

This discussion of domestic violence highlights the complexity of the relationships between gender, race and ethnicity. Rather than seeing these in any fixed order of priority, as some authors suggest, it seems more appropriate to consider their relative strategic merits in a given context. Implicit in Mama's review of the history of domestic violence is the need of all women, at certain historical moments, to acknowledge a shared experience of domestic violence, and the failure of the state to make an adequate response. In other contexts, black women may need to emphasise their particular experiences of the police, the housing department and other agencies, in order to increase their access to adequate alternative housing and to defend their right to freedom from harassment.

The above discussion suggests that there will be times when black women themselves will want to make demands on the basis of their ethnic backgrounds, partly in response to culturally specific forms of stereotyping within the dominant culture, and partly as a means of expressing their own cultural needs. Mama makes clear that the appropriateness of different mobilising categories depends on the political context, what the issue is and how to pursue it. June Jordan makes this point in an interview with Pratibha Parmar when she says identity and unity mean nothing unless they are linked to a winnable political struggle (Parmar, 1989: 55ff.). It is the relationship between allegiances and identities, on the one hand, and contexts on the other, and the assessment of both in strategic not abstract terms, which is at the root of Jordan's point and implicit throughout Amina Mama's work.

CONCLUSIONS

Throughout this chapter, the 'family' has been defined as the dominant, middle-class white norm, as well as in terms of its alternative, oppositional or 'other' forms. Cultural processes which define white western nuclear families

as the norm end up defining alternative family forms as deviant or pathological. Lone parent families, lesbian and gay relationships with children and black
extended families, all fall into these 'other' categories. As far as African-
Caribbean and Asian families are concerned, these pathological constructions
take on ethnically specific forms which are based on distinct sets of stereotypical assumptions regarding both women and men.

Despite evidence confirming an increase in the numbers of lone parents,
divorce rates and children born outside marriage throughout the 1980s, the
new right persisted in promoting and defending traditional family norms, as
if nothing had changed. This highly selective version of British culture inevitably heightened the sense of 'otherness' experienced by those who lived
outside the alleged norm. This experience was compounded for black
families, who were reminded of their outsider status in numerous other
contexts. Added to this was the depletion of public resources and the privatisation programmes carried out during the 1980s, backed up by the rationale
of self-help and the sovereignty of the consumer and the market-place. The
scope for improved child care arrangements for lone parents, or adequate and
culturally sensitive public provision for the victims of domestic violence, was
thus reduced.

These new market-led conditions did not provide the basis for increased
consumer freedoms and opportunities. On the contrary, markets surrounding
the employment of social and community workers, the selection of adop-
tive/foster parents, are profoundly structured and influenced by an array of
cultural processes and policies. Markets do not operate in a cultural or policy
vacuum: in that sense they are never 'free'. Attempts to suggest that they are
only serve to conceal mechanisms of unequal distribution and access. Adoption and domestic violence provide two examples of how cultural assumptions
articulate with institutional practices to the disadvantage of black parents and
women respectively.

In the case of adoption, the initial tendency to place more black children
in care, the failure of social work departments to recruit more black parents
and assimilationist assumptions underpinning transracial adoption policies,
have all fundamentally affected the lives of black children caught in the care
system and those placed with white families. Whatever the merits of same-race
placements, the struggle for the principle was as much about contesting
dominant, pathologised versions of the black family, as well as the over-
representation of black children in care and the under-representation of black
parents and black social workers, as it was about the matching of black
children with black parents. It is important to see the campaign in these wider
political terms rather than just as a conflict around those promoting mystical
absolutist notions of blackness or ethnicity.

In cases of domestic violence against black women, similar processes are
at work. Prevalent notions of black people in terms of their shared blackness
and in terms of their ethnic particularities, in the context of cutbacks and the

privatisation of public housing all help to shape black women's experience of domestic violence. Bryan's argument that 'if you're a black woman, you've got to begin with racism. Its not a choice, its a necessity' (Bryan *et al.*, 1985: 174) has been the focus of debate within the black feminist movement. However, more recently there has been a growing acknowledgement that the issue of prioritising one struggle over the other is less relevant than the need to prioritise different elements of struggle in different situations. In an interview with Pratibha Parmar, Trinh T. Minh-ha talks about fragmented identities and the need to see these as ways of living with difference rather than turning them into opposites (Parmar and Minh-ha, 1990: 71–2). Black lesbians, whose struggles against homophobia, racism and sexism make for a further level of oppression, fragmentation and allegiance, have also stressed the need to work in different political contexts and not to essentialise any one of them.

This chapter has sought to develop an analysis of the articulation of cultural forms, institutional conditions and political practices, taking the family as its general focus and using case studies to illustrate the complexity of particular connections. The implication of both case studies, of adoption and domestic violence, has been to suggest the inappropriateness of resolving conceptual questions regarding race, ethnicity, gender and sexuality in an institutional vacuum. It is only through an analysis of different institutional contexts that it becomes possible to make sense of, and assess, different political strategies. The rightness or wrongness of the latter cannot be gauged without reference both to political objectives and to specific historical conditions.

4

CONSUMING EDUCATION[1]

Within the broad theme of forms of representation and their inscription in institutional practices, the specific aim of this chapter is to explore the impact of recent educational developments on forms of racial and ethnic demarcation and contestation, developing the theme of the state's promotion of market-place values in the public sector. In education, one consequence of this wider trend has been the construction of new parental identities, defined increasingly in terms of 'consumption'. This represents a step beyond what Claus Offe (1984) suggested when he distinguished consumers from their other roles, for example as voters, workers and family members. Now, through recent educational reforms, parents are being brought directly into the sphere of consumption.

This new political terrain in education has also been the contested site of reconstituted struggles over minority rights, forms of cultural expression and educational racism. Here, parents have not acted as individuals, as their consumer status suggests and, indeed, encourages, but around collective and communal forms of identity. Whilst the idea of a single constituency of parents has served to suppress differences based on ethnicity, race and gender (David, 1993), these latter distinctions have been reasserted and redefined through struggle. The importance of such localised struggles (which, in this case, have served to challenge the universal, yet highly atomised, category of the parent consumer) has been noted by Stuart Hall, when he talks about their importance as counter-movements and forms of resistance (1991b: 61).

With all this talk of parents, the idea that pupils or young people might also be thought of as educational consumers is easily forgotten. Once remembered, the differences between parents and young people in terms of issues of culture, identity and race become an important focus of concern. For example, how different constituencies of parents represent and express cultural needs on the one hand, and how their children, as pupils/students, may express more transient, fluid and displaced forms of 'ethnic' allegiance on the other, is one potential difference to consider. I sometimes use the terms 'black' and 'ethnic

73

minority' together in what follows by way of acknowledging the different identities around which educational struggles have been waged and groups defined. Elsewhere I use one or the other where either has become the main form of mobilisation, expression and definition. In the case of pupils, as it will become clear, neither of these forms of identification will suffice.

Following these general lines of interest, the chapter begins with a discussion of recent policy changes in education with particular reference to the changing status of parents: why, in particular, have parents become the focus of, and stated rationale underpinning, so many recent educational reforms? Government attempts to construct a universal, highly individualistic category of parents, in terms both of cultural uniformity and equality of rights and access have been challenged by black and ethnic minority parents from outside the formal educational system. In the section which follows, I will look at two collective attempts to promote alternative forms of educational provision, through supplementary and community school initiatives and the struggle for separate schools for Muslims. This will be followed by a more detailed case study of a predominantly Muslim school in inner city Birmingham, which opted out of local authority control in 1989. In so doing, it invoked a clause of the 1988 Education Reform Act which, on the face of it, appeared least applicable and suited to black and ethnic minority parents and pupils. To what extent the decision, supported by the majority of parents, has worked for or against their stated interests will be the focus here.

Pupils, like their parents, do not always do what they are told and one of the drawbacks of recent debates is the way they have tended to eclipse some important differences and forms of resistance amongst, arguably, education's real consumers. To conclude this chapter, therefore, I shall illustrate these by looking at the particular significance of Creole and some south Asian languages amongst young people in Britain, and black English in the United States. The use of language, as both a conscious and an unconscious form of resistance and opposition, has also served, in some instances, to challenge traditional forms of ethnic allegiance and identity. How parents, schools and officialdom have responded, or can respond, to such developments is a question left open for debate.

PARENTS AND THE STRUGGLE FOR A NEW EDUCATION CONSENSUS

Conservative educational policy during the 1980s mirrored reforms in other areas of social policy. Thatcherism's wider political project, aimed at rolling back the public sector (albeit on a selective basis) and disempowering local Labour councils, was skilfully executed through a combination of legal sanctions and more subtle cultural means. Strategically, this project entailed building an alliance between central government and groups of 'new consumers'. Hence the gradual 'empowerment' of parents throughout the 1980s coincided with a set of reforms designed to reduce the formal powers of local education authorities and teachers. I shall return to the apparent contradictions implied here shortly, but in specific terms this entailed increasing parental participation on governing bodies and the strengthening of the powers of the latter through the delegation of financial management and the control over school budgets; spelling out parents' rights to information; open enrolment which, nominally at least, increases parental choice of school, and finally, the right to opt out of local authority control. Steven Ball has suggested that recent policy has been a massive experiment, concerned less with education than with markets (Ball, 1990: 1).

The background to attempts to incorporate parents into the formal apparatus of educational management can be seen to date back to the late 1960s and 1970s. The social democratic consensus, dominant in the 1950s and 1960s, was associated with a commitment to equal opportunity, the ending of selection and the principle of comprehensive schooling. However, from the late 1960s and 1970s onwards, this broad agreement, which included an acceptance of existing power relations in education, became the object of a protracted attack. This was mounted by a powerful bloc of political and educational pressure groups committed to the return of selection, the expansion of the private sector, reinforcement of traditional teaching methods and a re-drawing of political boundaries in education. Their projected allies in the struggle for a new educational hegemony were parents. In his analysis of these changes, Ken Jones suggests that a key element was a shift in the meanings attached to parents from the idea of a single parental constituency committed to equality of opportunity and state-funded comprehensives, to a view of parents as individuals and, in particular, consumers. Associated with these new consumer identities were to be notions of variety, choice and self-respect (1989: 49).

One extremely influential landmark in the history of these developments was the crisis at William Tyndale School in Islington, in 1976–7. In their attempts to develop radical forms of pedagogy and practice at the school, the headteacher and some of his staff lost the support of parents and the educational establishment. Their teaching practices were also opposed by a minority of vocal staff dissenters at the school. The fracas, which was reported widely in the national media, eventually became the subject of the Auld Committee of inquiry and led to the dismissal of the head and his supporters. Events at Tyndale were used, both at the time and subsequently, to mobilise and give prominence to those views expressed in the Black Papers, which had been demanding greater parental involvement and central control of education from the late 1960s onwards (CCCS, 1981: 200ff.).[2] By way of making the connections between Tyndale and more recent reforms, Anthony Flew, a key spokesperson on the right, speculated on the difference that open enrolment (a key principle of the 1988 Reform Act) would have made, had it been adopted in the mid-1970s:

Suppose. . . that the parents in William Tyndale ha[d] the. . . legal right
to withdraw their children, taking them to some other institution perceived as superior, and that every such withdrawal [was] immediately
followed by a substantial transfer of funds to that preferred alternative.

(1987: 100–1)

In other words, open enrolment would have either brought about Tyndale's
closure through lack of pupil take-up, and hence resources, or it would have
forced the school's management to change its ways to make it more responsive
to market demand.

In a European-wide study of parent participation, Nicholas Beattie (1985)
has also attempted to make sense of these changes. He stresses the important role that initiatives on parental participation have played in helping to legitimise changes imposed by central government. This, he argues, was true in
Germany in the period immediately following World War II, in France and
Italy in the aftermath of the political protests of 1968 and in England and Wales
in the 1980s (Beattie, 1985: 229). This would appear to give only partial support
to Miriam David's argument that government support for parental participation
can be understood largely as an attempt to win popular support for measures
designed to make education better tailored to the demands of the economy
(David, 1980). In Beattie's account, political crises play a more significant, if
not independent, role in provoking an interest in parental participation.

Such has been the growing importance of parents in this struggle for a new
educational consensus that one writer, Philip Brown, has characterised the
recent period in terms of the emergence of a parentocracy which, he argues,
has superseded the idea of meritocracy. It is no coincidence, he argues, that
the idea of parentocracy grew from the 1970s onwards, at a time of high youth
unemployment, concern about educational standards and the failure of state
education to secure equality of opportunity. The shift in responsibility for
education from government to parents took place in the context of a wider
crisis of political legitimacy (Brown, 1990).

The idea of a parentocracy, however, serves to conceal some important
conflicting tendencies in recent educational reforms. Hence, in contrast to the
principle of parental power, the elements of which aim to devolve power from
the centre, the national curriculum attempts to centralise control. For Richard
Johnson, this seeming contradiction, ironically, is the key to understanding the
popularity of Margaret Thatcher's Conservative governments in the 1980s.
These two strands reflect the two dominant themes of the new right: the
emphasis on the parent as educational market-place consumer, embodied in
neo-liberal values, and the emphasis on traditional conservatism, reflected in
the national curriculum.

The reconciliation of these two strands rests on the twin assumption that
the state is both the source of (public) oppression and the guarantor of
(private) freedom. Proposals and reforms across a range of public sector

services, including health, housing and, in a different way, welfare benefits, as well as education, have been designed to promote a culture of enterprise, within a centrally controlled framework. The case for such reforms rests on the following assumptions: that they give consumers greater freedom of choice; that they make the public sector more cost conscious and accountable for what it spends;[3] that they encourage a spirit of conscious activity rather than passive dependency, and that the terms and conditions within which these policy areas operate, including their levels of spending, are the responsibility of central government.

The changing significance attached to parents has been part of a wider climate of cultural change which characterised the 1980s and in which social constituencies based on gender, class and ethnicity were denied in order to reaffirm identities based on national belonging, family status or simply the individual (Johnson, 1989). Parents, in their role as consumers, have been encouraged to act as individuals and discouraged from thinking about the social consequences of their actions, for example in terms of the distribution of resources between schools within their locality (ibid.). The denial of social inequalities has had the serious effect of trivialising everyday oppressions or robbing them of remedy (Johnson, 1991: 101). The shift to 'market accountability', as Stuart Ranson (1988) calls it, has been attacked for the limits it sets on local democratic control. The aim of such manoeuvres, according to Richard Johnson, would appear to be to do away with politics in education and turn it into economics (Johnson, 1989). The construction of parent identities around educational consumption as well as family leadership has had the further effect of hiding social oppressions around race and ethnicity (in addition to those linked to gender, disability and sexuality).

To sum up the discussion so far, parents, at least nominally, appear to have emerged empowered as a result of policies designed to re-draw political boundaries in education and thereby to build a new educational consensus. The background to these changes has been a concerted attempt by Conservative governments and their political allies to break up the old political order in education based, at least in their judgement, on non-accountable, bureaucratic, state monopolies. The latter were held responsible for eliminating choice, reducing educational standards and turning parents into passive recipients of public provision rather than active citizens. These views were propagated in a steady stream of publications from the late 1960s onwards, including the Black Papers, the *Salisbury Review*, *The Times*, those of the Adam Smith Institute and the Hillgate Group, as well as being disseminated in books and at conferences, for example those organised by the National Council for Educational Standards. Now, as a result of the successful impact of this political pressure and the legal changes that have resulted, parents have direct responsibility for the hiring and firing of teachers, for spending school budgets and for matters concerned with the curriculum, via their representation on governing bodies. If they are unhappy with the way the national curriculum is being introduced they now have the right, at least in principle, to appeal to their local education authority and, if enough of them so wish, to 'opt out' of local authority control.

The limits of these powers in practice, their subordination to market-place economics and the denials of collective social experience that new consumer identities imply, will now be explored in more detail with reference to the role and potential role of black and ethnic minority parents and the general implications of the 1988 Education Reform Act for black pupils and students. These limits have been the focus of a growing number of articles, all of which foresee potential disadvantages for black and ethnic minority parents and pupils (Ouseley, 1988; Troyna, 1990; Hardy and Vielar-Porter, 1992). I shall summarise some of the main concerns to have emerged from this growing body of work.

In the first place, there is a danger that the procedures and traditions surrounding both parental involvement and local electoral politics will make it easier for white articulate middle-class parents to dominate 'parent' constituencies, at the expense of working-class, black and ethnic minority parents. According to Hardy and Vielar-Porter, intervention by black parents will be possible in those schools where they are well represented and organised. Otherwise white parents with 'an understanding of school processes and an easy facility with such institutions' will determine 'parental community interests' (Hardy and Vielar-Porter, 1992: 179).

Moreover, when black and ethnic minority parents are elected to governing bodies, they will be responsible for overseeing a national curriculum which expresses a particular version of Anglo/Eurocentricity at the expense of their own diverse backgrounds and perspectives. These backgrounds reflect global diasporas and in some cases long-standing settlement in Britain; there are groups who regard themselves not only as African, African-Caribbean, Jewish, Indian, Pakistani, Bangladeshi, Indian-African and Chinese, but also in many cases as English, British and European. Such richness and complexity is glaring in its absence from the national curriculum. The teaching of history, if government strictures are anything to go by, will be built around a chronological, celebratory account of Britain, Europe and the West's ascendance to world leadership (ibid.: 183–4). For example, John McGregor, in his role as Education Secretary, criticised the national curriculum history syllabus 'for not reflecting sufficiently the British experience' (Hatcher and Troyna, 1990: 3). If he and his colleagues had their way, then other cultures, if they appear at all in the teaching of history, could only expect to do so as temporary blips along the way to western global dominance.

The emphasis on a centrally co-ordinated national curriculum, introduced under the 1988 Education Reform Act, along with explicit references to the traditional forms of pedagogy referred to above and expressed in ministerial interventions and national curriculum statements and documents, work against developing a curriculum which is tailored to the needs, and reflective

of the traditions, of a particular locality, and the experiences of its communities. The expressed bias towards the teaching of an Anglocentric
curriculum will reinforce the experiential gap between schools and local black
and ethnic minority communities. Hence in the case of the teaching of English,
Kenneth Baker warned the National Curriculum English Working Party that
the proposals for the English curriculum should draw on the English literary
heritage and promote the reading of 'great' literature.

Other reforms, again introduced under the 1988 Act, notably 'open enrolment' and 'local management', will inevitably create different classes of
schools with some, often those attracting a predominantly white middle-class
intake, better resourced than others. Not unrelated to this is the prospect of
creating *de facto* segregated schools, made possible by a white exodus of
the kind successfully attempted at Headfield school in Dewsbury in 1988,[4]
where white parents withdrew their children in protest against the multiracial character of the school. They organised meetings in a room above a
pub where their children were taught by voluntary teachers for about a year
until Kirklees Council finally gave in to parental demands. This action was
applauded in the media under the guise of freedom of choice and educational standards as well as made legal under the 1988 Education Reform
Act.[5]

In 1991, the principle of *de facto* segregation was given further legitimacy,
this time by the courts, in a case in Cleveland. There, a mother successfully
transferred her daughter from a multicultural to a predominantly white school,
on the grounds that her daughter had been exposed to languages and cultures
considered threatening to her educational chances. Racist motives, the court
argued, were of less importance than the principle of the mother's freedom of
choice. The examples of Cleveland and Dewsbury demonstrate the need to
qualify the term 'freedom'. In both cases, the freedom that was legally sanctioned was the freedom to act in racially discriminatory ways. The threat of
the exercise of this freedom on the freedoms of black parents and pupils (for
example, freedom from racial harassment and abuse) is strategically omitted
from this discourse.

In fact, attempts to tackle the specific problems of racial harassment and
abuse in schools, within the framework of local education authority equal
opportunity and anti-racist policies, have actually been weakened under the
Education Reform Act, a fact which could not have escaped the Act's architects.
'While the effectiveness of LEA race policies has always been in doubt, there
is little question that the Act will further widen the gap between LEA policies
and school policy and practice' (Hardy and Vielar-Porter, 1992: 180). For all
their limitations, local education authority efforts did provide a framework for
school-based equal opportunity and anti-racist developments. They also provided an important level of moral jurisdiction to which schools, committed to
these principles, could appeal, thus legitimising their actions (Troyna, 1990:
412).

Popular tabloid attacks on local authority anti-racist initiatives were couched in terms of white victims and, from the mid-1980s onwards, the press catalogued its martyrs with great regularity. Notable amongst these was the Bradford headteacher, Ray Honeyford, who resigned with a golden hand-shake after being 'persecuted. . . by a nasty bunch of parents, councillors and race agitators' (*Sun*, cited in Searle, 1989: 69). In another case reported in the *Sun* under the headline 'Outcast', a mother removed her (white) son from his class, which was all black/ethnic minority, because he couldn't learn his ABC (cited in Searle, ibid.: 64). Finally, the local press came down in support of white parents at Montgomery Junior and Infant School in Small Heath, Birmingham, whose revered symbol of English culture, the pig, was removed from images and stories as a mark of respect for the Muslim parents and pupils at the school. Under the banner headline 'Pork Chop', Conservative MP, Roger King, was reported as saying: 'the pig is a major part of British life' (*Birmingham Mail,* 26 October 1991).[6]

The above cases illustrate the inconsistent and selective way in which parents were invoked (or not) to support the new education agenda. In Bradford, for all the apparent tabloid media and government support for parents, the views of minority parents were dismissed in favour of those of a white headteacher. In Bradford, what proved decisive in terms of media allegiances was the stand Honeyford took against the alleged threat posed to 'British culture' by anti-racism and multiculturalism. Bradford's white parents and pupils were thus cast as victims of the lunacies of anti-racism and left Labour authorities. The other side of this strategy, of course, was to trivialise and undermine those attempts, by black teachers and local authorities, to promote anti-racism (Searle, 1989: 74).

It is clear from the above that parental empowerment is meaningless unless it is discussed with reference to specific constituencies of parents and under particular circumstances. The Conservative governments of the 1980s universalised their national parental constituency as they did other consumer groups, with the predictable result that real differences within these groups were concealed. Moreover, these consumer groups were used to front the attack on areas of the public sector; its work-forces, local administrators as well as local politicians. In one sense, then, parents were integral to the wider political project of Thatcherism and the new right. The parents at William Tyndale school in Islington in the mid-1970s had proved their potential in challenging radical and progressive teaching methods and curricula. Unwittingly, perhaps, they were auditioning for a role that parents were to play on a larger stage in the 1980s. In the next section I will explore attempts to express real differences within the allegedly single constituency of parents and how efforts have been made to suppress, sideline and subordinate such differences. I shall do so with reference to two kinds of intervention: the supplementary school movement and the struggle for separate Muslim schools.

SUPPLEMENTARY PROVISION AND THE STRUGGLE FOR SEPARATE ISLAMIC SCHOOLS

As its name suggests, the supplementary school movement has historically sought to augment, as well as contest and provide an alternative to, mainstream provision. Whilst the movement is thought about largely in terms of black and ethnic minority community initiatives in Britain from the 1970s onwards, their history is longer and by no means confined to this country. Such schools have played an important cultural, educational and political role, both in this country and in the United States. For example, early Sunday schools in the United States were associated quite openly with radical political movements. In Rochester, New York, pupils at one school run by the Socialist Party recited after all their lessons, 'I shall always remain a red rebel as long as there is poverty in the world' and sang 'The Red Flag' and 'Song of the Capitalist Squeezer' (Teitelbaum and Reese, 1983: 435). In Britain such schools have been established by newly arrived immigrant groups – Irish, Jewish, Polish, Italian, Chinese and Greek – with the primary aim of maintaining cultural, notably religious and linguistic, ties with their cultures of origin (Tomlinson, 1984: 68).

In the most recent post-World War II period of immigration, schools have been set up in Britain by, amongst others, Greek Cypriot and Japanese communities, but the most extensive network of provision has been made by African-Caribbean and south Asian communities. In general, these schools grew out of a concern expressed by black parents and community organisations about their children's education. The emergence of black organisations and campaigns from the 1960s onwards included a successful struggle against the local authority's dispersal policy in Haringey, in which children were bused around the borough to ensure that no school had in excess of 30 per cent black pupils on its roll. Another issue, the numbers of black pupils who were being classified educationally subnormal, became the focus of an important book by Bernard Coard (1971). The Caribbean Education Association, which formed in 1969:

> waged campaigns against police treatment of our children, the practice of placing most black kids in the lowest streams, blaming home for what schools and the DES were patently failing to do, and most historic of all, against the nation-wide placing of vast numbers of black children into schools for the educationally sub-normal.

> (John, n.d.: 2)

The numbers of supplementary schools for African-Caribbean children grew in the 1970s as parents and community groups turned their concern into action. It was against this general background of dissent, agitation and frustration that the Black Parents' Movement was formed in 1975. Based in London and Manchester, but with links across the country in Nottingham, Rugby,

Northampton, Reading and Ipswich, it began to establish, campaign for and support the setting up of supplementary schools. The purpose of these supplementary schools in the early and mid-1970s was 'to correct the damage the schooling system was doing to black children and to give those children opportunities to develop a positive attitude to themselves, their educational potential, their families and their history' (ibid.: 3).

These schools were thus primarily concerned with improving standards and developing basic skills. Datchwyng Saturday School was the topic of a BBC programme on multicultural education in 1979 and was written up as a case study by Sally Tomlinson (1984: 73–5). The initiative to set up the school came from black parents who were dissatisfied with state schools and concerned that their children were not realising their educational potential. Traditional core subjects, that is, reading, writing and maths, were available, but so, too, was a range of other subjects. Black Arrow, another school, taught basic curriculum subjects, but was also concerned 'to provide information about the rich cultural heritage of Afro-Caribbean people' (ibid.: 75).

One of the schools set up by the Black Parents' Movement, in 1985, was the George Padmore Community School (named after the political activist from Trinidad who worked for African liberation struggles in the 1950s). Like Black Arrow, it combined the three Rs with the 'history, languages, and cultures of black people in Africa, the Caribbean, the USA, and Europe' (*Battlefront*, February 1987). It ran on Saturdays for children of primary school age. The school's independence, both financial and political, enabled parents and teachers to retain control over decision-making.

In a survey of Asian supplementary schools in Coventry, J.S. Nagra identifies four aims: to encourage communication between children and their parents and community; to build a sense of identity; to create an understanding of, and participation in, their particular social and cultural environment, and to communicate and express their religion and culture (cited in Nixon, 1985: 129). Educational provision has been made at mosques, gudwaras (Sikh temples) and other places of worship. Whilst the emphasis has been on using schools to maintain their communities' cultural identity, primarily through community language instruction and religious teaching, they have also helped to counter the experience of discrimination and racism in the wider society, including that found in mainstream education. In common with supplementary provision within the African-Caribbean community, the existence of these schools implies a dissatisfaction with state schools, and in particular their inadequate response to cultural diversity and more overt forms of racism. That black and ethnic minority parents have felt prompted to take such initiatives is a reflection of their sense of exclusion from, and related failure to influence or participate in, mainstream schools.

This last point raises the important question of the relationship between supplementary schools and mainstream education. Jon Nixon has made the point that many supplementary schools regard their independence from the state sector, both politically and financially, as a precondition for their effectiveness. In her study, Maureen Stone (1981) described contact between supplementary and mainstream schools as spasmodic, but amiable and supportive, although no details were provided. The widespread failure of mainstream education to accommodate the demands of black and ethnic minority parents in the ways in which these are expressed through supplementary schooling can be attributed to a number of factors.

The first factor is teachers' professional identity, which, all too readily, interprets the existence of a supplementary educational system as a threat to their already beleaguered sense of expertise and autonomy. In the second place, the existence of such schools suggests a high level of dissatisfaction on the part of black parents and a failure to use existing channels and institutional options to express their grievances or exercise their choice. Such dissatisfaction has been easier to suppress than to respond to in any meaningful way. Third, such initiatives do not fall within the framework of consumer/parent power laid down by Conservative governments, nor, since they challenge schooling in many inner city authorities under the control of the Labour Party, do they win political support from that end of the political spectrum either. Last, and by no means least, is their status as black and ethnic minority initiatives; a status which has won little support in a climate supporting individual over collective concerns and majority over minority forms of cultural expression.

The issues surrounding the setting up of separate Islamic schools, like the principle of same-race fostering and adoption discussed in Chapter 3, has largely been framed in terms of a media-led debate in which only two positions seem possible: we are invited to align ourselves either for or against the existence of such schools. Rather than work towards a resolution in these terms, I am more interested here in how this debate has been constructed and with what effects. In this sense it can be used to explore educational discourses and institutional practices as well as their materialisation in lived culture.

There are a number of conditions which have helped to set the terms of the debate. The first, already mentioned, has been the 1988 Education Reform Act and the wider political cultural strategy of which that law formed a part. Overall, the Act gave a new impetus to demands for separate schools, its contradictory strands only serving to crystallise the debate. The twin goals of laying down a national curriculum and promoting the principle of parental choice had the effect of alienating sections of the Muslim community and giving them a potential voice. To those aspects of the curriculum already mentioned, it should be added that languages often spoken in the homes of British Asian, Chinese, African-Caribbean and Jewish communities were denied a slot in the national curriculum. Instead, the national curriculum included a 'modern European' language, as if the above languages were neither modern nor widely spoken in Europe. Likewise, its stipulation that school assemblies 'must be of a wholly or mainly broadly Christian character' contributed to the overall attempt to use the national curriculum, as the name implies, to construct and cement a sense of national identity, on this occasion by defining it in Christian terms.

The idea of parental choice, expressed specifically in the principles of open enrolment, 'opting out' and the local management of schools, was intended, I have suggested, to bolster government plans. However, the voices with which parents were expected to speak were individual ones and not collective expressions of alternative political/cultural interests. Nevertheless, the principle of parental participation has created a terrain on which black and ethnic minority parents have found new opportunities to articulate their demands, as the well publicised cases of the Sikh College in London, Stratford School in East London and Small Heath School in Birmingham confirm. The last two are inner city schools which used the provision to opt out, not, as the Conservative Government had hoped, to escape profligate Labour authorities or their anti-racist dogma but for other, more complex reasons. In both cases, concerns centred around the educational performance of black and ethnic minority pupils, as well as political divisions along, and within, ethnic boundaries. The climate thus became ripe for renewed claims for separate school provision for Muslims.

I have already suggested that the concerns and educational experiences of black and ethnic minority parents and pupils pre-date the 1988 Act by a good twenty years and that educational racism has been one important feature of that experience. How the 1988 Act will affect levels and forms of racism depends on the outcome of different kinds of political struggle. The demand for separate schools is one, but by no means the only, strategy for cultural expression and/or contesting racism within the parameters and conditions created by recent changes. Before looking at these strategies more closely, it is important to identify some of the most decisive forms of educational racism. I shall mention five: racist harassment and abuse; language policies; school organisation; policies on religion; and the tokenism of some forms of multi-culturalism.

Racist incidents have a long and undistinguished history in Britain, from the Teddy boy attacks in the 1950s through 'Paki-bashing' in the 1960s and 1970s to the attacks perpetrated by the extreme right in the 1970s and 1980s (see for example, Fryer, 1984). The1980s, in fact, witnessed an escalation of such incidents. Reflecting on this upward trend, it has been argued:

> The quantitative data adduced in this period by local monitoring projects, trades unions, the Commission for Racial Equality, local authority housing and education departments and specialist inquiry teams set up in the Home Office and Department of Education and Science (DES) leave no doubt that racist harassment is one of the most 'frightening realities' for black citizens and their children in Britain.
>
> (Home Affairs Committee, cited in Troyna and Hatcher, 1992: 188)

Although much of this evidence appears to suggest that such incidents are directed at young people of south Asian and African-Caribbean origin, there has been growing evidence of an escalation of attacks on Jewish pupils and students, partly related to an upsurge in anti-Semitism across Europe. (I shall discuss this more fully in Chapter 7.) Pupils of Irish background living on mainland Britain have also been the object of attacks, which reach their peak during and after IRA bombing campaigns. Racist incidents against Chinese communities are also likely to rise in the run-up to 1997, when Hong Kong loses its dependent territory status with the United Kingdom and officially becomes part of China.

These incidents are clearly feeding off racist discourses, which may not be part of an official educational discourse, but which nonetheless enter the school gates and move onto the playground and into the classroom in more informal ways. The Rushdie affair has already been cited as an important catalyst in the escalation of verbal and physical abuse of young people of south Asian background (not just Muslim). The case of Ahmed Ullah who was murdered in the playground of Burnage school in Manchester in 1986 illustrates not only the significance of racism within the ethos of the school (both staff and pupils) but also the culture of violence and bullying that is present. In the subsequent inquiry into the incident, the school was criticised for the manner in which it sought to implement its anti-racist policies without the involvement of parents, notably white working-class parents (see Macdonald *et al.*, 1989).[7] Elsewhere, the failure of schools and local authorities to develop policies and procedures for dealing with such incidents may not be the direct result of an explicitly racist discourse (at least not one expressed officially). Nevertheless, the persistent failure to intervene in the face of growing evidence, the willingness to accord racist incidents such a low priority, is hard to explain except in terms of some latent racist undercurrent. In any event the non-institutional response of schools is as much a part of the problem of racist incidents as are the incidents themselves.

Educational racism is also reflected in the response to ethnic minority languages. In her study of black girls, Audrey Osler (1989) found evidence of a systematic devaluing of black and ethnic minority languages, both by fellow pupils, who laughed at those who spoke in minority languages, and staff, who reinforced these attitudes through their association of Patois with bad English. Asian languages, if they were taught at all, were often fitted in after school or on a Saturday on a voluntary basis; the kind of supplementary provision described above. A limited number of mainstream schools do provide south Asian languages as part of their timetable but the unsupportive framework provided by the national curriculum for the provision of languages other than French, German and Spanish has already been acknowledged. In contrast, an expertise in European languages is valued by pupils, parents and staff. It would have been interesting to know how the Cleveland mother might have responded had her daughter come home singing nursery rhymes in French or even ancient Greek.

The third condition which has helped to set the terms of the debate on separate schools relates to the way schools are organised. This includes questions concerned with employment. How many black and ethnic minority staff are in post and at what levels? This, in turn, depends on recruitment promotions policies and practices, which may not depend on an explicitly racist discourse (this would be illegal) but which nevertheless couch their resistance to increased black employment in more acceptable terms. Again the unwillingness to take positive measures to redress under-representation can only be interpreted as evidence of racism, buried, maybe, under a set of more acceptable discursive rationalisations. In some cases, institutions work with seemingly neutral rules, for example on streaming, but when these rules are implemented in a discriminatory way it can lead to the exclusion of black and ethnic minority pupils. Cecile Wright (1987) demonstrates how black African-Caribbean students were channelled into non-examination sets and streams despite, in some cases, getting better results than their white peers. Such decisions taken by teaching staff were always made on the basis of negative stereotypical evaluations of pupil behaviour and took no account of academic merit. Similarly, the disproportionate levels of suspensions and exclusions of pupils of African-Caribbean background take place within a set of neutral rules within which there is considerable scope for discrimination.

The fourth condition relating to the setting up of separate schools, of more direct relevance to Muslim communities, is the issue of religion. Prior to the changes introduced in 1988, there had been provision for the state to fund voluntary aided denominational schools. In fact almost a third of all state schools are voluntary, either Church of England or Catholic, and there are five secondary Jewish schools. Some private Muslim schools have applied for voluntary aided status, but so far all have failed. The decision to grant voluntary aided status is up to the Secretary of State for Education, although in the past he has taken account of the advice of the local education authority (LEA). So, the question remains: why has the law been used to create Catholic, Church of England and Jewish, but not Muslim schools? How is it possible to justify favouring Christianity and Judaism over Islam? Educational racism in this case stands for decisions which systematically favour one group over another and the social exclusions and inequalities that result from the arbitrary, or rather discriminatory, exercise of state power.

Another factor shaping the debate has been the gestural nature of some attempts to promote cultural diversity which have served to reinforce educational racism and, in other instances, hinder positive developments. For example, efforts to acknowledge other cultures, associated with policies and practices commonly known as multicultural education, are often implemented in a patronising way or in a way which marginalises the knowledges built around these cultures. Hazel Carby (1982) provides a powerful critique of such practices. So, too, does Audrey Osler through her interview with pupils who were asked to do a project on Pakistan. Anyone who opted to do it was dubbed 'a typical Paki', i.e. 'absolutely dumb' (Osler, 1989: 18). So long as such knowledges are subordinate to mainstream curriculum and tacked onto it (in this case as a project option), it is much easier to associate cultural differences with cultural inferiority, in terms both of the knowledges themselves, which are regarded as low status and, by implication, the pupils and parents who possess them.

One final effect of the way in which the issue of separate schools has been framed has been to oversimplify a variety of positions not easily accommodated within the alleged polarisation. In this case the arguments for separate schools have been attributed to a whole 'ethnicity' without taking account of important political differences which cut across traditional ethnic lines and other social boundaries, for example gender and class. The same, of course, applies to majority ethnic communities, however hard governments attempt to construct a 'national identity'. There is therefore, every reason to suppose that other cultures reflect differences and divisions along numerous axes. The principle of separate schools is but one strategic response to the pressure to assimilate, arising particularly in the wake of the Rushdie affair and the failure of the educational system to meet the cultural aspirations of many Muslims.

Another strategy, in this instance opposed to separate schools, has been pursued by the organisation Women Against Fundamentalism, whose aim has been the secularisation of education, on the grounds that Muslim traditionalists have exploited the principle of separate provision to provide an institutional basis for the maintenance of the oppression of Muslim women. Elsewhere opposition has come from those who have argued that separatism, by simply withdrawing from mainstream education, leaves intact and unchallenged the latter's institutionally racist structures and practices. The principle of separate schools also implies that young Muslims see themselves exclusively in terms of their Muslim identity, whereas recent evidence suggests much more fluid, complex forms of identity, cutting across different ethnicities and aligned to different sub-cultures, sexualities and gender-based affiliations (Khan, 1992). Thus, the idea of separate Islamic schools can only be fully understood in terms of both the relationship between the Islamic community and mainstream education and culture, and relationships within the Muslim community.

STRUGGLES ON THE NEW EDUCATIONAL TERRAIN: 'OPTING OUT' AND THE CASE OF SMALL HEATH SCHOOL

In this section I shall explore one further struggle, this time not on the margins or outside mainstream provision but firmly located on the terrain created by recent educational changes: that of Small Heath School in Birmingham and its decision, in 1989, to go grant maintained or 'opt out' of local authority control. Critics of the principle of opting out have objected to it on a number of grounds: that it takes schools out of the democratic control of local authorities; that it makes pupil recruitment more selective; that it exacerbates inequalities in resources between schools; and that it puts teachers' and other school employees' jobs at risk. Alongside other recent reforms, opting out, its critics claim, will polarise the educational system into sink and swim, second- and first-class schools, with the latter attracting predominantly white middle-class pupils and the lion's share of the resources while the former remain under-resourced, unpopular and non-white.

Advocates of 'opting out' saw it as an opportunity to escape from the wastefulness, inefficiency and doctrinaire policies of left Labour LEAs. Parents, assuming enough of them supported the idea, could vote to remove their school from LEA control against the wishes of both the LEA and the teaching staff. Parent or consumer 'empowerment' was seen as integral to this provision. The local state was rolled back to make room for the idea of a school as market-place, subject of course to the approval of the Secretary of State and the imposition of a national curriculum.

In fact, from the outset the picture became considerably more complex than either side predicted. Schools opted out for widely differing reasons and in varying circumstances. The motives have included avoiding merger or closure; promoting Islamic values in a single sex school; avoiding comprehensive status; and finally, in Stantonbury School, Milton Keynes, maintaining a community comprehensive in the face of pressure to reintroduce grammar schools by the Conservative County Council (*Observer*, 15 August 1989).

The case of Small Heath School in Birmingham is interesting for a number of reasons. In terms of this chapter it can be used to assess the role that parents played in what happened, given that the opting out clause is regarded by the government as part of its general move towards parental empowerment and consumer choice. Linked to this, the case also illustrates the complex motives for opting out, since it does not readily fit into the most common interpretations cited above. Irrespective of parental involvement in the decision to opt out, it is also important to look, as far as possible, at the consequences of opting out for black pupils, parents and 'communities'. The use of these last two terms raises a final point: the problems entailed in talking about 'the parent body' and 'the community' as if each spoke with a single voice. In Small Heath, both terms have come to embrace widely differing, sometimes conflicting, sets of constituencies, with identities and allegiances shifting around political affiliation, religious background and country of origin, as well as economic location.

In 1992 the school was 90 per cent black and ethnic minority with the majority of pupils coming from families of Pakistani and Bangladeshi origin. It is situated in an area of Birmingham once famous for manufacturing motorcycles and weapons and home to skilled workers and successful entrepreneurs. Now it can only boast one of the highest levels of unemployment and crime and the highest perinatal mortality rate in the country. Sixty per cent of the pupils are from homes on income support (interview with headteacher, March 1992). In September 1989, the school went grant maintained after a long and extremely bitter campaign. Labour MPs Dennis Howell and Roy

Hattersley, in conjunction with the local Labour council and teacher unions, led a campaign of opposition against the proposal to opt out. The two MPs wrote to all parents (on House of Commons notepaper) warning them that a yes vote would be a vote for a Conservative school. The National Association of Schoolmasters/Union of Women Teachers (NAS/UWT) produced a leaflet, *What Every Parent Should Know*, in which they also warned of the dangers of opting out. These included: loss of job security of the teachers; difficulties of attracting staff; possible reduction of income which might result from the loss of LEA support, and the absence of financial guarantees by central government. Opponents also sought to discredit the headteacher and challenge the procedures both he and the governing body (the majority of whom supported opting out) followed in the period leading up to the parental ballot. The case went to judicial review and to the High Court before Kenneth Baker intervened, enabling the school to formally transfer to grant maintained status in time to begin the new school year in 1989; just one year after the governors had voted by nineteen votes to two to set in motion procedures to opt out.

It has already been suggested that grant maintained schools 'opt out' for different reasons. According to Small Heath's headteacher Cecil Knight, the school had been subjected to unfair publicity designed to attract local pupils away from Small Heath to outer ring secondary schools, with damaging consequences for the school and its surrounding area. Furthermore, he felt that the school would make better use of its financial resources acting autonomously than it had been able to under Birmingham's LEA, which not only had a very poor spending record on education but was also not particularly renowned for its efficient or progressive management of schools in the city.

Hence, the background against which the school opted out was a complex one and not containable within a clear-cut division between (Labour) advocates of local democratically controlled state education and those (Conservatives) seeking to promote selection and an extension of consumer choice through the creation of new educational markets. The complexity of conditions at Small Heath can be illustrated with reference to the impact of opting out on the school's predominantly black pupils, their parents and the surrounding community.

There was a widely accepted view, held by parents and staff at the school, that parents were not at the forefront of the opting-out campaign. Indeed, it has been claimed by some parents that since the ballot paper was not translated into what for many was their first language, few understood it. Nor had there been an organised campaign against the school in terms of curriculum or management issues prior to opting out. Ultimately, those parents who voted 'yes' were persuaded by the headteacher, who saw it as an opportunity to express the school's general disaffection with the local education authority. The quality of educational provision at Small Heath never really became an issue for debate during the opting-out campaign. In view of these circumstances, it was not altogether surprising that the campaign left parents divided. Out of 970 parents, 80 per cent of whom voted, 56.3 per cent voted 'yes' and 43.7 per cent 'no'.

Divisions within the Muslim community over the issue reflected different national and political identities. From the early 1980s, Pakistani Muslims had begun to enter representative positions in local politics at the behest of the local white Labour activists. For these Muslims, the Labour Party provided an opportunity to articulate demands and exercise influence. Not surprisingly, this group remained loyal to the party, and hence opposed to 'opting out' throughout the campaign. The political links forged here, between Labour and this section of the Muslim community, threw up a small group of co-opted 'community leaders', who emerged as spokespeople for the whole area. On the other hand, the Kashmiri community's sense of exclusion and disaffection with the Labour Council and the school was expressed, not only by their absence from local organisations, but also by young people themselves, who left school without qualifications, sometimes unable to read or write their own name or address. The splits which emerged in the campaign reflect these ethnic and local political affiliations and serve to highlight the difficulty of talking about 'communities' (in this case Muslim) out of a very specifically defined political context.

It is interesting to reflect on the idea of 'community' in the context of what has happened to Small Heath since 1989. One of the arguments against opting out was that school would no longer be democratically accountable to its local community, a principle which, it was argued, had been guaranteed through local political representation. In other words, the decision would, in effect, disenfranchise those who would otherwise have had some say in education via local elections. However, as the experience of the Muslim community indicated, its sense of active involvement and potential influence was by no means unanimously felt. For some parents, opting out seemed to provide a rare, if not unique, opportunity to influence the character and destiny of their local school.

According to the head, opting out of local control has, if anything, led to a strengthening of community ties. What was, prior to opting out, a 'community' school has actually become closer to its community since it lost its formal community status. The school's control over its own budget has enabled it to buy goods and services from local businesses. Work placements, where pupils gain experience in local firms, banks or shops, further these links with the local economy. So the idea of opting out of local control has, arguably, meant closer local links. However, the sense in which the term 'local' is used here is all-important. For example, the high unemployment rate in the area means that many local people will remain unaffected by these local economic ties. Neither will these links affect those working in the 'black' (which is also predominantly black) economy, who cannot formally or publicly admit to having employment services or goods to sell to the school. Hence, there are many local black businesses which are effectively excluded from school–community links (discussion with local Muslims, July 1991). Despite the outward attractiveness of the principle of 'community links', the term 'community' would seem to be more elusive and exclusive than at first appears to be the case.

Nevertheless, the school has been able to develop local links in other ways. Additional government resources, made available since opting out, have been spent, in part, on additional black/ethnic minority staff including a home school liaison teacher,[8] and investing in a broader curriculum including Bengali. The recruitment of community language speakers has made communication with parents easier and may also explain the increase in attendance at parents' evenings. 'Communication', however, is another slippery term. It can range from the passing on of information and feedback to parents, to more reciprocal forms where parents are actively involved in school life, including its curricula and decision-making. Whilst parents are welcome visitors at the school and some black parents clearly feel involved through their role on the governing body, many continue to feel excluded and powerless in terms of influencing the direction and character of the school (interview, ibid.). The continuing dominance of white staff at senior levels (the chair of governors is also white) has compounded this sense of exclusion and revived local calls for the creation of separate Muslim schools.

A good example of this continuing sense of exclusion from the school can be illustrated with reference to the use of the adjoining library and community centre. Prior to opting out these facilities were linked to the school through the LEA's community education policy. Even then, there was a strong social control ethos running through the community facilities which had the effect of estranging many young people. The shift towards private contracting, tendering out, 'cost-effective' management exacerbated this sense of distance between the facilities and the local users. These so-called 'community' facilities now come under the city's Leisure and Recreation Department, but pursuit of profitability has meant that the sports facilities are used increasingly by people from outside Small Heath and local youth are deterred from participating, by over-zealous policing, excessive use of lighting around the car parks and talk of the instalment of video cameras.

In conclusion, Small Heath School cannot be attacked with the usual left rhetoric which sets the debate in terms of either opting out or remaining within local democratically elected Labour control. Nor can all opted-out schools be accused of seeking to avoid city-wide anti-racist/multicultural initiatives. On the contrary, the parents who voted for opting out partly did so precisely because they felt disenfranchised from a supposedly democratic local political system. Their significance, if anything, increased, as did, albeit in quite limited ways, the school's multicultural curricula provision and community links. Why the school could only fund these appointments out of additional government resources available to opted-out schools and not under mainstream LEA funding, however, is less clear. Moreover, the 'community links' which the school has been able to forge since opting out have, arguably, been at the expense of other community ties which have remained unaffected or weakened.

On the other hand, the increased funding, which would probably have gone to schools in more prosperous areas and/or with a predominantly white intake has, in this case, gone to a school in one of the poorest (in material terms) areas in the country. This has provided opportunities not only to give the school a face lift (literally) but also to re-equip it with better facilities including new laboratories and computers. However limited such resourcing is, however short-lived the benefits and however inequitable the principle of opting out is in the context of the country as a whole, it created a sense of empowerment and ambition in Small Heath, the like of which many black and ethnic minority parents had not experienced before.

EDUCATION'S OTHER CONSUMERS: LANGUAGE AND ETHNICITY IN PUPIL CULTURE

The aim of this chapter has been to locate ideas of cultural difference in education within the context of a broader political agenda in which parents have been assigned a key role. In according them a privileged status, governments have created a new terrain for the articulation of minority parental interests and demands. Consequently, conflicting definitions of culture, ethnicity and even racism have so far been couched largely in terms of the perspectives of adults: politicians, minority parents, majority parents and community activists. Education's real consumers, pupils, have largely been silent, or maybe silenced. There are numerous ways to rectify this. I have chosen to return to the issue of language, this time as perceived and practised by pupils themselves. There are two main reasons for this choice: the role that language has already been seen to play in previous chapters in processes of subjectification and institutional power (Fanon,1986; Fairclough,1989), and the significance of language within the school setting as a mechanism for producing and reproducing cultures, including peer group sub-cultures and identities.

In an article on the teaching of Black English to a group of African-Americans in New York, June Jordan records an incident in which the brother of one of her pupils was killed by the police. Her class decided to send messages of condolence to the press. The dilemma they faced was whether to use the language of the police, standard English, or to use Black English. In Jordan's words:

> If we sought to express ourselves by abandoning our language wouldn't that mean our suicide on top of Reggie's murder? But if we expressed ourselves in our own language wouldn't that be suicidal to the wish to

communicate with those who, evidently, did not give a damn about us/Reggie/police violence in the Black community? In the end the class decided to write it in Black English even though Black English had doomed our writings, even as the distinctive reality of our black lives had always doomed our efforts to 'be who we been' in this country.

(Jordan,1987: 36)[9]

In the case of June Jordan's class, the teacher and students decided together to use their language to express their views most powerfully and precisely. I want to extend this example to consider different ways in which school pupils and students make use of different minority languages outside of the formal teaching context, breaking down traditional linguistic boundaries. I shall focus on African-Caribbean and southern Asian languages, primarily because of the existence of research evidence. It is possible that other languages, for example Greek, Hebrew and Cantonese, have been appropriated in similar ways.

The first conclusion to be drawn from existing research is the way language has been strategic in processes of identity formation, often in ways which serve to break down traditional ethnic boundaries. In other words, language has been instrumental in constructing identities but not always along racial or ethnic lines. One example of this is given in Ben Rampton's study of pupils in London schools. Black African-Caribbean and white pupils drew on Punjabi to make friendships and hence develop shared peer identities. In one example Peter, a white boy, used the Punjabi word *gora* which means white man: 'I always call people who didn't go to Southleigh middle school goras yet I'm white myself – 'cas we reckon you know they're a bit upper class!' This shows not only how languages are being used across traditional ethnic boundaries, but also how class can act as a common denominator in the sharing of a particular language (Rampton, 1989: 29).

In another study by Roger Hewitt (1986), the acquisition of Creole by white pupils was found to be almost involuntary and used as part of normal conversations and banter with black friends; as a form of abuse, an expression of emotion and in discussions about sex.[10] Likewise, Simon Jones (1988) found that Patois was used by young whites, both as a way of expressing identity with black friends and as a way of displacing racist attitudes. Both these uses served to express an affiliation with black culture in general. In his research in Birmingham, Jones also shows how music, particularly reggae at the time of his research, was an important source of new catch-phrases. Patois thus became an important cultural mediator of black and white interaction and, in all white groups, a mark of prestige. It would be interesting, in this respect, to look at speech styles amongst young people of mixed parentage, since this was not something specifically considered in Tizard and Phoenix's study referred to in Chapter 3.

Language has also been used to promote an oppositional culture to the dominant school culture. Adrian, a black African-Caribbean in Rampton's study, learnt Indian songs in Punjabi from his friend Iqbal. He learnt them in economics lessons:

(Q): And what do the teachers say. . . when you're doing that?
(A): Teachers just tell us to be quiet 'cos they don't understand what we're saying.

(Rampton, 1989: 30)

The defensive and hostile response of teachers to the use of languages in this way is clearly part of the languages' attraction. Jones illustrates the reaction of teachers to the use of Patois in his study. 'Stop that mumbo jumbo' was one response of a teacher to an all-white group's use of Patois. In both Jones' and Rampton's studies, Patois and Punjabi were used to abuse teachers, as collective and individual acts of defiance. The fact that young whites used it reflects the oppositional resonance of black cultural forms for them. In these instances, language was employed as a means of closure; jokes and teasing could be communicated in 'other' languages to construct new divisions, not just along traditional ethnic lines but in effect creating new 'us' and 'them' distinctions around class and the hierarchy of the school.

This last usage is linked to an idea developed by Manning (1990) in her study of a multiracial primary school in which she uses the metaphor of territory and space to explain the role of Patois in school. Patois was used to reinforce or to redefine group boundaries, to exclude, or even include, outsiders. Its success in drawing in a wide range of traditionally defined ethnic groups lay in its ability to accurately reflect inner city urban life. Rampton's study of the use of Punjabi also shows the way language was used to include black African-Caribbean and white pupils. The idea of language functioning as a means of controlling territory and space echoes a point made by Paul Gilroy (1987) in his discussion of the uprisings of 1981 and 1985, which he argued could be understood partly in terms of control of a highly localised area: a street or an estate.

The kinds and varieties of languages used by pupils and students by no means always coincide with parental concerns nor, as I have suggested, do they accord with school priorities. Edwards (1986) found that the prevalence of a strong black peer network was an essential precondition for competence in Patois precisely because, in the majority of cases, it was discouraged in the home. Parents, older brothers and sisters often encourage younger children to speak in standard English (ibid.: 130). This evidence of parental views on language was in marked contrast to south Asian parents who not only encouraged the use of ethnic minority languages in the home but, as we have seen, have exerted pressure to include them in the school curriculum. However, even they, in their commitment to language maintenance, could not have anticipated, or necessarily approved of, its various uses and users.

The above research on pupils and languages illustrates, above all, the dangers of making assumptions about the relationship between culture, ethnicity and educational 'consumption' while omitting the perspectives and practices of pupils themselves. It suggests a much less straightforward pattern of ethnic allegiance and identity than perhaps the literature on education and ethnicity and race suggests. In addition, it opens up the prospect of new, more fluid affiliations, which question and challenge dominant ethnic majority *and* minority constructions. If any attempt were made to incorporate these languages into the mainstream curriculum, then the question of how young people might respond remains unknown. The very incorporation of these languages into the formal curriculum, for instance, might undermine their role as forms of resistance, and even lead to new (counter) cultural expressions and strategies.

CONCLUSIONS

The unifying constructions of both 'parents' and 'consumers' in education were used throughout the 1980s by central government to lend support to attacks on both LEAs and teachers. According to the government and the right, parental rights of freedom and choice had been undermined by the imposition of an unwanted, wasteful and sub-standard educational service provided by so-called professionals and local (Labour) politicians. At, or near, the top of the list of examples that were said to symbolise the decline of English education was the left's apparent obsession with anti-racism and multicultural education. The parents at Headfield School in Dewsbury were proof, if proof were needed, that white parents were capable of orchestrating a powerful campaign, with press backing, against both multicultural education in general, and more pointedly, against the presence of black pupils. The reforms of the 1980s sought to mobilise and formalise such pressure.

Clearly, when the government uses the rhetoric of parental choice and involvement, it is constructing parents as individuals, thereby denying any collective exclusions and oppressions they may experience. However, this fraudulent attempt to universalise the entire constituency 'parents', while at the same time effectively only empowering a minority of parents, has not gone unchallenged. A variety of interventions has been made to subvert, contest and reject the educational agendas of successive governments, particularly those since 1979. In this chapter I have examined a number of these strategies with particular reference to black parents of different ethnicities.

The contradictions within the government's position were highlighted in the case of separate schools. On the one hand, parents were being encouraged to exercise their rights of choice, on top of which the Secretary of State, himself, was proclaiming the virtues of schools offering a wide variety of specialisms. Add to this that strand of government thinking which has favoured separatism and it can be seen how, on the face of it, these would seem appropriate conditions for Muslims supporting separate schools to make their demands or, within the rhetoric of government, to exercise their rights. Why, then, in view of these favourable conditions, have successive governments denied Muslims' demands, despite the existence of such schools for Catholics and Jews? The difference, I have argued, can be found in another discourse, invoked in the wake of the Rushdie affair and drawing on older Orientalist themes. The proposed solutions by government and much of the mainstream press to the 'threat' posed by Islam and its 'outsider' followers has been expedient and crude: assimilate or repatriate. On top of this, the Muslim community itself is not at one on the issue, as the arguments of groups like WAF clearly show. In such contradictory circumstances as these, the climate for the provision of Islamic schools appears both ripe and unripe for change.

Likewise, the experience of Small Heath presents a complicating picture, especially when put in a wider context. On the one hand, it could be argued that, for every inner city school with a predominantly black pupil population thinking of opting out, there are many more predominantly white middle-class schools opting out in order to promote old grammar school values. The resistance of the latter to anti-racism and multiculturalism will now gain official backing. Opting out, in the long run, could well work against these principles and the demands of the majority of black and ethnic minority parents. Moreover, educational markets are undoubtedly being rigged by government in order to provide financial incentives for schools to opt out. On the other hand, the case of Small Heath does raise some important questions, which cannot be easily swept aside. There is no doubt that many parents had felt excluded and powerless during the time that the school was under local authority control. They experienced real grievances and a sense of disenfranchisement from the local educational system prior to opting out. When the decision came to opt out, many parents felt a unique sense of empowerment on being asked to decide the future of the school. There is also no doubt that the multicultural curriculum, such as it was at the time of opting out, has since been given additional resources, and has been expanded, albeit in quite limited ways, for the 90 per cent Muslim pupils at the school. The case of Small Heath can certainly be used to highlight some of the weaknesses of the old local state system and to resist the temptation to reduce the 'opting-out' debate to a simple yes or no.

Small Heath also highlighted the problems of talking about 'a community'. The 'Muslim community' stood for a section of the population divided nationally and politically. The 'community' with which the school sought to develop commercial links was also divided, with black businesses often excluded from the post-opt-out partnership. At other times, the idea of community was imposed on groups to legitimate consultation with co-opted leaders. The term also runs the risk of attaching groups to some ascribed absolute identities: the 'Muslim community', as if that were the only way to talk about its members. Nevertheless, there have been times when the term community, elusive as it may be, has provided an important basis for identification. The strategy of mobilising around 'community' has arguably been necessary because it has enabled groups to define their own needs, collectively, in the face of attempts to pick them off through individual consumer definitions.

The initiatives taken by schools do not exhaust the range of responses and strategies pursued by black parents and groups. Organisations like the Black Parents' Movement and the plethora of supplementary schools across the country are indicative of the failure of mainstream education to convince black parents that the system is adequately providing for their children. Once again, these parental and community initiatives are not what the government had in mind when it sought to increase parental choice and freedom. Despite its commitment to parents and to self-help, little tangible support has been given to such initiatives from government. So black and ethnic minority parents and organisations have sought to develop a variety of strategies, which in the present climate seek to reclaim definitions of consumer choice and parental rights. They have done so in ways which further their collective educational needs rather than consenting to the prejudices and privileges of the majority white community.

Both the debate on separate schools and the discussion of language usage by pupils and students highlighted the dangers of attributing identities and strategies to groups on the sole basis of traditional ethnic demarcations. The complexities and divisions within minority communities are as real as they are within white majority culture. Attempts to construct walls around these affiliations cannot hope to capture the multiplicity of forms of identity and allegiance and the importance of contextualising their various forms of expression.

5

'UNDERNEATH THE ARCHES': McDONALD'S, MARKETS AND EQUALITY

The idea for this chapter originally came from a Radio 4 programme broadcast in 1989, *The McDonald's Generation*, from the series, *After Dread and Anger*, written and presented by the black journalist Ferdinand Dennis. The programme made a personal impact for a number of reasons. In one sense it surprised me. I had expected Ferdinand Dennis to attack working conditions and low rates of pay for black workers, but instead the progamme heralded McDonald's as a beacon for future minority employment opportunities. Part of its success, in this respect, was attributed to the absence of well-developed equal opportunity programmes. McDonald's, it was claimed, had no need to take steps to eliminate discrimination and promote black employment, since unlike other UK firms, it was 'unfettered by British traditions and prejudices'. Since racial discrimination only interfered with the rational operation of market forces (for instance it inhibited recruitment on the basis of aptitude for the job) then leaving markets to themselves offered the best prospects, or so it was argued, for eliminating discrimination. My specific interest in McDonald's thus arose out of this programme and particularly its suggestion that this global fast food chain had the answers to problems incapable of being solved by legislation and political means.

I am especially interested in the ways in which the cultural phenomenon of McDonald's embraces ideas of the market and consumption which serve to conceal discriminatory and exclusionary practices. I shall begin with a discussion of global and societal significance of McDonald's as a cultural icon. This will be followed by a review of a number of intellectual arguments which have lent support to McDonald's opposition to special policies which seek to protect the rights of black and ethnic minority workers. I will return to these arguments in the light of a discussion of work-place culture and practices at McDonald's UK with some additional evidence from the US. The final section will look at class struggles, both work-place and consumer protests, by way of concluding this assessment.

In many respects, my selection of McDonald's appears arbitrary. I could have chosen Coca-Cola or Kentucky Fried Chicken, for example, as a case study to explore many of the above themes. All these companies have prospered in the same market-place culture described in this chapter and elsewhere in this book and in many ways they reproduce many of the cultural, including work-place characteristics associated with McDonald's. However, what has interested me in the latter is the particularly aggressive and self-congratulatory way in which it has presented itself as an egalitarian employer and service provider. On top of this is its claim that equality is more effectively realised *in the absence* of any attempt to promote it through law, policy, regulation or other forms of state interference.

Its arguments for leaving the market to its own devices are particularly reflective of a dominant trait in political and intellectual culture throughout the 1980s, which left public interventions on racial equality, via equal opportunity policies etc., weakened and beleaguered. Whether this makes McDonald's more or less typical than other work-place institutional settings is outside the scope of this book to claim. The more important concern here is to show how work-places, whose primary concerns are economic, are not immune to important political and cultural dimensions. Equally, economic arguments, which have been used to reflect on, and sometimes explain and justify, the organisation of work, should be brought within the domain of political and cultural analysis. In this general respect, there is a strong case for extending this case study of McDonald's to other companies or work-place settings.

Resources for this chapter have been collected from both sides of the Atlantic. I have used my local community organisational contacts to establish links with a number of McDonald's employees, who have been willing to talk freely to me, although some expressed a desire for confidentiality. I have respected this concern by changing their names. I have had contact with a community-based project, organised by the regional Commission for Racial Equality, which looked into equal opportunity policies and practices in the retail sector in the Midlands. I have also been in contact with two organisations, the Service Workers' Advisory Group and the International Union of Food and Allied Workers, with whom I have discussed issues around working conditions and unionisation. My main reason for extending my research to the US was to compare McDonald's opposition to equal opportunity policies in the UK with the situation in the US, where the development of affirmative action programmes is a legal requirement. To complete this part of my research, I visited the US and collected material on McDonald's unavailable in Britain and held interviews with a member of McDonald's Affirmative Action Unit, the president of the Black Workers' Group in Chicago and the registrar of Hamburger University, in Oak Brook, Illinois.

McDONALD'S: ICON OF THE 1980s

The origins of McDonald's are now written into twentieth-century capitalism's folklore. It is the classic tale of an entrepreneur by the name of Ray Kroc, who had exclusive rights to a milkshake machine. He visited a restaurant in California that had managed to install eight of them, to see what had created such a high demand. The restaurant had a sign outside advertising its name, 'McDonald's', and offered a 'Speedee Service' inside. Inspired by its name and its work practices, Kroc opened the first of his McDonald's restaurants near Chicago, Illinois in 1954. By 1988, there were 10,000 restaurants in 50 countries. By 1989, McDonald's served 20 million customers a day and sold 65 billion hamburgers. The original restaurant in Illinois is now a museum, complete with original cooking equipment and models of the staff wearing the 1955 uniform. In Britain, the history of McDonald's is more recent. It opened its first restaurant in Woolwich in 1974 and, after a shaky start, it began opening up between 35–40 new outlets each year. By the late 1980s the total number was in excess of 300.

The 'Big Mac', or hamburger, which has become such a powerful symbol of late twentieth-century North American culture, actually has its origins, not in Germany, but on the Russian steppes. It is the Tartars to whom the Big Mac owes its biggest debt. The steak tartare was eventually refined into a patty shape in Hamburg, from whence German emigrants took it to Cincinnati in the early 1800s. Since then, McDonald's has more than reciprocated its debt to its global origins. In January 1990, McDonald's opened its first restaurant in Pushkin Square (*Daily Mirror*, 30 January 1990). Such is the universality of McDonald's that in 1991 *The Economist* magazine compared Big Mac prices in the 54 countries where it was sold in order to construct a global cost of living index.

As the title of his book, *The McDonaldization of Society*, implies, George Ritzer (1993) sees McDonald's as part of a wider set of socio-cultural changes. In particular, McDonald's represents all that is efficient, calculated, predictable and over which we can exercise control. For some authors, Jean-François Lyotard and Allen Shelton, McDonald's is an example of a new state of society: postmodernity. The automation of the customer, the compression of space/time (you can eat at McDonald's anywhere, any time) and niche advertising are all features of this new condition. Ritzer, however, argues that McDonald's exemplifies modernity and takes capitalism to new rational heights. What authors characterise as postmodern Rizter argues is just on a continuum with what preceded it. The McDonaldisation process can be witnessed elsewhere; in credit cards, plastic cutlery, chat lines, mass teaching, tabloid newspapers and films with roman numerals after their names (ibid.: 184–5). His book goes on to critique the assumptions underpinning this process. In other words, society may not be as efficient, predictable or calculable as the process implies.

McDonald's projects itself, primarily through its advertisements and promotions, as a fun, clean, cheap place to eat, offering a fast service and a friendly staff. Its recent marketing has targeted consumers of all ages and backgrounds, although traditionally it is associated with young people and young families, typified by its Ronald McDonald houses. These are located near children's hospitals and provide accommodation for the families of children who are seriously ill. In one survey in the United States 96 per cent of schoolchildren were able to identify Ronald McDonald, making him second only to Father Christmas as the most recognised figure (Ritzer, 1993: 5)! Its facilities for children's parties, competitions, and the décor of many of its British restaurants all reinforce its young family image. McDonald's advertising campaigns reflect this, although in the United States there has been much more vigorous niche marketing, that is targeting different ages and ethnic groups separately. In Britain it has constructed a more universal image, although in practice this has meant targeting the youngish, white, middle-class, nuclear family. There are similarities here with the early Benetton, Coca-Cola and Pepsi-Cola advertising campaigns which projected the idea of a 'global youth', thus cleverly concealing real differences, including inequalities, between those it claimed to represent.

As an employer, McDonald's promotes itself as dynamic, expanding and youthful. It consciously rejects what it describes as old management traditions in Britain associated with hierarchies, deference and prejudice. It is also less concerned with formal entry qualifications.[1] Instead, the emphasis is placed on 'general disposition' for part-time staff. The mistrust of mainstream educational institutions is carried over into management training, which is in-house. In the United States, much of the training takes place at the 'Hamburger University', in Oak Brook, Illinois. From here, two-week courses are simultaneously translated into fourteen languages, available world-wide for McDonald's management. (The university has accreditation links with other degree-awarding institutions, so that courses successfully competed at Hamburger University can be accredited elsewhere.)[2] The very idea of a Hamburger University, particularly to a British audience, challenges both elitist and anti-vocational traditions in its educational system.

It is against this background that McDonald's 'strategy' on equal opportunities can be placed. According to UK management, McDonald's is, already, an equal opportunity employer. This is reflected in the work-force, half of whom are from minority groups. Moreover, it is alleged that these minority group employees are not just in the lowest-level jobs; it is claimed that 50 per cent of supervisory staff are from such groups (personnel manager, McDonald's UK, interviewed in *After Dread and Anger*). This apparent success is attributed, first, to the transfer of US recruitment practices, which are claimed to be more open than in Britain, and second, to the visibility of black staff, which encourages more blacks to apply (ibid.). McDonald's does have a formal equal opportunity statement, but no monitoring and no formal policies on training, investment, marketing and contracts. In other words what 'equal opportunity' means in principle and practice can and does vary enormously. I shall return to these questions later in the chapter.

Two of the black staff interviewed on Dennis's programme had indeed reached positions of management and in 1989 were earning £27,000 and

£15,000 respectively. Both were women who conveyed a strong sense of the 'it's just down to me' idea, which McDonald's has clearly encouraged its staff to internalise. This catch-phrase draws on Ray Kroc's dictum, now etched in glass at the McDonald's Plaza in Oak Brook, Illinois: 'Luck is the dividend of sweat: the more you sweat the luckier you get'. By way of confirming the programme's critique of equal opportunity policies, McDonald's staff interviewed by Dennis contrasted their current experience with previous employment, in one case the relative security of the Civil Service, in another, the stop-gap employment of a post-Youth Training Scheme. In general, they spoke of less discrimination, more career opportunities at McDonald's and being treated as an 'equal'.

The above thumbnail sketch will be followed up, shortly, with a closer look at working practices and consumption struggles at McDonald's. Before doing so, my aim is to consider the wider political and intellectual climate which has proved favourable to the global expansion of McDonald's, particularly through its endorsement of the McDonald's strategy on equal opportunities. In fact, resistance to policy and political intervention around affirmative action and equal opportunities has come from all sides of the political spectrum. In the next section I shall examine three sets of arguments which, though intellectually and politically distinct, effectively condone, if not outwardly support, the stance taken by McDonald's.

THE MARKET AND CLASS AS MECHANISMS FOR EQUALITY: THE INTELLECTUAL RATIONALE

In this section I will look at three critical assessments of the terms 'affirmative action' and 'positive discrimination' carried out by three writers on race, Thomas Sowell and William Wilson in North America, and John Edwards in Britain. The particular meanings attached to the above terms are less important, at this stage, than what they generally stand for: forms of policy intervention which aim (with varying degrees of commitment and practice) to secure equal rights to employment, promotion, equal pay for equal work and freedom from discrimination for groups hitherto disadvantaged in the above ways.[3]. Although there are some important differences (reflecting the conservative, Marxist and liberal viewpoints respectively of each author), they share important points of convergence in terms of the implications of their writing. In this sense, McDonald's could take comfort from all three positions, by way of justifying its own stance on equality. I shall discuss each briefly now and return to them towards the end of the chapter.

Thomas Sowell on affirmative action

Thomas Sowell's argument against affirmative action is built on a series of assumptions and propositions (Sowell, 1981, 1987). History, Sowell argues, has confirmed that ethnic groups that have sought advancement through political channels have ended up worse off, economically, than those who have eschewed politics. North American Indians, for instance, are still under-privileged, despite using the political system to make their demands. On the other hand, Japanese immigrants, who have not sought to use political means to secure their prosperity are, nevertheless, amongst the most successful. Sowell argues that political demands on the part of minority groups encourage a culture of dependency rather than self-help; of continued poverty rather than fostering the 'it's down to me' spirit.

In making this claim, Sowell disregards the possibility that other factors, besides levels of political mobilisation, might have influenced levels of prosperity between groups. These factors include, for instance, the compatibility of minority with majority cultures, the willingness on the part of minority groups to assimilate and last, and by no means least, the different levels of capital and wealth of different ethnic groups. Sowell's second point is equally contentious since it overlooks the fact that we are all socially dependent: some of us on employers to give us work, others on customers to buy our goods and all of us on the state (the police, courts, education) to protect and secure our rights. Hence, the question begged by Sowell's argument is how it is that these latter kinds of dependency are rendered invisible, or at least considered legitimate, whilst 'dependencies' which arise from minorities, making political demands and exercising their legitimate rights, are both highly visible and consistently called into question.

Whatever the processes of legitimation involved here, and I would argue that both Sowell and McDonald's, in different ways, play their part, one important effect is this: it becomes easier to interpret concessions to minority political demands as a favour rather than as a right. Structured relations of 'dependency' thus remain intact but they result, not from the actions of the minority, but from the values and actions of the majority culture. Furthermore, in appealing to an apparently universally desirable proposition, 'it's down to me', Sowell is working with a culturally specific as well as ideologically laden judgement. The assumption that this is a realistic, or desirable, outlook for everyone to have, remains questionable and unproven. Certainly, the growing disparities of wealth in the US and in Britain and the differences in educational rewards suggest that the 'down to me' attitude cannot, on its own, secure success for all, and that the majority are bound to fail in terms of educational qualifications and economic success. It is also clear that individual failures will originate from some social groups more than others.

According to Sowell, government affirmative action programmes actually reduce both choice and the incentive to 'get on'. He gives the example of slum clearance schemes which, he argues, eliminate people's preference to stay where they are and spend their money on something else. The argument that no one should be expected to live in a slum, or have to choose between that and something else (health insurance?), is rejected in favour of one justifying existing inequalities in order to provide incentives and the motivation to 'get on'. Sowell's logic leads him to associate the culture of affirmative action with patterns of behaviour incompatible with the desired ethos of modern industry, characterised by punctuality, discipline and co-operation (Sowell, 1981: 110).

Another form of statutory intervention, the setting of minimum wage levels, Sowell argues, would actually provide employers with an incentive to discriminate on racial grounds, through the shedding of surplus labour. In other words, according to Sowell, since minority groups are amongst the least skilled and qualified, it is likely that they will be hardest hit in the event of the introduction of a statutory minimum wage. (Similar arguments were expressed in the UK by the Conservative Party against Labour's proposal for such a wage in the 1992 general election campaign.) An important inference of Sowell's argument here is that, faced with the choice of employing black and white labour at the same price, employers are likely to choose white. Instead of demanding legal redress in such circumstances, Sowell's message for blacks is that it is better to have poorly paid work at discriminatory rates of pay than to have no work at all. In essence, therefore, Sowell's argument restricts our options; we have to choose between discriminatory redundancy policies and discriminatory wages levels. Faced with this 'choice' (a choice structured by Sowell's argument and oversimplified view of labour market conditions), we are invited to accept the latter, presumably because it would appear to cost less, both to the employer and the taxpayer.

Finally, Sowell questions the motives of those pursuing affirmative action through politics. 'Discrimination thus becomes an interest, a means to pursue political career ends' (ibid.: 103). This claim is made regardless of whether or not discrimination exists, or whether formal political responses might help. In an essay entitled 'Preferential Treatment' he argues that preferences end up helping those who are more fortunate to begin with and increase polarisation and inequalities within the black population (Sowell, 1987: 198). It is hard to respond to the argument that affirmative action can best be understood in terms of the career intentions of those promoting it, since it relies on attributing motives to individuals which are well nigh impossible to prove. It could be argued, if such arguments were resorted to, that any nests feathered over the last ten years, in the US and UK are more likely to have belonged to those intellectuals, like Sowell, whose contributions have helped to justify, excuse and generally provide moral sanction for Reaganite and Thatcherite policies.

Sowell's arguments can thus be understood within the context of a broader attack on affirmative action in the US and on equal opportunity programmes in Britain. The US, a climate which has permitted the restructuring of the Civil Rights Commission; a succession of Supreme Court decisions which rejected employers' decisions based on the affirmative action principle, and a popular backlash against affirmative action, is more than compatible with Sowell's own pronouncements. In fact, he, like other academics, has provided the intellectual gloss which has legitimised a retreat on affirmative action. Shelby Steele and Walter Williams, both black academics, have also argued against affirmative action. In all three cases, their blackness, linked to their success, can also be used to undermine the principle.[4] Steele (1990) suggests that affirmative action only heightens African-Americans' sense of failure. The views expressed by both Steele and Williams challenge the idea that racism is responsible for economic inequalities. On the contrary, it is argued, Jews have been discriminated against but have been economically successful. One reason for the relative economic failure of African-Americans has been their concentration in the public sector, a fact Steele also blames on affirmative action programmes which have promoted (wasteful?) public sector employment.

The nomination and selection of Clarence Thomas, another black conservative, to the Supreme Court (see above, p. 49) is a fulfilment of Presidents Reagan and Bush's desire to use the Supreme Court to endorse their brand of free market conservatism. Thomas was an outspoken critic of affirmative action, even during his time as head of the Equal Employment Opportunity Commission. I shall return to Thomas's case shortly.

John Edwards on positive discrimination

Britain, too, over the past decade has experienced a backlash against its (much weaker) equal opportunity policies. These attacks, which have already been referred to (see p. 26) have been well documented elsewhere (Gordon and Klug, 1986; Gordon, 1990). I do want to discuss one contribution to this debate, by John Edwards, an academic who has critiqued the concept of positive discrimination on similar, although not identical grounds to Alan Goldman's critique of reverse discrimination (1979). In discussing Edwards' work, I do not wish to suggest any direct link with McDonald's stance on equal opportunities. However, I would argue that many of his ideas coincide with a wider culture of resistance to policies aimed at redressing group inequalities.

Edwards defines positive discrimination as any action which gives preferential treatment to someone just for being a member of a specific group (1987: 26). He goes on to distinguish two ways of distributing goods and resources in society: according to market criteria and according to social justice. In the latter, he argues, for goods to be distributed on grounds of social justice it is necessary to apply one of the following: merit, needs, deserts, rights, or consequential benefits. If there is a basis for positive discrimination, Edwards argues, it has to be shown to be socially just.

So, for example, when applying the principle of merit as a basis for social justice, he argues that IQ is a crucial qualification for the receipt of benefit in order to meet the needs of technology and professional requirements. The idea of quotas, according to this argument, interferes with the allegedly rational, efficient allocation of resources. In the case of needs, Edwards argues, like Goldman, that these are best met if resources are distributed on an individual, rather than an ethnic or racial basis. The danger with distribution on a group basis, according to Edwards, is that you can end up giving to privileged members of one group at the expense of needy members of another. The argument against linking positive discrimination to deserts is similar. Edwards claims that compensating members of a minority for past injustices is unjust on two grounds. First, he argues, white people living today cannot be held morally responsible for actions of their imperial great-grandfathers. Second, and again underlining his rejection of the needs principle, he contends that if you compensate on basis of race, affluent blacks would gain at expense of poor whites. Finally, he maintains, the principle of positive discrimination cannot be justified on grounds of its beneficial consequences because it would provoke a backlash (the argument is very similar here to that of US conservatives and British writers like Lewis, 1988) and also because, ultimately, rewards come as a result of motivation and hard work, not by quota-guaranteed places in higher education. Once again this point is identical to that made by Thomas Sowell and others in the US.

Ultimately, Edwards rejects positive discrimination because it benefits undeserving (i.e. affluent) blacks at the expense of some deserving poor and innocent whites and, further, that it is unworkable because it would create a backlash. My own view is that Edwards' book has helped to fuel this very backlash and, like the arguments of Sowell, Williams and Steele in the US, has played a part in the retreat on race equality programmes. I will now consider the arguments of William Wilson, who offers a Marxist perspective on affirmative action, but whose conclusions are not so different from those already discussed.

William Wilson's critique of affirmative action

Wilson's extremely persuasive argument (1980) is built on the assumption that affirmative action programmes do work, but only for the black middle class. Affirmative action has thus polarised the black community, the vast majority of whom remain in low-paid, insecure employment if, indeed, in work at all. The most effective way to improve black employment, according to Wilson, is via class-based strategies, since class, and not race, is the real divide in terms of employment opportunities and rewards (ibid.: 150ff.). Wilson develops this argument by examining evidence of employment opportunities in the manufacturing and service sectors of the economy (ibid.: 126). In the 1930s and 1940s, important improvements in pay and conditions for black workers were secured by trade unions. By the 1950s and 1960s, manufacturing was declining at the expense of the service sector, the consequences of which were most heavily felt by black workers (ibid.: 129). The 'crisis' of the inner city (over which the local state had little control,[5] since it was macroeconomic growth and sectoral expansion and decline that dictated local circumstances) weakened the role of the unions.

In contrast, the expansion of the corporate government sector created a demand for skilled labour and this, combined with the impact of affirmative action programmes initiated in the 1960s, provided the basis for a growth in the black middle class. The civil rights movement, with its focus on race, did not address class subordination and 'tended to operate with little direct relationship to the black ghetto' (cited ibid.: 136). Consequently, the black community has been split between a small middle class who have benefited from affirmative action in the context of an expansion of the service sector of the economy, and a much larger working class, for whom affirmative action has been no match for the unemployment, low wage rates, lack of union organisation and residential segregation.

Wilson's analysis of economic trends leads him to conclude that class is a more useful term than race because it more accurately reflects the problems facing the majority of North American blacks, and hence provides a more effective basis for mobilising to improve their position. Whilst Sowell sees black employment in the public sector as holding back black advances in the private sector, Wilson sees the former as having benefited blacks, but only a privileged few. Whilst Sowell sees the solution in terms of markets, Wilson envisages solutions more in terms of political strategies around class. A broadly similar argument was put forward, in the British context, by Malcolm Cross on Radio 4's *Analysis* (25 March 1989). Demographic trends and economic upturn, he argued, would prove more significant than government policies in countering racial discrimination.

What all these arguments do, as I have suggested, is to endorse the McDonald's stance on equal opportunities. If black people are going to get on, it is because the market allows them to. No amount of institutional tinkering on equal opportunities will help; only, maybe, a small black middle-class elite. Together these arguments span the political spectrum from right to left. McDonald's, therefore, is very much part of a wider culture of resistance to affirmative action for which the above arguments provide an important basis. The institutional forms of this resistance and how they are experienced will now be discussed.

McDONALD'S

The cultural significance of McDonald's in Britain in the last quarter of the twentieth century can partly be understood with reference to global shifts in production, transfers of capital and labour and the political structures integrally bound up with these movements. In three articles, Sivanandan has identified a new underclass in Britain, made up of Third World refugees, fleeing from persecution (Sivanandan, 1988, 1989, 1990b). He locates this class in Britain beneath indigenous black labour, both in terms of employment (pay, conditions and security) and political rights. Political repression has created the conditions for the emergence of a new migrant underclass of refugees, who amongst other kinds of work, 'serve in the up-front kitchens of McDonald's' (1988: 16). I shall return to the specific point about the role of refugee labour at McDonald's later, but what Sivanandan's analysis identifies, in broad terms, are the conditions which make the use of such labour possible. It also helps to explain the use of indigenous black labour. The decline in manufacturing and the expansion of foreign multinationals in Britain can also be seen to play a role in shaping local employment opportunities and conditions in the UK (Martin and Rowthorn, 1986: 266; see also Massey, 1986; Gamble, 1981).

The role of government has not been insignificant in these changes, a fact which in itself undermines the idea of 'free market' conditions. In two key respects governments have shaped the market in ways detrimental to black people. First, since 1979 they have switched the targets of aid from regions to industries and, in particular, the 'sunrise' high technology industries such as microelectronics. These have expanded in places like the 'western corridor', that is to say in the predominantly white areas of Berkshire and Wiltshire, and not in the former industrial heartlands like the Midlands. Support for economic regeneration of these latter regions has come through local enterprise boards like the West Midlands Enterprise Board and what was the Greater London Enterprise Board. Second, the UK government has, through its abolition of exchange controls and relative absence of planning restrictions, facilitated the movement of capital in and out of the country. The prospect of a strong European economy after 1992 encouraged Japan and the United States to invest in Britain. Multinationals now account for 21 per cent of net manufacturing output in Britain. Finally, the state has played an important role in shaping the work-force. Legislation on part-time work, wage restrictions and employment protection has encouraged McDonald's to employ young people on part-time contracts, thus ensuring a cheap and disposable work-force. Consequently, 75 per cent of its work-force is under twenty-one (Transnationals Information Centre, 1987: 9).

Many of the above trends manifest themselves in localised settings. Birmingham, England's 'second city', is an old manufacturing centre. Its wealth was built on steel and slaves. The people and traditional industries of Birmingham were particularly badly hit by recession of the late 1970s and late 1980s, and none was more affected than the city's black and ethnic minority population. Service sector work has thus become an increasingly important source of employment, from fast food outlets to multinational hotel chains and from private security firms to international conference centres. McDonald's has its fair share of restaurants in Birmingham and has its regional headquarters in one of Birmingham's northern suburbs, Sutton Coldfield.

McDonald's restaurants in Birmingham are not situated in areas of high black African-Caribbean or south Asian population, with the result that the only restaurants to attract significant numbers of black staff and customers are the two in the city centre. Decisions about locating restaurants in one part of the city rather than another are important for a number of reasons, one of which is their effect on recruitment. McDonald's staff will often live locally, since rates of pay are low and have to be offset against travelling expenses, and because part-time employees are often expected to turn up for work at short notice. In fact, there is a question on the 'crew information' form which asks applicants to state how close they live to their nearest McDonald's restaurant, indicating that McDonald's takes proximity to work into account in recruitment decisions.

Location may well partly explain the representation of black staff across Birmingham's restaurants. In predominantly white localities black staff were barely represented at all. In more mixed areas they made up between 20 and 25 per cent of the work-force, equivalent to the level of their representation in the city as a whole. The above figures give no indication of job level, although it was clear in some restaurants that higher-status jobs went to clean-cut young white men and exceptionally, to a woman. These figures were collected in 1989,[6] but given the time lapse, the large numbers of part-time staff and the high turnover, they can only be used as an approximate guide. What *was* marked was the under-representation of black and ethnic minority staff at McDonald's regional head office in Sutton Coldfield. Out of a total sample of 51 employees, there were two of south Asian background, one male and one female. There were no other visible members of ethnic minority or black groups. Of the 49 white staff, 26 were female. In other words, 96 per cent were white. Even without information regarding job levels, it is reasonable to assume that most jobs at head office, in contrast to part-time restaurant work, are full-time clerical, secretarial or managerial, that is, of higher status, better paid (for the most part) and certainly characterised by more favourable working conditions. In other words, taking black employment in McDonald's in Birmingham as a whole, the higher the job level the less likely you are to find a black worker. Moreover, even at the lowest levels, McDonald's does not rely disproportionately on black labour, but attracts youth labour from a variety of backgrounds.[7]

It is clear from the data above, however approximate it is, that most McDonald's workers of black and ethnic minority background are in low-paid work with minimal skill requirements. Janet was sixteen when she started working for a McDonald's restaurant. She had an interview and was offered the job there and then: 'he [the floor manager] just wanted to know what my interests were and that I knew what working for McDonald's entailed'. A black manager, of African-Caribbean background, based at one of the city centre restaurants confirmed this: 'Smart appearance and an ability to get on with the public were the most important criteria'. Janet earned £1.67 per hour, including Sundays, and £1.87 after 5.00 p.m.[8] In addition to weekends she worked three days a week, after school, from 4.00 p.m. to 9.45 p.m.

The work of crew members seemed initially (and superficially) varied, reflecting the division of work: preparing dressings (sauces on lettuce and buns); frying chips; filling baskets of chips; cooking and salting the bags of chips; checking the pies and fillet of fish; cooking the burgers at the grill station; serving at the tills, and cleaning, which meant tidying the back room, bringing down food from the stock room and tidying the front of the restaurant, including the toilets. Crew members rotated these jobs, although how this was done depended on the particular floor manager. According to Janet and other interviewees, the work seemed varied for a while, although the limited skill demands it made on its young work-force soon became apparent.

The staff are graded by coloured badge and stars: green badges for the period of training, which lasts four weeks, and then yellow badges with the chance then to gain up to five stars. Stars are important. They were used to decide aptitude and opportunities in management training. Janet had no stars after working for over nine months. She was never really sure when or whether she had been assessed in terms of performance. This had not been made clear to her, nor were the criteria for the assessment of performance. Once again the floor manager has considerable discretion to assess and select criteria with no procedure for feedback or accountability. At Janet's restaurant there were five floor managers, all of whom were white. After nine months Janet handed in her notice.

Despite Janet's eventual loss of interest, she had clearly internalised the belief that anyone can get on at McDonald's, so long as they are dedicated. In common with other young black people, she believed that McDonald's, in contrast to other employment fields, did provide management opportunities for black eighteen-year-olds. In fact, her store manager was black. Although she felt that opportunities were there for young women as well as young men, it just so happened that those getting on in her restaurant were men. It could be that whilst the rhetoric appeared to be working sufficiently for staff like Janet not to have become disillusioned, there could well have been more informal incentives encouraging young men to get on, and young women like Janet to leave.

It should be stressed, though, that very few black young men make it either, even when they start out with a positive commitment to work and to success. At sixteen, Monji joined McDonald's on a part-time basis in 1987. After only two weeks (it normally took four) he gained his yellow badge. At first, he opted to work very long hours, in one week he grossed over £100, which is a lot of hours at £1.58 per hour. Like Janet, however, his enthusiasm subsequently waned, a process which he attributed to different forms of pressure, including close supervision and sometimes victimisation by white floor management; the speed and intensity of work; an extremely competitive ethos; and racial harassment by other staff with no recourse to support from management. Monji left after only three months to work for a night club.

Floor managers were crucial in influencing the work experience of staff. They did so primarily through the discretion they were able to exercise over staff. Sometimes different managers would issue staff with conflicting instructions and expect both to be carried out. 'It was like they were playing tennis with you,' according to Michael, who worked as crew member over a period of eight months when he was sixteen and seventeen. On another occasion, a white staff member invited Monji to the toilets for a cigarette, then promptly reported him to the management, who gave him a verbal warning. When Monji asked why the white staff member had not been treated in a similar way, the reply was, 'We don't care about him.' On another occasion Monji was singled out for 'eating up' at the end of the day, something commonly practised by most staff and generally condoned by management. Similarly, informal rules about drinking were applied in a discriminatory way. In the absence of minimal protection provided by trade unions, complaining often merely invited further pressure: docked pay, warnings, failed assessment and blocked career aspirations; until, in the end, you leave. According to Sonia, 'If they don't like you or they've got too many staff (sometimes this happens after a peak like Christmas) they just start putting pressure on people until they leave.'

The pressure of work was enormous, made palatable, at least initially, by the games show ethos of the working atmosphere. So much of the work was organised around competitions, sometimes on an inter-ethnic basis and spurred on by management with gift vouchers for clothing shops, night club tickets etc. for the winning team or individual. There were also prizes for 'crew member of the month'. The competitiveness was not just within the restaurant, either. Restaurants competed regionally and, nationally, for even bigger prizes. *McNews*, McDonald's staff newspaper, carried photographs and write-ups of 'crew members' and, every three months, 'hostesses' of the quarter. The work was demanding, not so much in terms of skill, although turning over two dozen burgers with a spatula, basting them, putting on the sauces and putting them in buns all in the space of a minute and a half did involve some measure of dexterity. However, the competitive ethos could only conceal the speed, physical demands and monotony of the work for so long.

The pressure of this competitive edge to the work generated a rivalry amongst staff which often turned to racial abuse. Monji and Jas were often called 'Paki', 'Ding Ding' and asked, 'Does your father own a corner shop?' Taunts and racial comments were part of their daily routine. On one occasion, Monji's head was held in a basin of water. 'At the time I thought it was funny. It's only since I've left that it makes me angry when I think about it.' Management took no action to eliminate these practices. In fact, the competitiveness they fostered, sometimes along racial lines, was strengthened by this 'off the field' hostility.

So why do young people, and young black people in particular, work at McDonald's? Clearly one reason was cash: supplementing pocket money and, in some cases, a family income. But the attraction of McDonald's went beyond this. It evidently had something to do with the continuities in young people's lives. From children's parties to an after school hang-out, McDonald's became a haven spanning the years up to employment. Seen from the customers' viewpoint McDonald's appears a friendly, youthful, clean, fun place to work.

According to Michael, 'It's the glamour, you know, that advert for McDonald's with the black guy with the hat. . . it's a big company – it's where your friends go. . . there are people who get on, managers at eighteen, it's young and dynamic.'

Virtually all of its restaurants had the atmosphere of a children's party: free flags, seats shaped like toadstools, colourful tiled murals and the inevitable pictures of Ronald. The staff play hosts and hostesses to a day-long party. The sense of fun rubs off on staff, which again has a usefully diverting effect. The take-away leaflets on diabetes, nutrition and the environment, not to mention Ronald, all give the impression that McDonald's and its staff really do care. The significance of McDonald's in young people's lives partly helps to explain why McDonald's successfully recruits staff from its own customers. The initial attraction is built on the idea of being paid to turn up at what has been a place of leisure and pleasure. The restaurants encourage this by advertising on their walls: 'More Than Just a Saturday Job' and 'Jobs Galore at the New Olton Drive Thru'. 'Flexible part-time hours (not only Saturdays) with the possible prospects of a five star career'. The 'party image' of McDonald's, 'the place to hang out', are what attracts young customers to work the other side of the counter. Those I spoke to soon came to appreciate the transparency of the image. 'The glamour wears off when you're actually working there. . . the pressure gets too much. . . people leave all the time' (Sonia).

For the most part, McDonald's is a highly pressurised working environment. Crew members run around taking orders to drive-thru customers and back across the kitchen to scoop another portion of fries, all the while shouting orders to those cooking at the back of the restaurant. While this is going on, they are also packaging and bagging food and performing routine jobs, many of which would, under normal circumstances, be regarded as unskilled. The element which somehow inflates the skill or at least detracts from the repetitiveness of the job is the sense of urgency.

Some, though not all, of these findings have been borne out by a study of McDonald's, carried out by the Transnationals Information Centre: TIC (1987), based on evidence from around the world. It was particularly concerned with wage levels and conditions of work amongst McDonald's employees. Low pay and part-time conditions attract the most vulnerable and exploitable sections of the work-force: young, female or black or a combination of these. McDonald's ability to exploit its work-force has been helped by management's success in keeping McDonald's non-unionised. Interestingly, there are exceptions to this. In Nicaragua, the company not only agreed to the union acting as sole negotiator, but agreed to 90 days' paid leave for all employees, including an allowance to attend union education programmes (TIC, 1987: 15)![9] Elsewhere, however, management has mobilised against the unions in a variety of ways. In Chicago, for example, when a worker asked for a union to be recognised, management threw a party for employees, gave them a free meal every day as well as other perks. Eventually the union's attempt to organise the work-force collapsed (ibid.). Elsewhere employees were subject to lie detector tests and risked dismissal if questions on union activity or sympathy proved positive (Boas and Chan, 1976: 93).

A further difficulty faced by union organisations is the high rate of staff turnover. McDonald's does not expect its work-force to stay long. Seven out of ten drop out within a month of starting. According to one manager cited in the TIC report,

> No one ever stays more than six to nine months unless they want to go on to management. It's the pressure, heavy hours, awful pay and it's a degrading job – having to clean tables and scrub floors in front of the customers – and always having to smile.

> (ibid.: 10)

The pressure is compounded by the long hours that part-time workers are sometimes expected to work. Although overtime is supposed to be paid for any time worked over 39 hours, many only receive the basic rate. TIC cited the case of a woman who was working 12-hour shifts, 12 a.m. to 12 p.m., six days a week, who was sometimes asked to work on her day off and still only paid, for each of the 70 hours she worked, at the basic rate.

'Flexible' working conditions means rotating around a series of jobs that have been designed to minimise the skill content through computerised technology and detailed task sub-division described above. 'There is no room for creative chefs in this factory' (ibid.: 14). Despite this comment, McDonald's did appoint a chef in their head office in Illinois in 1990, who had formerly worked as chief chef at Café Provençal, one of Chicago's few 3.5 star restaurants (Forbes, 24 December 1990)! It seems unlikely, however, that employees or customers across the McDonald's empire, or even within the United States, are likely to benefit from his culinary creativity.

In the United States, the company and government have actively worked together on minimum wage legislation. President Nixon, who once wrote to Ray Kroc congratulating him on his burgers (which, he claimed, came a close second to Mrs Nixon's), consulted Ray Kroc on the minimum wage bill which enabled employers to continue to pay less to students. In appreciation for Nixon's efforts, Kroc donated $255,000 to Nixon's 1972 presidential campaign. On the subject of political donations, there was a rumour (unfounded as it turned out) circulating in Britain in the late 1980s that McDonald's was supporting Noraid, the US fund-raising body for the IRA. This was vigorously denied by McDonald's and The Economist magazine subsequently explained that the confusion had arisen when British viewers tuned in to CNN news on satellite television to hear that McDonald's gave generously to the IRA, which, in the United States, was an acronym for Individual Retirement Accounts. Despite this explanation, the rumour continued, notably amongst members of the British armed forces in Northern Ireland, some of whom continue to boycott McDonald's restaurants.

MARKETS: THE GREAT EQUALISERS?

So, in the light of the evidence above, are Sowell and McDonald's UK management right to assume that market freedom is the most effective way to achieve equality? Is McDonald's a testimony to this kind of intellectual and corporate rationale? My view is that Sowell's argument is flawed, both in its logic and in the face of overwhelming evidence to the contrary. First, in all the market-based arguments, there is a subtle conflation of two distinct ideas. The first is that more employment opportunities for all will inevitably improve employment opportunities for black and ethnic minority employees: in other words, opportunities will increase in absolute terms.

Whilst this may or may not be the case, it cannot be assumed from the idea of *absolute* improvement that black employment opportunities will improve *relative* to white. This latter idea, however, is decisive, since it is the relative difference which defines the level of racial inequality. Bhat *et al.* (1988) make the point simply when they argue that, irrespective of market situation, black and ethnic minority groups have suffered adversely. In other words, since racism takes different forms under different market situations, the market itself cannot determine whether racism exists or not, although it can help to structure its forms. In the 1950s, when the economy was expanding and black labour was recruited to sectors where labour was in short supply, racism did not take the form of a lack of job opportunities, but expressed itself in the kind of work available to black immigrants, their treatment by employers, trade unions and other workers.

The expansion of particular sectors of the economy, like demographic trends, is only part of what contributes to greater employment opportunities for black people. Which sectors are expanding? Where are there labour shortages? At what levels? What is the pattern of geographical location? What are the skill requirements? Answers to these questions are bound to begin to complicate the simple equation that expansion by itself equals opportunities for all. The idea, moreover, that all these factors are shaped by some invisible market hand, rather than produced by political processes inside and outside the private sector, is based on a seemingly highly convenient fallacy. It allows those who preach this market forces doctrine to keep their hands out of potentially muggy political waters while at the same time allowing their arguments to be used to serve very definite sets of political interests.

There is a second flaw in these arguments: the assumption that rational capitalism needs equal opportunities. It is identical to the argument used in South Africa. At one time, apartheid was thought of as a dinosaur that would reform itself away with the development of capitalism. The latter, it was argued, needed a flexible, skilled, mobile work-force that only free labour, recruited on meritocratic criteria, could meet. For all the formal dismantling of apartheid, considerable political and economic inequalities remain intact. Moreover, what change has been secured has been in no small part due to the role of black struggle and international pressure rather than egalitarian capitalism. In fact, there always have been as many 'rational' reasons for maintaining as for abolishing apartheid. Both the fear of a white backlash and the idea of so-called 'intrinsic' differences between groups have been appealed to in the past to justify the maintenance of the apartheid regime even when some (by no means all) business interests were pressing for reform.

Similarly in Britain, concern about customer reaction to black sales staff and work-force reaction to black superiors have both been used to discriminate on allegedly 'rational' commercial grounds against black people. As Stuart Hall has pointed out, capital has always been able to work with and through sexual divisions as well as ethnically and racially inflected labour forces to accomplish the commodification of labour (1991a: 29). The point is that there are many, sometimes conflicting, interpretations of what rationality entails when it comes to employment opportunities for black people. These interpretations may increase or reduce opportunities but there is certainly nothing intrinsically anti-discriminatory about the operation of market principles.

This is an important moment to reflect on John Edwards' case against positive discrimination. The argument is built on the idea that merit, established through IQ, is a fair basis for distributing jobs, income and wealth unequally. The reality is somewhat messier, as Mason (1990) and Jenkins (1987) have rightly suggested in their discussions of recruitment. There is the question of how schools come to evaluate pupils, how curriculum, in a broad sense, works to the advantage of white middle-class males and how qualifications reflect these discriminatory processes within education. There is also the question of what qualifications are really necessary for a particular job and how employers use a much more ambiguous set of criteria, centred around whether the 'face fits'. It is interesting that McDonald's US acknowledges the dangers of reproducing a top class of executives modelled on Ray Kroc and his original team of predominantly white men (interview, Affirmative Action Unit, July 1991). In the terms of Edwards' argument, where is the social justice or fairness in that?

These processes affect not only who gets appointed but what happens to black and ethnic minority staff when they are appointed. The case studies from Birmingham, and elsewhere, suggest that there are mechanisms operating within the dominant cultural ethos of the company which exacerbate racist practices. Edwards' idea of denying the collective experience of black workers, of individualising their problems (in order to avoid benefiting the better off amongst them) only serves to maximise their vulnerability to further exploitation. Needless to say, the failure of Edwards' argument to acknowledge the institutional implications of its abstract dismissal of positive discrimination has not been lost on companies like McDonald's, who are only too willing to abide by its implications.

Empirical evidence from McDonald's adds weight to the logical flaws in these arguments. The reality of black and ethnic minority employment at

McDonald's cannot be reduced to a handful of successful managers. The vast majority of black employees are working part-time, without any job security or trade union rights and on extremely low rates of pay. Moreover, the work is tiring, repetitive and stressful. The personnel manager may boast employment at all levels of the organisation but, without monitoring, there is no evidence for this. My own, albeit limited, evidence from Birmingham confirms a multiracial work-force at the lowest employment levels, in contrast to regional head office employment, which is virtually all white.

If, for a moment, we assume that McDonald's is a desirable place to work, then it is worth noting that there are no McDonald's restaurants in the city of Birmingham in areas of high black settlement. Handsworth, Lozells, Sparkbrook and Saltley, might consider themselves fortunate to have been spared a McDonald's. However, the consequence of a decision to locate a restaurant in Northfield in a predominantly white area will have important employment implications for black people. There were no black or ethnic minority staff in the Northfield branch. This suggests that, other factors being equal, a 'rational' consideration when it comes to recruitment decisions might well work against those living in predominantly black or ethnic minority areas which are not near a McDonald's restaurant.

Black employment is not just about getting work. Racial inequalities are a factor in the quality of work itself. The experience of those black and ethnic minority workers with whom I spoke confirmed that McDonald's by no means escaped on-the-job discrimination, including physical and verbal abuse by white co-workers and managers. The emphasis on black–white or inter-ethnic rivalry in the context of a predominantly white floor management, which is itself capable of exercising considerable discretion over day-to-day work experiences, helps to foster discriminatory practices of the kind described above.

McDonald's cynicism with regard to policy intervention in this area is evident in three further ways. The first, ironically, can be illustrated with reference to the company's Equal Opportunities (EO) statement and its attempts to begin collecting ethnic data on its work-force. The Equal Opportunities statement is not so much a commitment to change existing practices but an endorsement of them:

> McDonald's is an Equal Opportunities employer. We ensure that employees and job applicants are selected, trained, promoted and treated on the basis of their relevant skills, talents and performance and without reference to race, colour, nationality, ethnic origin, sex or marital status.

The statement does go on to place responsibility for implementing the policy with the personnel officer, although all employees are held responsible for its day-to-day application. However, policies need objectives and frameworks for implementation and evaluation. So, what does McDonald's offer in this respect? The policy limits its purpose to non-discrimination, a principle to

116

which McDonald's is already committed on strict commercial grounds. The EO statement thus sanctions what already happens at McDonald's. Its implementation is left, very vaguely, to personnel and to all employees, who are expected not to discriminate. If anyone feels they have been discriminated against, they are encouraged to use the grievance procedure.

The point about record keeping is that it provides the data to identify patterns of under-representation, and hence provides a basis for positive intervention (for example targeted recruitment, a reappraisal of promotion criteria) in those areas and levels of work where black staff are under-represented. Since McDonald's has never been committed to any kind of intervention in this sense, only to non-discrimination, there was no basis for the introduction of monitoring at McDonald's. It was against this understanding of, and limited commitment to, equal opportunities that McDonald's management approached staff with the idea of monitoring. Given its views, management could not help but present the idea of monitoring as unnecessary (since McDonald's was an equal opportunity employer anyway) and/or, if it were introduced, say that it would inevitably favour ethnic minorities over the ethnic majority, regardless of ability.

In the event, it was not at all surprising that staff, including black and ethnic minority staff, expressed their opposition to the idea, and it was dropped (interview, Commission for Racial Equality, June 1989). So long as EO is restricted to non-discrimination, then, monitoring, which is linked to positive intervention, will be interpreted as preferential treatment or reverse discrimination. Black and white staff, faced with the option of recruitment and promotion on merit, or reverse discrimination, are unlikely to opt for the latter. In the end, it was management's interpretation of EO that secured the failure of the monitoring attempt and not, as management claimed, grassroots, including black and ethnic minority, opposition.

The above interpretation of EO developments is backed up by management comments. The UK personnel officer, according to the Commission for Racial Equality, believed 'the company was already an equal opportunity employer'. Data, it was claimed, was unnecessary because a level of awareness already existed and because of the reality of a multiracial work-force at all levels. Similarly, the programme in the *After Dread and Anger* series contrasted British business practices which were described as hierarchical, 'fettered by prejudice and tradition', with McDonald's UK's informal, non-hierarchical, meritocratic, 'it's down to you' ethos. The inference here is that British firms may need elaborate equal opportunity policies to create equal opportunity but McDonald's does not.

McDonald's record at industrial tribunals bears testimony to the company's attitude towards racial discrimination. By 1989, there had been three tribunal cases in the UK involving alleged racial discrimination at McDonald's. One case involved two applicants, D. S. and K. S. Dhatt, who were asked whether or not they had work permits. They did not, for the simple reason that they did not legally require them. They were nevertheless refused work. The case went to tribunal and, although the error was drawn to the attention of McDonald's, they proceeded to defend their decision. Even more surprising, or perhaps not, was the decision of the tribunal, which found in favour of McDonald's (interview, Commission for Racial Equality, June 1989).

In contrast to the views of McDonald's management in the UK, the US corporation has a long association with affirmative action. A number of factors have contributed and given shape and substance to initiatives in this area. The first of these has been legal pressure brought about by the Civil Rights Acts of 1964 and 1984, which required corporations to submit records on recruitment patterns to the Equal Opportunities Employment Commission. The fear of adverse publicity arising from legal action undoubtedly galvanised McDonald's, as it did other major corporations, in the US.

A second factor has undoubtedly been the size of the black and Latino populations in the US, and hence their importance as consumers and as employees. Areas with high black populations have been amongst the biggest moneymakers (Boas and Chan, 1976: 161). If for no other reason than commercial profitability, franchises have been awarded to black businesses. It is worth noting here that McDonald's receives over 20,000 applications for franchises each year, of which only 200 are eventually successful (*New York Times*, 12 May 1991).

Third, a key factor prompting many initiatives on affirmative action has been to pre-empt opposition, from customer boycotts to union recognition disputes. McDonald's has created a number of consultative forums, an acknowledged function of which is to diffuse such protest. The rapping sessions, in which employees have an opportunity to air grievances, were originally designed to monitor potential agitators and infiltrators (Boas and Chan, 1976: 86). Other forums include groups of black operators, who meet with management to discuss issues and areas of concern, and the networks of black and Hispanic staff which also provide forums for expressing dissent.

Beyond these in-house forums, there are also links established with minority organisations (including civil rights groups) through the McDonald's Community Trust Bank. This body gives financial support and/or advice, in return for which organisations refer possible staff recruits and support the corporation in the case of a boycott (interview, Affirmative Action Unit, 23 July 1991). Maintaining links with minority communities, given their significance in numerical terms, is clearly part of a wider marketing strategy that aims to add to McDonald's 60 million customers per year.

The affirmative action process therefore has a strong expedient thrust to it. Its various forms have reflected the overriding concern to maintain profit levels by avoiding disruption. However, since the late 1980s, prompted by the wider political and intellectual climate and reflected in Supreme Court decisions, the writings of Thomas Sowell and others and a popular Reaganite backlash against intervention, McDonald's has developed a revised version of affirmative action, which fits more closely with the views of McDonald's management in Britain. According to this view, the overriding focus of corporate America has been the rapidly changing population. In a Department of Labor report, published in 1988, it was claimed that by the year 2000 almost a third of new entrants to the labour force will be minorities, that is twice their current share (Department of Labor, 1988).

This projection has encouraged McDonald's to consider the increasing need to employ from minority populations, particularly as these groups are growing fastest at the younger end of the age spectrum. The reality of a multi-ethnic work-force has given rise to a new McSpeak. This new discourse has been incorporated into training programmes under the title, 'Managing Diversity'. According to the corporation, there is an urgent need to take account of cultural differences in values, language and methods of learning. Such training begins at the interpersonal level, with all participants encouraged to discuss their perceptions of themselves and others with the group. 'Painful' is how this process has been described by McDonald's management, but 'necessary for future advance' at the same time. Painful it might be, but how such forms of training secure 'future advance' is less obvious.

In the US, therefore, McDonald's has moved away from a traditional understanding of affirmative action in the sense of recruitment, franchising, career opportunities, and monitoring for quotas or targets, towards a concern about how the corporation will cope with an ethnically mixed work-force. 'It [affirmative action] is going to happen anyway' seems to be the new credo. I have already questioned the reliability and inevitability of this kind of forecast in my discussion of Thomas Sowell's work. For centuries, a numerical minority in Britain and in the United States has maintained its privileged position in terms of occupation and wealth. The fact that in the US it is possible to talk about minorities becoming a majority cannot, by itself, guarantee the elimination of discrimination. Moreover, whatever shape the economy, even if everyone has a job there is no guarantee that employment opportunities, admittedly for all, would be distributed fairly. On the contrary, without some form of policy or regulatory intervention at a minimum, it is highly likely that old divisions will reproduce themselves, whatever the demographic trends.

The debate surrounding the nomination of Clarence Thomas to the Supreme Court provides a good example of my argument. In a very powerful response to Thomas' rejection of affirmative action, Rosemary Bray, an African-American writer, wrote an article 'The Hands that Fed Judge Thomas' in the *Chicago Tribune*. In it she emphasised the importance of positive educational programmes in the 1960s for her and her mother, which helped her to get to Yale College. (The college, recognising the under-representation of black students, offered fee waivers, in some cases, to make possible their entry.) She contrasted this, her own experience under the era of affirmative action, with fading opportunities for minorities in the present climate. Clarence

Thomas, who had entered Yale a year earlier and hence also benefited from Yale's positive intervention, was now apparently against it. She continued:

> Clarence Thomas and I. . . were born in time to participate in a movement to ensure our rights as American citizens. . . . We, Judge Thomas, were given the chance to change our lives, a chance that fades for more and more of our citizens. . . helped along by the very people who nominate you to the high court.
>
> (25 July 1991)

CLASS STRUGGLES

The historical connections drawn between racism and capitalism were touched on in Chapter 2. One important consequence of this debate has been a continuing interest in the relationship between class and black or ethnic minority status. The point of production has traditionally been regarded as the dominant site for class struggle, although sites of consumption, for example housing, education and welfare benefits, have been taken more seriously as terrains for new forms of class engagement. (I shall return to this below.) Recent developments in Eastern Europe and in what was the old Euro-communist strand of western Marxism sought to question the continuing reliance on class as the dominant site of struggle. Debates and disputes around class, let alone its relationship to race, remain as contested as ever.

It seems evident that black and ethnic minority employment in McDonald's does not neatly follow class lines, however the latter are defined. Each locality has its own peculiarities in terms of labour markets. Sivanandan (1990b) could well be correct in stating that, in London, McDonald's employs a high percentage of refugees, the 'new underclass'. However, this group of workers, part-time crew members, are certainly differently placed to those young black executives interviewed on Ferdinand Dennis's programme earning in excess of £15,000 per year, or ethnic minority supervisors who, according to McDonald's, make up 50 per cent of the total supervisory staff in the UK. In Birmingham the employment profile of black staff was different again. Here, McDonald's was attracting young people, many of whom were white, with the exception of the McDonald's in the city centre. At the regional head office only two out of approximately fifty were black. In the United States, where different institutional conditions again pertain, African-Americans and Latinos are certainly better represented among franchisees. At the same time, McDonald's itself acknowledges that there is an under-representation of minorities at chief executive level (interview, Affirmative Action Unit, 23 July 1991).

While it is undoubtedly true that the closer to the bottom of the organisation you get, the more black workers you find, it is not the case that black workers have simply replaced white workers. The semi-fracturing of the black work-force in this way throws up important questions around identity and interests, both of which are culturally constructed. In some restaurants in Birmingham, and elsewhere no doubt, the competitive ethos, often defined around ethnicity, made for a divisive work context. In others, depending on the make-up of the staff and floor management's role, interracial identities and interests were fostered. Age, a shared work situation, shared schools and localities brought staff together, with the factor of ethnicity cutting across and working itself into these identities and interests in quite varied and complex ways. In the US the situation of black workers is also fractured along class lines. Take, for example, the older, well-established class of black franchisees in the US, some of them multi-millionaires, who have experienced racism in their efforts to secure loan capital from banks, struggled to secure a franchise and continue to experience racism from a predominantly white corporate management at McDonald's (interview, Black Operators Group, 26 July 1991).

Their shared experiences of racism may be analogous, but a multi-millionaire franchisee is clearly not, economically speaking, in the same position as Janet or Michael or the other part-time black and ethnic minority workers. These complex economic locations are shot through with cultural forms, such as the racially structured ethos of an inner city restaurant and the 'you can do it' mentality of the upwardly mobile young black executive. There is a contingency and indeterminacy as to where and with whom black (and white) workers perceive their interests to lie and, relatedly, what forms the basis of their allegiances, for example age, gender, class and/or ethnicity.

The distinction between class *location* and class *formation* is one way of reflecting on the above discussion of locations, identities and interests. Whilst the absolute size of the working class is declining, thanks to McDonald's and the expansion of the service sector (arguably, McDonald's crew members are not in the working class if the latter is strictly defined in terms of the production of surplus value), it is important to consider the processes by which classes are formed (Gilroy, 1987). This introduces a dynamic into this debate which is often missing when classes are talked about as fixed locations. Groups like the International Union of Food and Allied Workers as well as individual national trade unions have tried to develop a sense of collective class experience against a background of non-union recognition and highly individualised work experiences. In most countries they have been largely unsuccessful but where there has been government support for trade unions (in contrast to recent developments in the West), in Nicaragua for example, a stronger collective ethos and commitment to securing better working conditions through collective action worked for a while, at least before the country's only restaurant changed hands and then, in 1992, finally went out of business! On the other hand, the environmental and the nutrition lobbies have developed a consumer class consciousness, although the precise nature of the concessions, who participates and who benefits from them are all questionable. I shall come back to this shortly.

Likewise, the presence of a black owner/management class in the United States has come about as a consequence of one or more of the following: affirmative action and/or the threat of litigation, the *de facto* application of equal opportunity principles and the concern for black custom and pressure from black organisations. The emergence of a fractured class, not only at McDonald's but elsewhere, has encouraged writers like Wilson to dismiss race and to focus on class as the real determinant of outcomes. The problem with this is that it denies the *continuing* not *declining* significance of 'race' for black people at whatever level they work for the company. Situations ranging from Monji's experience of harassment to the existence of a black operators' group, made up of black franchisees in the US and working towards the representation of its members' interests, both indicate the continuing significance of race.

In terms of his socialist objectives, Wilson is right. It is not enough to aspire to maintain existing forms of production, work organisation and conditions, and simply aim to improve the job levels of black workers. The success of black enterprise in the US will depend on what that success brings, not just to those individuals, but to the black community as a whole. The struggle for affirmative action and equal opportunity in their radical forms has never been just about replacing one elite with another. They have been seen as strategic tools *en route* to more fundamental change. As it is, recent political pressure to dilute already weak versions of both has further restricted their impact and encouraged those on all sides of the political spectrum, including Wilson, to turn against the principle of state political intervention itself.

The principle of affirmative action or equal opportunity or whatever term is chosen (the choice of term seems less material than its substance) should not simply imply the replacement of white managers by black ones. Rather affirmative action could, potentially, be linked to a wider struggle for workplace democratisation and more open forms of decision-making about product development, investment and location. There is nothing inherently capitalistic about terms like product development or investment. Their meaning will result from cultural struggles waged on economic sites, amongst others. The aim of these struggles will be to recapture those terms and to inscribe them in new sets of working practices.

Class struggles based around consumption have, on the face of it, been more effective in pressurising McDonald's management than those seeking change through traditional forms of class action. Over the past twenty years or so, McDonald's has become the *bête noire* of the environmentalist movement, which has accused McDonald's of using ozone unfriendly packaging, of playing a part in the destruction of the tropical rain forests to clear space for cattle farming, and of selling high-fat foods associated with heart disease and obesity (Cannon, 1987).

It is worth reflecting on the impact of the health lobby in the US on McDonald's. After years of resisting criticism from nutritionists, McDonald's eventually succumbed and brought out its McClean de-luxe burger. Perhaps they were eventually persuaded by a fall-off in sales and a damaging advertising campaign mounted by Philip Sokolof, an independent entrepreneur, who took out full-page adverts with the headlines 'McDonald's, your Hamburgers have too much fat 'and 'Your french fries still are cooked with beef tallow'. The adverts went out in April 1990 and by the following year McDonald's had reduced the fat content of their hamburgers by adding water (which is presumably considerably cheaper!) and a water-retaining gum that comes from seaweed (*Newsweek*, 25 March 1991; *Time Magazine*, 25 March 1991). Attempts to introduce whole-food variations, as well as gourmet hamburgers with oysters and anchovies, are part of this attempt to head off such attacks.

In the US, McDonald's has also apparently given in to pressure from environmental groups like the Environment Defence Fund to replace its polystyrene packaging, not only because of its CFC content which McDonald's had already allegedly removed, but because of its waste effects: polystyrene takes ten years to decompose. McDonald's had intended to respond to this by entering into an agreement with its polystyrene suppliers to build seven recycling plants. However, under continuing pressure from the National Toxics Campaign, who got schoolchildren to send their empty clamshell containers back to McDonald's with angry letters, McDonald's agreed to replace its polystyrene packaging with polycoated paper. However, this, too, has its disadvantages for McDonald's, its customers and for the environment. It is not as efficient a heat retainer as polystyrene, takes more energy to produce and creates more pollution in the process.

It is interesting to compare the impact of consumer campaigns in the US with McDonald's restaurants outside the US. Apart from the fat and packaging campaigns, there is a much healthier menu in many US restaurants, including salads, carrot sticks, bran muffins and cholesterol-free fries (which McDonald's now claim are fried in vegetable, not meat, oil). The fact that these healthier alternatives are not as widely available in Britain suggests that McDonald's has only been won over to the environmental/nutrition lobby only when under pressure. In the US pressure also has to do with sales. In contrast to some of its rivals, whose sales increased in the 1990–1 period, McDonald's fell by about 3 per cent. 'The Halcyon days are over', according to a report in the *New York Times* (12 May 1991). Competitors, like Taco Bell, are selling cheaper, healthier more varied fare. This, more than external pressure, may have forced McDonald's to make these changes. In the process, it has also cut some of its prices to remain competitive with its rivals.

So can we say, in conclusion, that consumption struggles are more effective than orthodox forms of collective action? Such questions are fraught with uncertainty. The political climate in both Britain and the US is undoubtedly more favourably disposed to consumption demands than to those of trade unionists. The legal framework in both the US and UK has, indeed, been reformed to diminish the powers of trade unionists while the status of the consumer has been enhanced. Moreover, consumption struggles potentially cut across national boundaries. The implications of corporate policies on the environment affect those living in North and South, West and East, and so the wealthier nations have a potential stake in making some kind of response to environmental pressure. Of course, such global struggles would need to go beyond the highly individualistic, privileged strands of the present environmental movement. In this respect, there have been clear limits to consumer politics, including, it must be said, McDonald's own concessions to consumer pressure.

McDonald's efforts, both in Britain and the United States, to make its menu more 'ethnically' diverse make an interesting footnote to this discussion. In 'Round the World with McDonald's', in 1990 and 1991, British restaurants were offered Italian and Chinese alternatives to the standard menu. Meanwhile in the US, McDonald's were serving Mexican burritos and chicken fajitas to their customers. There is an irony in this global food chain with McDonald's, having built its reputation on selling slices of US culture,[10] which actually originated in Europe, now appropriating foods from elsewhere and selling them back, in some cases, to their original creators. This irony is all the more striking in Russia, which was responsible for both the first steak tartare and now plays host/outpost to McDonald's global market empire. At the same time, McDonald's strategy of packaging ethnicity and of celebrating difference and variety, effectively reduces variety to a version of the dominant culture. In this case ethnicity is OK as long as it comes in a polystyrene box, or rather in polycoated paper.

In reality, the emphasis that McDonald's apparently puts on diversity clashes with its dominant corporate identity. The 'family', as McDonald's management refers to it, has a set of values handed down by Ray Kroc, which provides the basis for corporation policy and practices. No amount of 'difference' will interfere with this identity since it is intimately bound up with the white male identities which created it. This goes for franchisees, too, who are bound by constraints of the corporate ethic. The latter was aptly summed up by Ray Kroc when he spoke of his competitors: 'If they were drowning to death I would put a hose in their mouth' (Moser, 1988). The extent to which McDonald's, as part of its 'response to diversity', incorporates alternative values emanating from its black franchisees or workers, on the one hand, or consumer protests, on the other, remains to be seen.

CONCLUSIONS

McDonald's golden arches and its Big Mac have become enduring symbols of western popular culture in the latter half of the twentieth century. Penny Moser, in her eulogistic testimony to the company (1988), suggested a number of possible reasons for the corporation's success, the first of which was to capture and retain the custom of the post-war baby boomers, like herself, who still have Big Mac attacks mid-afternoon. But why for a burger? Is it the 'quality, service, cleanliness or value'? Is it McDonald's relationship with its franchisees, which is considered to be more supportive and less exploitative than that of other corporations? Is it just knowing what to expect, the familiarity, security and safeness of those red and golden signs lighting up main streets all over the world; from Birmingham to San Jose to Toronto to Pushkin Square, you know what you are getting. Or maybe it really is actually what you get that draws customers in such large numbers: the addictiveness of the fat (or the seaweed?) and sugar in its food. Or is it, more simply, that McDonald's stays open long after most shops have closed and the staff gone home? Maybe, from a consumer's perspective, there is a snobbish reaction to McDonald's (witness the local outcry at the proposal to base a restaurant in Hampstead, London), which prejudices many against its possible virtues.

The prospect of extending the activity of 'eating out' to the masses is linked to Ritzer's (1993) acknowledgement of the wider process of McDonaldisation. The expansion of the service sector at the expense of manufacturing industry and the growth of new leisure classes from the 1950s onwards captured in the idea of the affluent, classless society. . . Television, shopping centres ('cathedrals of consumption'), personal stereos, cash-points, vending machines, EuroDisney, computer games and telephone advertising (the list is endless), are all part of this phenomenon, which gathered a particularly frenzied pace during the1980s. However, behind the myth of an affluent society has been the harsh reality of part-time work in the low-paid, unskilled service sector of the economy. Big Mac's 'value for money' has always been at the expense of those who work behind the counter. The use of labour at knock-down prices – part-time, young people, people of colour and migrant refugees – is a feature of employment in both the West and in the Third World. The struggles over unionisation at McDonald's bear witness to the problems in securing adequate working conditions, security and rights for employees. Debates about post-Fordism and postmodernity, whether the above conditions reflect distinct societal shifts and whether McDonald's typifies modern or postmodern conditions, seem less important than the issue of exploitation evident from the above discussion.

The forms of racism discussed in this chapter can be seen to work at a number of levels. It took the form of *under-representation* of both black staff in full-time positions in Birmingham in England and African-American staff at top management levels in the United States. Elsewhere racism took the form of *over-representation*, when black labour was used disproportionately to work long hours, often without overtime, at risk of instant dismissal with no security, let alone holiday entitlement or sickness pay. Hence, inequalities can be linked to both under- and over-representation of black staff, depending on the local circumstances. Processes relating to recruitment and working conditions have worked against black people in different ways, sometimes to exclude them, sometimes to over-represent them in low-paid, stressful insecure work. Racism has also enmeshed itself in the highly charged competitive ethos of McDonald's working practices. The discretionary role assigned to shop floor management has worked against black staff who remain vulnerable to discriminatory treatment with little, if any, redress.

The idea that the market and demographic trends will eliminate these discriminatory practices has little evidence and less logic to support its claim. Class privileges have been passed down to a minority for generations without anyone suggesting it would be more rational to open the class system up because the non-privileged were numerically superior. Without some framework of policy and monitoring, the system will leave itself open to precisely those abuses practised in institutions that operate a colour-blind policy at present. 'Merit' is by no means a culturally neutral term and it has been used in the past to ensure the maintenance of white male supremacy.

In the current climate, still very much living with its Thatcherite and Reaganite legacy, the idea that we can trust employers and corporations to implement equal opportunity because it makes sound market sense or because there will be an increase in the non-white population is a nonsense, and a convenient one at that for those seeking to dismiss political strategies around equal opportunities and affirmative action. By the same token, the relative increase in black unemployment over the past ten years has more to do with institutional factors, including government industrial and training policy, education and the absence of effective equal opportunity strategies, than it does with some invisible law of the economy or hand of the market.

Part III

GLOBAL THEMES

6

GLOBAL JOURNEYS

Sweet Honey and the Rock, a black African American a cappella group have a song in their repertoire called 'Are My Hands Clean'. In it they describe the production, distribution and sale of a blouse, including the role of cotton pickers, a multinational oil company, fabric manufacturers, pesticide producers, and a big department store where the blouse is bought at a 20 per cent discount. The song ends with the line, 'Are my hands clean?' Global journeys of this kind are very much at the heart of this chapter.

It is not just commodities that travel, however, but people (workers, refugees, tourists) and information and ideas, too. Clearly there are far too many journeys to write about them all. My purpose in this chapter is to look at how we, in the West, are encouraged to think about the Third World in particular ways. I am also interested in exploring how common-sense understandings of the so-called 'problems' of the Third World have changed over time and the role that the mass media have played in such constructions. I want to look at how these constructions affect ways of living both in the Third World and in the 'First'. Precisely who or what is the 'Third World' is a central question running throughout this chapter. Does it stand for a geographical area or a people? Is it a myth serving to reinforce the idea of a global ranking in terms of civilisation and backwardness, or a reality designating a common experience of oppression and struggle?

The chapter begins with a discussion of the notion of 'civilisation' and looks at the historical significance of black civilisations. All such attempts, including my own, are value-laden. What does 'civilised' mean exactly, which cultures are 'civilised' and which are not, and where does 'civilisation' originate, are all questions reliant on some preconceived standard. Since this standard itself is European in origin we must call into question all subsequent claims based on its use. As I suggested in Chapter 2, we can learn a lot about the emergence of ideas of civilisation from Edward Said's analysis of Orientalism and Martin Bernal's study of the black origins of western civilisation. Frantz Fanon's discussion of the internalisation of racism and the role of language in the process of constructing colonised subjectivities is also important in this respect.

Ideas about 'civilisation', in turn, underpin assessments of the 'problems' of the Third World. 'Over-population' is one such 'problem', the perception of which has, in turn, helped to sanction a variety of birth control programmes, some of which have been introduced coercively whilst others have relied on drugs that have been banned on health grounds in the West. The problem of over-population has also served to justify large-scale investments in agribusiness. In practice, however, in ways I shall discuss later, such investments and the economic practices associated with them have arguably helped to create the very food shortages (not to mention other hazardous effects) they claim to reduce. The problem of over-population and the solutions put forward by the West reinforce and are reinforced by other stereotypical characterisations ('ignorant', 'dependent') associated with the Third World. The latter have, in turn, helped to frame the West's response to the famines, disasters and coups that have provided the staple diet of media representations of the Third World fed to the West. In order to illustrate these processes, I shall look at the response to the Bhopal chemical disaster in India in 1984 and the 'aid' responses of the 1980s (Band Aid, Live Aid, you-name-it aid) to famine in Africa.

As tourists or would-be tourists we are also invited to experience the Third World by tour operators, travel companies and international airlines. I shall examine some of the ways in which Third World tourism plays on nineteenth-century explorer/adventurer themes and, in so doing, helps to cement the West's sense of its own superiority. Part of this has entailed the packaging of the Third World in the West's image, drawing on versions of 'authenticity' which bear little resemblance to ways of living then or now. The other side of these constructions is the material consequences of western tourism in the Third World. Although these cannot be reduced to a simple formula, there are important benefits which accrue to the West which are worth noting, just as there are destructive consequences for Third World countries. There are numerous manifestations of these effects, from didgeridoos to game parks to Thai brothels.

The circulation of assumptions and ideas surrounding the Third World takes place in a global economy dominated by western multinationals and post-colonial powers, notably the United States. The inequalities and injustices alluded to by Sweet Honey in the Rock and the corresponding journeys of capital as well as peoples to find work and escape persecution fit comfortably within those dominant assumptions and explanations of the Third World. The purpose of the final section will be to locate such migratory processes of people and commodities within the context of a critical discussion of what A. Sivanandan calls 'circuits of imperialism'.

WHAT IT IS TO BE CIVILISED

The origins of the term civilisation give some clue as to its subsequent use. It derives from classical Rome, from the Latin word *civis*, meaning citizen. Its roots in western antiquity have guarantied its use as a Eurocentric yardstick against which all other cultures have appeared inferior. Eighteenth- and nineteenth-century colonialism helped codify that sense of superiority. The construction of 'otherness as lesser than' through cultural institutions has been described in Edward Said's *Orientalism* (see Chapter 2). It continues to permeate our post-colonial world, from tourism to charitable events like Band Aid and Comic Relief, through multinational advertising to the Gulf War. It pervades our educational system from school curriculum (see Chapter 4) to higher education courses on 'business administration' and 'planning' for students from 'developing' countries.

Ironically, Martin Bernal's impressive project, also discussed in Chapter 2, shares this Eurocentric definition of civilisation. His central point, it should be remembered, was that classical Greek culture, and hence western civilisation, is black, specifically black Egyptian. Thus Egyptian culture influenced developments in mathematics, philosophy, language, religion and engineering, all of which found their way into Greek and thence, more widely, into western European culture. But the very concern with western civilisation in this way still assumes that what has to be explained is the 'advancement' of the West. It is just a matter of acknowledging its African roots. Moreover, by crediting black Egypt with the creation of western civilisation he has to deny the role played by India in the development of the West. In this respect, Bernal's argument is based on pitting one black culture against another to decide which (black Africa or India) has the authentic right to claim the all-important, all-superior (?) heritage of the West.

If we stay with Bernal's assumption that the West is best, just not western in origin, it is possible to cite many other examples of 'advanced' cultures whose advances were denied, destroyed and distorted as a result of assault by the West in the period of European expansion. 'Civilisation', as the West chooses to define it, was well developed in many parts of the world before Europe claimed its monopoly on it from the eighteenth century onwards. Indian culture during the Vedic period, dating from the fifteenth century BC, was advanced in a number of ways: in the development of both the Arabic and Sanskrit languages; in philosophy, in which both Buddhism and Jainism offered highly sophisticated systems of thought and theories of knowledge; in mathematics (see Shan and Bailey, 1991), and in medicine, particularly in the field of plastic surgery. In the Madhubani region the centuries-old highly sophisticated, allegorical symbolic and often humorous wall paintings were the communal act of women artists belonging to a family or group (Chattopadhyay, 1985: 133).

Many other civilisations, too numerous to mention, pre-dated the Enlightenment period in Europe: some, like those in India, by many centuries. The indigenous Indian civilisations of central and southern America, the Aztec, Maya and Inca, were renowned for their advances in technology, irrigation systems, mathematics, astronomy and medicine (especially brain surgery). The Ashanti in west Africa, on the other hand, were noted for the sophisticated administration of their kingdoms (Rodney,1988). Hence, even if we accept western criteria of 'advancement' it is still possible to cite many examples of societies whose civilisations were in advance of the West by many centuries. How Europe managed to convince itself and much of the world of its unique capacity to civilise and be civilised is my next question.

In *Black Skin, White Masks,* Frantz Fanon describes a situation where he meets a German who speaks French badly and compares this with meeting someone black:

> I can hardly forget that he has a language of his own, a country, and that perhaps he is a lawyer or an engineer there. In any case, he is foreign to my group, and his standards must be different. When it comes to the case of the Negro, nothing of the kind: He has no culture, no civilisation, no 'long historical past'.

(Fanon, 1986: 34)

Fanon, a black African, struggling against French colonialism and oppression in north Africa, recognised the effects of racism on the colonial subject of the 1950s. Racism was internalised by the oppressed class and the more they learnt about the West, its languages and cultures, the more they understood their own identity though its inscriptions in 'texts of history, literature, science and myth' (Bhabha, 1986a: xiii). Fanon did not live to see the explosion of black consciousness in the 1960s, which challenged these assumptions through a reassertion of black culture. This followed shortly after his death in 1961.

However, Fanon's analysis of how culture, notably language, served to undermine indigenous culture goes far beyond the context of its conception. In India, for instance, under British rule, the process of devaluing indigenous Indian culture was reinforced through the imposition of the English language. Charles Grant, in his influential seventeenth-century text *Observations on the State of Society among the Asiatic Subjects of Great Britain,* had written enthusiastically of 'an evangelical system of mission education conducted uncompromisingly in English' (Bhabha, 1986b: 199). Likewise, the nineteenth-century historian Macaulay mocked Oriental learning (ibid.: 200) and suggested that the whole of the native literature of India and Arabia was worth less than a shelf of European history (Goonatilake, 1984: 95). The intellectual foundations were thus laid for replacing Arabic and Sanskrit with English, which became used as the medium of communication in education, as well as administration and commerce. Attempts to retain an Indian perspective in universities put forward by Annie Besant, amongst others, were rejected (Goonatilake, 1984: 96). The imposition of English served to undermine developments in history, metaphysics, theology and other disciplines and at the same time helped to build the cultural edifice of Anglocentrism (bearing in mind Bhabha's central argument in the above quoted essay on mimicry, that being Anglicised was 'the same but not quite' as being English).

132

Similar processes were at work in scientific and technical research. As Fanon wrote, 'A man [sic] who has language consequently possesses the world expressed and implied by that language' (1986: 18). In India, scientific and technological problems were increasingly defined by the West, regardless of whether they fitted with Indian paradigms of research or were appropriate to the Indian context. India, like other colonies, became dependent, imitative or satellitic in its relation to the centre, in this case Britain (Goonatilake, 1984: 39). As a result, its own development in these fields fell prey to distortion, manipulation and control by the West, while its own previous advances were lost, or effectively removed, from the historical record. The dominance of western science and technology and the cultural mechanisms by which such supremacy was secured provide a very important backcloth to an understanding of more contemporary events and developments, including those at Bhopal.

BHOPAL

At 1.00 a.m. on 3 December 1984, a greenish-white cloud of methyl isocynate (MIC) gas emerged from Union Carbide's chemical works into the atmosphere in Bhopal, central India, having passed through an apparatus designed to make it harmless. The wind blew the gas at low altitude through the densest part of the city. The effects of the leak on the local inhabitants varied, depending on where they were at the time, if and how they were sleeping and how old they were. The gas produced a number of physical symptoms including burning, an inability to breathe, nausea and vomiting. Many women suffered spontaneous abortions. Three months after the gas escape, one of the many thousands of victims gave birth to a baby with eye sockets but no eyes, whose sex was indeterminate and whose skin was scorched. The baby died within forty hours. Such were the effects of exposure to the gas that people were still dying in 1993, nine years after the initial disaster. Since MIC is a mutagen, teratogen and a carcinogen, its victims die from many different diseases, including those affecting the chest and lungs. For many thousands, coma and death were a relief from the excruciating symptoms of the poison. Although figures vary, which in itself is part of a much larger problem, the death toll was thought to be around 10,000. In addition, 200,000 were estimated to have sustained injuries and disabilities as a result of what happened (Dinham, 1987: 271).

The incident took place in a wider context of global uncertainty and disaster: famine in Ethiopia; civil wars in Sri Lanka, Cambodia and Afghanistan; the war between Iraq and Iran, and in India itself, religious violence and unrest following the death of Indira Gandhi. The balance of superpower domination at that time centred around events in Afghanistan, but the whole region, from the Middle East to south Asia, was considered by the US to be critical to future superpower relations. The subsequent story of Bhopal, capital of the state of Madhya Pradesh, can only be understood with reference to this wider context.

Another aspect of this context was the relationship between a US multinational corporation, Union Carbide (UC), and its Indian subsidiary company. This relationship was not purely economic, as we are sometimes encouraged to believe, but had an important political and cultural dimension. Ironically, Union Carbide's position in the world economy actually improved as a consequence of the disaster. To understand how this came about and to examine important cultural processes which secured UC's continuing dominance, I shall identify four reactions to what happened at Bhopal. Each of these both drew on and fed into common-sense understandings of the Third World and its 'problems'.

Recording these reactions, and thereby highlighting the significance of the company and the West's role, however, should not be used to eclipse the other, all too easily forgotten side of the struggle: the people of Bhopal and their allies. Their struggle, insofar as it has been told, has served to undermine one of the West's pervasive myths of the Third World – that it is peopled by victims, rather than by active participants in struggle. The idea of a 'victim' locks those designated as such into a passive role, which, in the case of the people of Bhopal, distorts and misrepresents the role they played in events subsequent to the gas leak of 1984. A steady flow of books, articles, reports and television documentaries is proof that their voices of protest were indeed audible above the cacophony of explanations, excuses and denials coming from the other side.

Self-absolution

From the outset, Union Carbide sought to downplay both the scale of the disaster and its own responsibility for what happened. Amongst its first reactions was to blame its subsidiary and the Indian government for not developing technical expertise to an appropriate level and failing to regulate safety levels at the plant. Larry Everest (1985), who carried out his own investigation, unpacks this 'official', almost knee-jerk, response to uncover a more complex picture of conditions and responsibilities at Bhopal. According to Everest's report, Bhopal's plant was not as well equipped as the plant in the US in terms of safety equipment. Moreover, UC took a number of risks at Bhopal that it had not taken in the case of other producers of MIC, including the location of the plant in a densely populated area; the use of toxic gases to produce MIC; its insistence that the storage capacity of the gas was ten times that of a German plant (ibid.: 29) and the reliance on the work-force in Bhopal to detect gas leaks, in contrast to France, where UC had installed sensor equipment to measure gas leaks automatically. Not only did all these practices have the company's blessing, it had the final say in introducing them, since it owned 51 per cent of the shares in its Indian subsidiary. What is more, it had a much greater knowledge of the design and safety standards than it admitted at the time. Contrary to its own claim, the plant at Bhopal was designed by a

US engineering firm under directions from UC, US. The latter has on record reports indicating the company's awareness of the deficiencies. Its response, as we now know, was deafeningly silent.

In another attempt to take public attention away from the company, UC (US) issued a report in March 1985, in which it was suggested that water was deliberately introduced into tank 610. Union Carbide's lawyer went further, making the explicit allegation that sabotage had been the cause of the accident. The company claimed that a Sikh terrorist group, calling itself Black June, had admitted responsibility. It even went as far as to identify a suspect who left the company shortly before the incident. The allegation was compatible with US foreign policy at that time which was based on the assumption that the Soviet Union was providing military support to Pakistan and at the same time looking for ways of destabilising India (Everest, 1985).

The specific allegation of Sikh terrorism was never substantiated. On the contrary, all the evidence pointed against it. Black June had not been heard of before the incident and has not been heard of since. The employee identified by Union Carbide was subsequently interviewed and it was established beyond doubt that he had nothing to do with the incident. To cap it all, an investigation carried out by the Indian Central Bureau of Investigation found water in all the connecting pipelines, a fact inconsistent with the idea of water simply being added to the tank at the end of the process (ibid.: 141). What the idea of sabotage did do was to deflect attention from the company and its responsibility for faulty equipment. To those in the West, whose common-sense understanding of India had been selectively constructed around the assassination of Indira Gandhi, Sikh nationalism and inter-ethnic violence (including the deaths of Sikh leaders at the Golden Temple in Amritsar), the idea of sabotage seemed perfectly plausible at the time, however far from the truth it actually turned out to be.

Building a wall of silence

One feature common to all parties implicated in what happened at Bhopal, with the exception of its victims, was a concerted effort to mask events and subsequent investigations in a shroud of secrecy. The State Government in Madhya Pradesh, the Indian Government and, of course, Union Carbide and their legal representatives, all colluded in this conspiracy (De Grazia, 1985). Even the press were discouraged from disclosing information in case it 'caused further panic'. In the words of one newspaper, 'A gas leak may have been acceptable but a news leak would be intolerable' (Everest, 1985: 149). The effect of this was to frustrate the legal process and, more generally, attempts to gain information. The People's Movement of Bhopal struggled against the background of this lack of information, a factor which clearly weakened their protests and undermined the legitimacy of their rights to redress. Despite this, they organised pickets and demonstrations outside the office of the Chief

Minister of the State. On 31 January, they organised a march in which approximately 10,000 participated, including many who had not been involved in political action before (ibid.: 147).

One important feature of this censoring process was the implicit way it was justified. The idea that information might turn to panic puts those in the know in a privileged position *vis-à-vis* those who are not. It assumes that one group, in effect, knows best and can decide what another group should know. At one point the US press made the comment that the people of Bhopal did not really understand what was happening (ibid.: 146). Of course, the people knew well enough what had happened and their protests and demands for justice were evidence of this. However, the deliberate attempt to withhold information as a way of exercising control over the protesters, and then to accuse them of ignorance, has proved, historically, a crude but effective form of control.

In one instance, this withholding of information or, more generously, the refusal to confront the truth for fear of adverse publicity, caused additional untold physical suffering. In this case, the company denied the widely accepted view that MIC had actually decomposed and transformed into hydrogen cyanide. (This decomposition was possible because of the great temperatures reached at the time of the emission of the gas.) Only when those suffering the symptoms, which were identical to those of cyanide poisoning, showed marked improvement when treated with sodium thoulphate (administered in cases of cyanide poisoning), was it accepted that those poisoned had, indeed, been inhaling cyanide, and their treatment was adjusted accordingly.

The fluctuating price of life

According to the *Wall Street Journal*, 'an American's life is worth about $500,000 but setting monetary value on damage inflicted in Bhopal US courts will take into account the differences between the US and Indian costs and standards of living. . . . Thus a court might award only $8,500 for an Indian's death' (Everest, 1985: 155). This comment reflects two important strands of thinking. The first seeks to justify the different prices put on the lives of an Indian and US citizen in terms of the different standards of life in the two countries. This ploy, which conveniently serves to maintain such differences, has been used elsewhere, for example in South Africa, to preserve wage differentials between black and white for the same work. Second, the Journal's proposal can be understood, in common-sense terms, as an almost inevitable consequence of living in the Third World. According to widespread perceptions of the latter, famines, earthquakes, floods and wars are so much a part of everyday life that fatalities on this scale, though regrettable, are to be expected. Compensation, according to this logic, should be adjusted accordingly. The dominance of this view in the West is made possible through a daily diet of Third World news reporting which serves up little else but death, famine and war stories (Hart, 1989). Small wonder, then, if we begin to see the Third World in these terms and fall in with the common-sense logic that argues for lower compensation.

The price of progress

There was another assumption running through the debate which suggested that Bhopal and incidents like it were the inevitable price to pay for economic progress. India, according to this argument, not only benefited in terms of employment opportunities (Bhopal's work-force was 800) but also because it needed the pesticides manufactured by companies like Union Carbide to increase the country's agricultural yield. The arguments regarding pesticides will be taken up below, but India is a very good example of the fallacy of this economic argument. Traditionally, pesticides have only been bought by the wealthiest of farmers, who have driven the small farmers off the land and into cities like Bhopal. Furthermore, crops grown with the aid of pesticides, like cereals, are exported and grown at the expense of more nutritious products, like beans, for domestic consumption. Lastly, since the pests themselves build up an immunity to pesticides, stronger pesticides are required to control them, which in turn become weaker as pests raise their level of immunity. In the meantime, the incidences of diseases like malaria have increased. Overall, the production of pesticides seems to have benefited multinationals who are looking for a high return on investment, but seems to be of little, if any, benefit to Third World countries.

In summary, Union Carbide sought to downplay both its responsibility and the scale of the disaster. In general, the company blamed what happened on the lack of technical expertise and the absence of a culture of safety. In this sense the company fed into a wider set of assumptions: that Third World peoples are ignorant and helpless; that life is cheap, and that disasters, wars, famines are to be expected and accepted.[2]

Moreover, it is revealing to note how the victims of such events in the Third World are constructed in 'mass' terms rather than, as in the West, as individuals. This can be seen by comparing Bhopal with the reporting of disasters nearer home and, more particularly, when they include British victims. Here, the tendency amongst British news reports is to give personal details of British casualties and invite us to empathise directly with individual loss. On the other hand, news of such events followed by confirmation of no British losses invites its audience to feel relief. The inducement of an almost schizophrenic response to domestic disasters and those in the Third World can be seen in the response to the plane explosion and crash at Lockerbie, in 1988. Here was an instance when we were invited to individualise suffering, rather than see it only in terms of numbers of dead (often counted in hundreds or thousands). As a result, 'solutions', in cases like Lockerbie, are defined and sought in terms of securing adequate levels of compensation through legal redress. In the case of Third World disasters, on the other hand, where responsibility is shared between fate and local inefficiency and incompetence, redress is conceived in terms of charitable handouts provided, not as of right, but out of a neo-colonial sense of philanthropy.

Both cultural constructions, of the kind described above, and economic factors help explain how UC actually came to benefit economically from the disaster. In the first place, the Indian Government, unwilling to put its relationship with UC at risk (and frighten off other multinational companies) agreed to an absurdly low figure in compensation and even to defend the company in the event of any further claims for compensation! UC also managed to avoid the spate of corporate take-overs in the years after the disaster. The fear of high compensatory payments during this period must have been a major disincentive to those corporations which might otherwise have been interested in UC as a possible take-over target. Once settled, the company's success was reflected in an increase in the value of its stock.

Union Carbide's ability to profit from Bhopal was also made possible by the way the explosion, put alongside all the other 'disasters', could be interpreted as just another act of God, or nature, rather than the result of human or corporate negligence. The Third World, with all the stereotypical baggage associated with that term, must therefore expect the odd Bhopal as a price to pay for all the alleged benefits of multinational investment. The advertisements of ICI and BP continue to remind us in the West of the contribution such companies make to the 'underfed', 'disease ridden' and 'backward' Third World.

In an interesting footnote on Bhopal, Tara Jones (1987) argues that, despite Union Carbide's consistent failure to maintain minimum safety standards in the face of local warnings of a likely disaster, the accident could have happened at any one of Union Carbide's plants, including those in the US itself. The reason for this had to do with the general fallibility of the technology used in all of Union Carbide's plants, irrespective of the particular deficiencies at Bhopal.[3] This highlights the need to consider the risks of working under such hazardous conditions all over the world. It also leads us to ask: who does work for companies like Union Carbide in the West; how do employment patterns here relate to the global migration of Third World workers and, finally, where does this leave us in terms of a definition of the 'Third World'?

CONSTRUCTING A THIRD WORLD COMMON SENSE

In this section I want to look at the processes by which Third World problems are defined and solutions prescribed. I shall take two examples: over-population/birth control and food. The ability of the West to define both problems and solutions in this way can be found in colonial discourses, of the kind illustrated earlier in this chapter and in Chapter 2. Underpinning such discourses, in both colonial and post-colonial contexts, has been the assumption that the West's superiority could benefit colonies and ex-colonies, as well as, of course, the West itself.

Over-population/birth control

It was Thomas Malthus, back in the eighteenth century, who first warned of the dangers of populations running ahead of technological advances. The argument proved unfounded then, partly because of the discovery of additional resources, including land. However, neo-Malthusian ideas have continued to preoccupy scientists, as well as economists and politicians, particularly with the emergence of the ecology movement and its concerns over finite global resources. *Limits To Growth* (Meadows *et al.*, 1974), the Club of Rome's sponsored research report, drew attention to the problems of land and fossil fuel exhaustion. Scientific knowledge was appropriated to support these ideas. Even the laws of thermodynamics, notably that energy transformed from one state into another entails a loss (whatever efforts are made to use recycled material), were incorporated into these early ecological arguments (Warnock, 1987: 39).

The resource argument converges with ideas about comparative rates of population growth. The idea that the least desirable populations tend to breed the fastest has been integrally bound up with these resource/population growth arguments. Historically, it was the focus of concern of the eugenics movement and informed the Nazi programmes of enforced sterilisation during World War II. Such concerns remain, although the emphasis has shifted from the lower classes of England and the Jews of Europe to the peoples of the Third World. Paul Erlich's *Population Bomb* (1968), following this cultural tradition, proposed that no food should be given to underdeveloped countries until they established programmes of birth control.

These resource arguments provided an important rationale for a powerful lobby advocating birth control programmes in the Third World. For instance, in the words of Alan F. Guttmacher, President of the International Planned Parenthood Association:

> Reckless population growth without parallel economic growth. . . makes for a constant lowering of the standard of living. Such a decline, with its concomitant mounting poverty and hunger, inevitably delivers a population into some kind of ism, whether it be communism, fascism or pan Arabism, and weans them away from democracy.
>
> (cited in Levidow, 1987: 46)

The implicit baby metaphor used in the above image of the Third World contrasts with the authoritative, parental/paternalistic status of the West. This in turn helps sanction Guttmacher's attempts to define the problems, of over-population and poverty, which then feed into the proposals for birth control. The elements of this argument, strengthened by the selective use of imagery and metaphor, is what Hall (1981a) has termed a racist chain of reasoning which, in this case, has been used to justify birth control programmes, including sterilisation. So, for example, sterilisation programmes have been carried out in India and Bangladesh, where in one exposed scandal women were denied food unless they agreed to be sterilised. Third World women have also been used as guinea pigs, and the Third World a dumping ground for contraceptives like the Dalkon Shield and Depo Provera. Both of these were previously found to be unsafe and banned from sale in the United States (Levidow, 1987; see also Davis, 1981: 202ff.).

Some of the above practices are not just happening in the Third World, but also to women living in the United States. Puerto Rican and black women in the US have been subjected to sterilisation campaigns and programmes, not to mention the native American female population, 40 per cent of whom were sterilised in the 1970s (Levidow, 1987: 47–8). This re-introduces a point made with reference to the working conditions of Union Carbide workers in the United States and the use of Third World labour in the First World. It suggests that 'Third World' could arguably be used to refer to peoples as much as to places. What links these geographical and social definitions is an attempt to grasp a commonalty of experience. The appropriateness of one or the other depends on the particular context in question. In the case of birth control, Third World women are working-class women of colour, whether they live in the United States or Central America. In another context, in Sweet Honey in the Rock's a cappella, it is the *difference* between Third World women and women of colour in the West that is being alluded to, with reference, in that case, to the making and buying of a blouse.

Western perceptions of the 'food crisis' – and solutions

Birth control is, of course only one solution to the problem of over-population. According to John Warnock (1987), the world rediscovered hunger in the mid-1980s. There had been food riots and demonstrations about food shortages in Brazil, Chile, Bolivia and Haiti, and famine in twenty-four African countries, including the one in Ethiopia that caught the world's imagination thanks to graphic and global media attention. Band Aid and Live Aid, which spawned a proliferation of charity projects designed to raise money for the famine's victims, are indicative of the West's philanthropic attitude to its former colonies. Moreover, it is part of a rationale which leads the West to believe that it is doing all it can to minimise Third World poverty and famine through aid, loans and emergency relief. What this rationale does not reveal and what, in fact, it helps to conceal, is that Africa's food crisis has been caused by the West and that the very idea of a 'world food shortage' is part of this mythology.

The Malthusian idea that famine cures famine and that the laws of nature help to restore the fine balance of population to resources was an early attempt to 'naturalise' so-called problems of food shortage and over-population. At the same time, the emphasis on 'nature' here helps to conceal explanations rooted in political and economic conditions while reinforcing cultural notions of western superiority. In recent times, a dominant model has been widely accepted as the basis for dealing with the 'problem' of food shortages. This model relies on the investment by the Third World in high-yielding varieties of grain, the cultivation of as few crops as possible or, preferably, monoculture, the use of pesticides and fertilisers to increase the yield and, finally, the use of mechanised equipment. These principles formed the basis of what became known as the first 'green' revolution.[4] In many ways the first green revolution has exacerbated rather than solved the problems it set out to tackle. These consequences can be discussed in both environmental and economic terms.

The effects of the first green revolution have been felt in a number of ways. First, biotechnology has developed high-yield variety (HYV) strains of crops which in turn have discouraged crop rotation and diversity. What HYVs have not done is to tackle the problem which encouraged the use of crop rotation in the first place: erosion and deterioration of the soil. Soil erosion has contributed to deforestation, which itself has contributed both to global warming and to the transformation of hitherto fertile areas into desert-type regions.

Second, the use of pesticides produced at plants like Bhopal have other hazards besides those associated with their production. The greater the use of pesticides, the greater the reliance on them. Not only do pests build up an immunity which calls for greater dosages, but the pests' enemies are also killed, which further increases the need for forms of artificial control. As a result, pest outbreaks are not uncommon in areas sprayed with pesticides, where the predators, but not the pests, are killed. The cotton boll worm is one such pest that has prospered in the era of pesticides.

Third, the toxicity of the chemical products, fertilisers and insecticides, has created what has been called a circle of poison: the export of toxic chemicals to the Third World to assist in food production and the importing of the contaminated food back from the Third World to the West. Pesticides, therefore, which are manufactured in the West (and as Bhopal confirms, increasingly in the Third World too) are then sold to the Third World for use on crops, not only endangering people in the Third World (one person is poisoned every minute in the Third World by pesticides) but also contaminating food products, which are then exported to processing companies in the US or direct to consumers (hence the increasing regularity of media scares concerning contaminated food). Pesticides, like contraceptives, found unsafe in the West have a way of ending up in the Third World. In fact, one quarter of all pesticides banned in the US, of which DDT is probably the best-known example, are to be found in use in the Third World.

Who actually benefits from such investment is a matter of considerable controversy. Apart from the many environmental effects, there are a number of economic dimensions to the problems arising from this kind of investment. Essentially agribusiness has to be paid for by economies already in debt, some of these, for example in Latin America, more in debt than others. Western banks and governments and international agencies like the International Monetary Fund have all been heavily involved in lending to the Third World. The current debt crisis has its origins in the oil crisis of 1973. The effect of this crisis was particularly felt in those parts of the Third World dependent on the West for chemical imports and exports of cash crops and raw materials. Upward pressure on both the costs of petrochemical-based fertilisers etc. and on rates of interest, in conjunction with downward pressure on the prices of imported raw materials from the Third World, squeezed the latter so hard that western banks and agencies refused further loans, or at least added further stringent conditions to loan repayments. In the mid-1980s, the total outstanding debt in Africa was $60 billion, over half the gross continental product (Sutcliffe, 1986).

The ability to invest in agribusiness products is generally only an option for the larger, richer landowners in the Third World. Their ability to finance capital-intensive programmes makes these too competitive for small farmers, who become an easy target for landowners looking to increase their land holding. The dispossession of the small landowner and the use of capital-intensive methods have created enormous economic and social dislocation, characterised by high levels of unemployment and migration to densely populated urban areas, like Bhopal. This process of dispossession and unemployment has been particularly damaging for women. In India, two-thirds of women cultivators lost their jobs between 1961 and 1971 (George, 1985: 51).

Moreover, the foodstuffs produced by large landowners are by no means those necessary for subsistence. On the contrary, they are often expendable products and of little or no nutritional value, like coffee and sugar, produced, largely, for a relatively affluent overseas consumer market and bought at relatively cheap prices. The effect of the concentration of ownership and production of food for export has been to reduce the capacity of Third World economies to produce their own means of subsistence. As it is, many countries in the Third World are importing food from the West in order to supplement foodstuffs for local consumption. This obviously makes these economies more vulnerable, not only to the vagaries of climate and crop blight, but to the fortunes of western economies which dictate the prices for Third World products.[5]

Other, related forms of pressure exerted on the Third World can also work in the interests of western economies. The encouragement to devalue Third World currencies in order to sell more products at a lower price has been characteristic advice given by agencies like the International Monetary Fund. Meanwhile, the European Community is stockpiling to keep its prices up. An example of this 'dual approach' is steel, the price for which was stabilised in the West, despite excess capacity, whilst coffee prices collapsed in the Third World (Singh, 1986: 110). This is a feature of Third World economies that are too tied to the West. The prices for commodities and raw materials depend on western economic policies, as do the imports of western capital and consumer goods. This dependence is a source of constant disequilibria for Third World economies. Even countries like India, who are more independent and less affected by growth trends in the West, at least in relation to food products, are indirectly tied to the West through other forms of multinational investment, of which Union Carbide is just one example.

Meanwhile, multinational investment, advertising and marketing, dissemi-nated partly via western-dominated media including television, western retail and food outlets, have created a demand in the Third World for western products. Susan George notes the irony in the fact that, whilst the Third World is imitating western patterns of food consumption (note the proliferation of McDonald's outlets throughout the Third World), there is a growing middle-class culture in the West which is actually imitating Third World food consumption patterns, including whole-food diets based on grains and pulses. Nothing, notes Susan George, is currently so *déclassé* in the West as a steak (George, 1985: 92). These forms of cultural appropriation can be further illustrated with reference to Third World handicrafts, which I shall discuss below with reference to tourism. Instead of appropriating its culture in this way, George argues, the West should be giving formal recognition to the Third World, paying officials to act as consultants on such matters as food policy, alternative medicine and specialist crafts. As it stands, instead of acknow-ledging the Third World's superiority in these cases, the West, through its appropriation of cultural forms and practices, adds to its own sense of superiority and economic security (ibid.).

In the ways described above, the West continues to dominate and monop-olise debates around the food crisis and its solution. It has developed its own economic language to articulate its common-sense understandings, explana-tions and solutions. If and when it becomes clear that its concepts do not 'fit' or work, they are replaced by new terms; new facades behind which lie old and familiar meanings (George, 1985). The terms 'take off' and 'trickle down' were key justifications for the imposition of the dominant model referred to above (based on maximum yields, monoculture, economies of scale, fer-tilisers, pesticides) on Third World economies. As their failure became apparent (for example in Brazil, where there were areas of growing poverty in the context of a relatively high growth economy) new terms were debated, but only within western academic and research circles (ibid.). Terms invoked by Third World leaders are always in danger of being reworked and appro-priated in western contexts. This process of cultural annexation is partly made possible by the West's cultural and institutional dominance in key academic disciplines and areas of research, for example economics, development

143

studies and biotechnology. This intellectual dominance has been a feature of the West's relations with its former colonies for centuries, as the example of India earlier in this chapter confirmed.

The academic language of 'underdevelopment' has served to underpin popular understandings of the work of charities and the Band Aid and Live Aid spectaculars of the 1980s. Although seemingly at odds with western governments, the latter nevertheless reinforced the dominant model described above. Bob Geldof, for example, openly criticised western governments for their failure to solve the problem of famine. As he pointed out at the time, while the world witnessed the effects of the famine in Ethiopia in 1984, there were food mountains in the EC, and the US was paying its farmers not to grow grain. However, at a more fundamental level, and embodied in the character of Geldof himself, Band Aid and Live Aid were extremely compatible with the anti-Europe, anti-statist, 'get up and do it' stance of Western neo-liberal governments in Britain and the US at the time. Charity events of this kind thus played a dual role, both in cutting through the bureaucratic red tape to make an immediate response to the famine crisis, and in confirming the West's philanthropic sense of itself.

The popular success of Band Aid and other similar events that followed can be partly understood in terms of the powerful convergence of values of self-help, philanthropy and enterprise culture on the one hand, with Geldof's attack on Euro-style bureaucracies, dominant throughout the 1980s, on the other. On top of this was Geldof's own successful pop image and the use of western popular music as a means of promoting the charitable cause in question. Where it was less successful was in making sense of the problem of the food crisis in terms of the debt crisis, the failure of the green revolution, the distortionary effects of multinational and financial investment on Third World economies, the downgrading of diets in the Third World and the failure of the West to allow Third World countries to define their own problems and solutions.[6] On the contrary, events like Band Aid and Live Aid in the 1980s not only served to perpetuate the 'West knows best' mentality, they elicited our sympathy and sense of charity at the expense of any alternative sense of justice and rights.[7]

It has been interesting to note that some of the largest aid charities, including War on Want and Oxfam, have sought to present stronger, more positive images of Third World peoples demanding their rights, rather than images of swollen-bellied young victims of the latest famine. In one poster, for example, War on Want used the caption 'It's not only droughts, floods and disease that are crippling the Third World', under which a (stereo)typical Third World victim was shown propping up the big four banks. Oxfam's Campaign for Justice not Hunger also included more powerful and assertive representations of Third World peoples. However, as Oxfam has itself conceded, it is the pathetic images which have provoked the biggest financial response, which may explain why War on Want continued with this image even as it tried to break with other, more problematic assumptions regarding the source of problems in the Third World.

This situation poses a real dilemma for such organisations in terms of fund-raising objectives.[8] The problem is not just Oxfam's, or War on Want's. It arises out of the strong paternalistic, philanthropic tradition in social intervention, which makes mobilising for rights an uphill ideological battle. Moreover, to do so would put the charitable status of the organisation at risk, since defending and securing rights could well be deemed political rather than charitable work by the Charities Commission. The loss of charitable status, and the tax benefits that go with it, could threaten the organisation itself. The dispute between War on Want and the Commission in the 1980s is a good example of these problems and risks.

It is also interesting to see how multinational companies seek to project a caring, almost charitable image in their advertising. The BP advert 'Colin can read by sunlight even after the sun has gone down', thanks to BP's investment in solar technology in Africa, and ICI's 'People shouldn't have to choose between dying of thirst and dying from cholera' both seek to elicit similar kinds of response from their western audiences. They read as worthy causes, pioneered for altruistic motives, almost without concern for profit. In the post Live Aid era, this was imaginative marketing, suggesting, as it did, that our own consumption of these companies' products (and even share investment?) could be seen as a form of pledge to some future 'charitable' project in the Third World.

'SEE A REAL MIRAGE': TOURISM AND THE THIRD WORLD[9]

The impact of western tourism on the Third World can be measured in terms of the ways in which tourism produces 'knowledge' of the Third World through holiday brochures, package trips, picture postcards, souvenirs and the kinds of knowledge produced as a result of these artifacts and experiences. The magazine *New Internationalist* has consistently warned of the dangers here. 'Far from reaching a deeper understanding of the Third World, the average tourists seem usually to have the worst prejudices confirmed by their jaunts' (*New Internationalist*, December 1984). But tourism's significance lies not just in how we are invited to see the Third World; it should also be considered in terms of its real effects, both economic and cultural, on the Third World itself.

A century ago Thomas Cook brochures enticed the wealthy few to embark on pioneering trips down the Nile ('Black Markets' touring exhibition, Wolverhampton, April 1991). Cook's motives were philanthropic. He organised day trips to Liverpool and Derby for the working classes to keep them away from the 'fiend alcohol'. His ideas for travel outside Britain were intended to bring international peace and understanding, although the idea from the outset was to adapt local conditions to make them more compatible with

British upper middle-class lifestyles. Anthony Burgess, reviewing Brendon's book, describes Cook's exploits, in a way which says as much about the reviewer as it does about Cook himself: 'Thomas Cook and Son went to Egypt, weeded out the dragomans, taught Cairo how to make tea, put boats on the Nile and ended by virtually running the country' (*Independent*, 11 January 1991).

Thomas Cook's son actually went as far as to provide boats to transport troops and weapons to assist General Gordon.[10] Cook's tours thus stretched the idea of 'cultural exchange' beyond its limits in countries where they promoted tourism (*Sunday Times*, 11 January 1991). The idea of the package tour, which again was Cook's invention, was based on the simple principle that more people cost less per person. However, the package holiday principle, with its emphasis on numbers, also put increased pressure on receiving countries to meet tourists' undoubtedly Eurocentric expectations. The knowledges that tourism produced thus reinforced the tales of explorers and travellers, which formed such an important part of the nationalist imperial project in the late nineteenth century.

The idea of tourists as discoverers or pioneers is a favourite theme of overland expedition holidays to Africa and South America. In order to experience 'the primitive', the effect of which is to confirm westerners' sense of their own 'advancement', the Third World must be packaged in particular ways. For instance, in Hawaii a dance of the Vestal Virgins was scheduled to begin at precisely 10.00 a.m. every Wednesday, to coincide with the arrival of a tour party (*New Internationalist*, December 1984: 8–9). Brochures abound with efforts to stage the 'authentic', from visits to Sioux markets to trips to the Sahara Desert. The search for the 'real' Mexico did not stop North American tourists from 'spending all their time in discos eating hamburgers' nor, in the case of one visitor, from remarking, 'they should speak English. After all they're in America' (Turner and Ash, 1975: 29). The 'authentic' in South Africa was summed up in its Tourist Board publicity, which invited its visitors to see 'the happy smiling Bantu' (*South*, April 1985).

Moreover, holiday advertising abounds with Third World people in subservient positions, from the waiter on a British Airways advert serving drinks to two white holidaymakers on what looks like their very own Caribbean Island, to an exotically dressed and deferentially posed air stewardess on an Air India advertisement. This image was powerfully juxtaposed alongside another image, a south Asian female cleaner at Heathrow airport, in the Black Markets exhibition referred to above. Likewise, one of Pakistan International Airlines' advertisements in 1991 included numerous representations of young girls in varying postures of subservience and subordination, collectively promoting passive, enigmatic and exotic forms of south Asian femininity (*Newsweek*, 18 November 1991).

In Guatemala, the National Tourist Commission entices tourists with the following:

From the monumental cities of the ancient Maya, through the heritage of the Catholic Spanish, who came ashore in the fifteenth century [the arrival of the Spanish brought new ways to Guatemala] to today's Guatemala, a blend of past into the present – the blending has made Guatemala the happy, colourful and friendly country it is today.

A different version of Guatemalan tourism is provided by Bob Carty: 'Twice a week tourists arrive. They pour out of buses, cameras ready, and surge through the town of Chichicastenango. . . . They [make for] St. Thomas church, ignoring the signs asking non-Mayans to keep out' (*New Internationalist*, December 1991: 12). Carty proceeded to describe the exploits of Pedro Alvarado, the Spanish conquistador who carried out eight major massacres, killing 3,000 Indians at a time, and the mass graves around the town of Chichicastenango, not of sixteenth but late twentieth-century origin; of Indians killed under the orders of Rios Montt in the early 1980s as part of a programme of genocide against the Mayan peoples. Meanwhile, western tourists flock to the town, lured by the 'official' promises of the authentic, quaint and exotic, not to mention cheap presents to take home from the town's famous market.

The economic impact of tourism can be felt in a number of ways, most of which damage rather than benefit the Third World. The first is the ability of transnational companies to monopolise the tourist market, from tour operators to airlines to hotel chains. Western tour operators, for instance, handle 80 per cent of Third World tourists. The twenty leading airlines have an annual turnover of £40 million. The twelve largest hotel chains own 5,000 hotels including one million hotel rooms (Ascher, 1985: 15)! *South* magazine's special report on tourism illustrated this process:

> If we cite the not untypical example of a US family on vacation in Java having bought their tickets in their home town, flown by a US airline, staying at a US-owned hotel, and spending a significant proportion of their food bill on items imported to suit their palates, we can see that the benefit to the Indonesian economy is minimal.
>
> (*South*, April 1985: 55)

The practice of using foreign currency also serves to bypass, and hence damage, the indigenous economy. At best, tourism helps to reproduce relations of dependency, offering low pay, low-status service jobs to indigenous labour. In doing so, it 'disseminates social and cultural models of industrial societies' (Ascher, 1985: 13). At worst, it can destroy indigenous cultures. One example, cited in this respect, is the small island of Saint Martin in the Caribbean, part of the Dutch Antilles, although constitutionally separate from it. From the late 1960s and early 1970s, the island, which had no customs inspection, became a centre for drug dealing and prostitution, primarily aimed at western tourist markets. Prostitutes were brought over from the Dominican

Republic. Hotel and apartment construction, necessary to accommodate in-creasing numbers of tourists, created massive social dislocation, with local black labour subordinate to, and dependent on, white-owned commercial enterprises. Western food outlets provided 'gristly fast food served at lightning speed and. . . Coca Cola flows like water'. Added to these dubious attractions for tourists, the island is English speaking, which means that tourists could give up any pretence at communicating in anything other than their only language (O'Shaughnessy, 1989).

What tourism does promote, in terms of local industry, is the mass production of tourist artifacts, which are often shoddy or are not functional in the way they were originally intended and involve workers in a much lower level of skill than when they worked in local craft industries. The manufacture of didgeridoos, the Aboriginal musical instrument, is an example of this. Ascher puts it bluntly: 'Tourists through their ignorance of local culture, their purchasing power and their stereotyped demands have encouraged the mass production of. . . trash' (1985: 13). While local populations make do with products manufactured in metal or plastic, tourists have them made in traditional materials, that is to say, as luxury items. At the same time, the mass production of airport art, bark and sand paintings from Australia for example, is certainly of inferior quality to what it attempts to replicate. The neon lights on the temples of Bali offend the tourists more than the Balinese. 'It interferes with the quest for maximum exoticism' (ibid.: 14). Even the staff at the Conrad Hilton are required to dress in traditional folk costume to match the facade of the building, itself designed in keeping with local architectural traditions. In these very superficial and contrived ways, multinational hotel chains attempt to stage authenticity for the top end of their affluent tourist market.

The above examples are not dissimilar, in form, to attempts to commer-cialise heritage in the West, sharing, as they do, the packaging of what is defined as historically 'authentic', albeit in highly selective ways. The cultural constructions of the 'Third World' in the late twentieth century, in terms of artifacts, traditions and relics of a bygone age have been particularly well suited to an era which has sought links with its Victorian, imperial heritage. It could be argued that contemporary attempts to construct a sense of English national identity rely as much on their ability to construct, control and possess notions of 'otherness' as did their nineteenth-century counterparts.

A further economic effect of tourism, again with cultural undertones, has been its impact on local food production. Local staple foods, rice and fish for instance, have been disrupted in order to cater for the palates of foreign tourists, who, it has been said, like their experience of 'the primitive' to come gift wrapped (*New Internationalist*, December 1984: 9). Local economies are distorted in other ways. In South East Asia, prostitution and pornography provide work for local labour, and women make up the most exploited group. Parts of some cities, of which Bangkok is the best-known example, have become brothels for western males, with 50,000 of them visiting prostitutes each year in the city. The Philippines, too, has become an important tourist centre for drugs and prostitution (*Maryknoll Magazine*, March 1991). Feminist groups have set up drop-in centres for prostitutes and, in Thailand, women's organisations like Empower and Friends of Women were formed in the 1980s to offer support including English language lessons and advice on AIDS (Enloe, 1989: 39). Under such circumstances, attempts to develop alternative forms of tourism in Thailand, for example those built around the importance of monasticism in Thai culture, have some ground to make up, despite their appeal to sub-cultures within the western middle classes.

Ayers Rock in Australia provides another example of how tourist experiences come gift wrapped at the expense of indigenous peoples. What is ironic in this case is that the Rock's significance stems from the fact that it marks the crossroads of dreaming tracks, or paths, taken by Aboriginal hero-ancestors. The Director of Welfare in the Northern Territory, however, sought to sever the Rock from its cultural context in order to make it 'presentable' to western tourists. He not only criticised local Aboriginals for their bedraggled and neglected appearance, but sought to remove them during the tourist season (Turner and Ash, 1975: 23)!

Attempts to preserve vast areas of game parks as living museums have also benefited foreign interests and at the same time threatened wildlife. Examples abound. In Uganda, for instance, crocodiles, on seeing tourists enter the water, flee their nests, leaving baboons to eat their eggs. Tourists arrive by the plane load and are guided across the parks by helicopter or Land Rover, the noise from which disturbs and disperses the wildlife (Mathieson and Wall, 1982: 58).[11] Game parks seek to 'preserve' culture in a somewhat fossilised form, one that is more concerned to meet the needs of affluent visitors from the West and their commercial providers than the needs of the wildlife, let alone indigenous peoples.

It has been suggested by Dean MacCannell (1976) that Third World tourism provides the international middle classes with an opportunity to scavenge the earth for new experiences in order to build up a single version of 'other' peoples and places, which in turn is linked to the ability to subordinate the Third World to their economy and culture. What tourists are looking for is linked to their backgrounds and how they came to know about 'other' places, usually 'through literature, cinema, television and travel books'. As Ascher writes,

> The absurdity is not that they end up seeing countries more or less as they imagined them, but that as a result of the actual measures taken by tourist operators, the countries visited end up by corresponding to the tourist expectations.
>
> (1985: 63)[12]

POLITICAL ECONOMY: THE MISSING LINK?

Whilst some attempt has been made to incorporate an economic dimension with reference to each of the examples above, I will now look at attempts to frame all such developments using the tools of political economy. In doing so, I am not looking for some global theory of capitalism to unlock all the doors of this chapter. General theories of this kind tend to reduce contradiction and variation to a simple formula and leave too much unanswered. A more detailed conjunctural discussion is required, and not one that can be read off from some grand economic theory. But there is an economic dimension to Bhopal, to the 'food crisis' and to the historical constructions of 'Third World otherness'. The difficulty is finding a way of acknowledging the significance of global developments without falling prey to the pitfalls of economic determinism. To illustrate these points, I shall look at A. Sivanandan's critique of world capitalism contained in his wide-ranging and provoking article, 'New Circuits of Imperialism' (1989). To begin, I shall summarise the article in five points.

(i) The world is divided into three types of country, each defined in terms of level and form of industrialisation. The first type is the 'developed countries' (DCs) which have moved beyond traditional forms of manufacturing to high technology industries, for example microelectronics. In Japan, 'robots make robots' (ibid.: 2). Even conventional manufacturing has been transformed with the aid of computerised technology, including robots in car manufacture. Service industries also play an increasingly important role in the economies of DCs. 'Newly industrialised countries' (NICs), the second type, have taken over the traditional manufacturing industries, notably shipbuilding and steel. Countries in South East Asia – South Korea, Singapore and Taiwan – and elsewhere, Brazil and India, are examples of NICs. Finally, there are the underdeveloped countries (UDCs), like Thailand, Sri Lanka and Malaysia, which rely primarily on food production and processing.

(ii) This 'hierarchy' of production is secured in various ways. First, governments of DCs, transnational banks and international institutions like the World Bank and International Monetary Fund regulate loans and aid to NICs and UDCs, so as to control their investment programmes and hence patterns of development. Second, the monopoly of different technologies and the resistance to export the knowledge required to transform production processes have also helped to limit the economies of UDCs. Finally, through overt and covert political means, DCs have been able to destabilise hostile regimes whilst offering support to 'friendly' regimes prepared to comply with terms laid down by DCs.

iii) Western political intervention plays a crucial role in these processes. Such intervention can be military, in the case of US operations in Central America, or more covert, low-intensity conflict, including disinformation and other psychological operations, insurgency and counter-insurgency programmes and military support. Examples of this can be seen in Central

America, southern Africa, Mozambique and Angola, the Far East, the Philippines and East Timor, and, of course, in the Middle East, in Libya, Iran and Iraq. These various forms and degrees of political intervention have, in turn, thrown up a variety of kinds of political regime, which range from dictatorships, mostly in NICs, to what Sivanandan calls parliamentary authoritarian regimes in UDCs.

iv) Such measures of control, both political and economic, are supported by cultural domination, particularly of the US; witness, he writes, the shift from coca colonisation to the global fetish for fast food. Cultural imperialism in different ways helps to secure the dominance of DC values. Of course, legitimacy based on 'persuasion' of this kind is backed up by the use of cruder economic and political instruments of the sort discussed above.

v) One important consequence of the above factors has been the emergence of a class of economic migrants and political refugees, the one searching for jobs, the other escaping persecution from authoritarian regimes. This new underclass, as Sivanandan refers to them, either enter DCs illegally (the migration of Central American labour to the southern US is a good example here), or as refugees, working for poor wages in hazardous jobs and with limited rights. The kind of work obtained relates to the pattern of industrial development in DCs: in nuclear power, in agribusiness, in the fast food sector and in the lower end of the service sector. Such conditions are graphically described by Günter Wallraff, a German investigative journalist, who took the Turkish Islamic name of Ali in order to experience the working conditions of migrant workers/refugees (1988).

Sivanandan's account, summarised schematically here, offers a persuasive account of global patterns of economic and political development in the post-colonial era. The role of multinational and transnational companies, international banks and agreements between governments have marked the latest phase in what Wallerstein has called the world capitalist economy, an example of what he calls a world system (1974; Wallerstein and Hopkins, 1982). Sivanandan's analysis goes beyond the simple developed–undeveloped axis of writers like Gunder Frank (1978) to describe, more fully, different degrees and forms of industrialisation.

He rightly acknowledges the importance of global shifts of capital and labour. NICs and UCs are both subject to forms of control by multinationals as well as tied to western governments' and/or IMF aid programmes. Bhopal is a good example of multinational dominance, illustrating the movement of capital to the Third World in search of cheap labour. A more recent example is General Motors' decision to move its car plant from Detroit, where it paid its workers $9 an hour, to Mexico, where it paid 69 cents, thus cutting costs and making it that much more competitive with its Japanese rivals.

It is important to remember, however, that the decisions of multinational companies like Union Carbide to invest in the Third World are taken on political and ideological grounds as well, which may or may not coincide with the economic calculations. Even the latter are not as straightforward as they seem. For example, there is an economic argument against relocation that has been articulated by some western economists. Even the 'offer' of a non-unionised work-force made by some Third World governments to attract investment can be offset by increased transport costs, communication difficulties and many other invisible costs. The general point here is that the movements of capital and labour are a messy business, complicated by numerous intervening factors. Even the economic arguments can be the object of dispute. Hence the patterns of investment and migration are much more complex than a simple model would imply.

Sivanandan also rightly recognises the key role of DC states in these processes, from direct military intervention, for example in the Gulf War of 1991, to its more covert role, for instance the role of the US in parts of Latin America. He uses this discussion to illustrate the ways in which states in developed countries help to shape political regimes in non-DCs, including dictatorships, and hence indirectly create refugee migrations which result from repression and human rights abuses often sponsored by western governments. In Chile, for example, political refugees fled the military coup of 1973, against a background of US covert operations that had sought to destabilise Allende's communist government and support the military under General Pinochet.

The impact of multinational companies has been well documented elsewhere. Tobacco is a good example. Discouraged by western governments from promoting smoking in the West, tobacco companies have diverted their advertising resources to the Third World with great success. Not only has smoking consumption increased in the latter at the same time as it has declined in the West, but it has also been reported that stronger and more addictive forms of tobacco are used in cigarette production for the Third World. The destructive and distortionary impact of multinational corporations on Third World peoples has been a recurring theme of this chapter, from pharmaceuticals to pesticides to prostitution. Equally significant is the role multinationals play through their dislocative impact on Third World economies by creating a pool of unemployed in the Third World eligible to work in the West.

What general theories of political economy, of which Sivanandan's is one example, provide is a broad and attractive theory of trends and developments. What they lack is a theorisation of politics and culture which can grasp the complexity of the contingency of outcomes (why Bhopal? why 1984?); the unevenness of development (for example the differences between and within DCs, NICs and UDCs), and the specificity of cultural and political processes, for example how do we make sense of events like Band Aid and Live Aid or of different governmental strategies in dealings with multinational companies? These general theories also take insufficient account of cultural and political interventions in economies, for example how we account for different forms and levels of political resistance. They can also gloss over conflicts and contradictions in institutional processes and forms of representation, for example how do we explain cultural struggles around education or alternative media representations of the Third World, or changes, some of which seem more, some less compatible with dominant forms and ways of thinking?

Whilst economic discourses and realities have often been neglected in cultural studies writing, such discourses have always eschewed the forms of complexity illustrated above, seeing them instead, as outcomes of some underlying economic logic. In sum, it is important to retain political economy without the trappings of a general theory; to incorporate an economic dimension into cultural studies without giving economics a monopoly status. At the same time, the opening up of economies and economic institutions to the frameworks and approaches of cultural studies is equally overdue.

CONCLUSIONS

Maryknoll, a Catholic organisation with global connections, calls for abandonment of the term 'The Third World' (*Maryknoll Magazine*, April 1991), which it claims is based on economic criteria and hence conceals enormous cultural diversity. There are other arguments against the term, including the fact that Third World economies themselves vary widely. Furthermore, the idea of a 'Third World' when the 'Second World' is, arguably, already dismantled, is another argument against its use. There has also been a reluctance to use any term which suggests a hierarchy, especially one in which the West comes out on top. In the course of this chapter, the term has been used to denote peoples as well as geographic areas of the world, thus adding to contentiousness of the term's use. At times, when the term is used in dominant discourses or when its status is being generally called into question, I have enclosed it in inverted commas. At other times, when it is used to designate a collective experience or to stand for forms of political/cultural mobilisation, I have removed the commas. This cumbersome practice reflects both my own uncertainty with the term and my desire to confer legitimacy on it in very selective ways.

In some senses, Günter Wallraff's experience as a migrant worker in Germany is closer to that of coffee pickers in Brazil than it is to members of the dominant industrial and political classes in Germany. So, why retain the term? Why not talk about individual countries in terms of the specificities of difference? The conclusion of this chapter is that there needs to be both. There has to be a way of examining particularities of difference while acknowledging the commonalties of experience. This will sometimes mean glossing over differences within Third World countries between, for instance, the rural dispossessed class and the urban bourgeoisie, in order to highlight dominant processes in the West. It may mean linking Third World peoples in the West with those in the Third World 'proper', even when there may be real differences between them, as Sweet Honey in the Rocks' 'Are My Hands Clean' testifies. The selection of focus will depend on the context and the (political)

153

point of making (or not making) the connections.

The dominant constructions of the 'Third World' have been culturally produced (with the proviso that cultural productions have important political and economic dimensions). This was the theme of the first part of this chapter. These cultural historical productions have been reworked and articulated with more recent discourses. Tourism offers one example of how the West is encouraged to see the 'Third World' and its people. Tourism is not just about a cultural construction. It is about the role of transnational airlines, hotels and holiday companies. It is about social relations between tourists and indigenous people. Different countries have resisted tourism in different ways, some more successfully than others, but what they are resisting is something they share in common: the cultural and economic power of the West.

Elsewhere, the intellectual hegemony of the West, examined historically by writers like Said, re-imposes itself in the West's ability to define and control the world's problems. The problems of over-population and food shortages were used as examples of common social processes. The West not only defines the problems using racist constructions, it uses such rationalisations to explain away discriminatory and exploitative practices, and in so doing creates another set of problems. Its failures make little dent on its ability to go on defining new problems and researching them within its own intellectual paradigms.

The extraordinary power of such explanations, and the West's capacity to absorb them into common-sense thinking, has made much of what happens in the Third World seem only natural. Disasters like floods and famine are perceived as natural even when they have been shown to be the result of human intervention, and sometimes non-intervention. This 'naturalising' of Third World history spills over into explanations of other kinds of disaster. For instance at Bhopal, 'ignorance', 'incompetence' and 'terrorism', the terms used to explain what happened, were widely regarded as 'natural' traits associated with the 'Third World'. In fact, the very idea of 'backwardness', commonly associated with the Third World, in contrast to the cultural and technological advances in the West, makes the Third World appear closer to nature, hence facilitating the kinds of common-sense explanation discussed throughout this chapter.

The global perspective in the final section helps explain the reasons why the struggle against such forces is an uphill one. The power of multinational companies to shift capital and labour around the globe, the abilities of western governments to intervene overtly and covertly and the power of states to reaffirm cultural superiority through education and the media, help explain the one-sidedness of these battles. What they cannot explain are the forms of resistance, or the links forged between oppressed peoples; how power is created through collective action and does not simply rest with the dominant political and economic classes of the 'First World'. The women on the picket line at Grunwick, who sought union recognition and improved working conditions, the people's movements in Bhopal, which sought more information, adequate compensation and greater accountability, and the 500 Years of Resistance Campaign in the Americas, which sought to give greater autonomy to women as well as to indigenous, black and popular sectors, are amongst the wealth of examples of localised, and not so localised struggles across the globe. Stuart Hall talks about a global mass culture originating in the West, which speaks English, but which never completes its process of homogenisation. Nor does it want to. Rather it works through 'local' differences, never quite destroying what is specific to them (Hall, 1991a: 28–9) The spaces that emerge here provide the basis for localised struggles and forms of expression, which in turn work their way back into our sense of the global.

For those in the West not directly implicated in such struggles, we have yet to discover and develop popular movements cutting across national boundaries. At best, support seems confined to attending a charity pop concert or sponsored sporting event; responding to television appeals using our credit cards; buying recycled clothes or Nicaraguan coffee from charity shops; recycling our beer cans and wine bottles; and, for a few, attending undercrowded meetings of anti-imperialist organisations with fragile alliances and small and overlapping memberships. In the main, our interventions resemble those of a critical, but largely passive, consumer. Moreover, it is largely individuals, not collectivities, that intervene and it is in their individual capacity that they choose the market-place to take up these issues.

7

EUROPE: 1992 AND BEYOND

1992 was a much talked about year in the history of Europe, marking as it did the legal 'opening' of the single European market, when capital, labour, goods and services could cross European boundaries freely without restriction or cost. Whether or not the single market will create equal levels of freedom for all 330 million people living in the 'new Europe' is an important theme of this chapter. More specifically, it will consider four aspects of recent developments in Europe, in terms of both cultural and institutional processes and their consequences for black and minority groups. I am using the latter term here to include temporary migrants, refugees and immigrants with citizenship rights as well as long-standing, well-established black and ethnic minority communities.

First, I shall look at the revival of Eurocentric thought in the latter part of the twentieth century, which has sought to transcend the individual nationalisms of Europe's member states. Whilst popular reactions to the Maastricht Treaty in the latter part of 1992 suggested that allegiances to Europe remained quite weak, in global terms the construction of a common European cultural identity is, arguably, as significant as – possibly more than – the sum of Europe's national chauvinisms. Second I shall examine the context of this revival, which entails, amongst other factors, growing evidence of the co-ordination and institutionalisation of European-wide structures on immigration and refugees, the promotion of stronger links between governments, security forces and civil servants, and the emergence of a common European consciousness on these matters. The relationship between these structures and forms of consciousness, on the one hand, and the recent revival of the far right across Europe, on the other, is complex. Support for the far right can be considered partly a response to the developments in Europe, notably the break-up of the Soviet bloc and the growth of European-wide networks of far right groups and organisations. At the same time, the far right remains fiercely nationalistic in terms of its aims; the third section provides evidence of its growth in support and impact on mainstream politics. In general, there are some ominous trends emerging out of the new Europe which will help to shape the experiences both of minorities living inside Europe and of those remaining in the Third World.

In the light of these developments, and by way of conclusion, I shall assess a number of emerging political responses from the left. These include opposition to, and in some cases direct action against the far right as well as opposition to measures like the Asylum Bill in Britain. This kind of politics has been expressed organisationally in the emergence, or in the case of the Anti-Nazi League, revival, of anti-racist organisations. However, the main focus of this section will be an assessment of the left's 'New Times' political agenda for the 1980s and 1990s which, it will be argued, is rooted in European intellectual debate and politics. Important intellectual influences on the politics of 'New Times', for instance, can be found in the disparate strands of postmodernist and poststructuralist thought. Within these broader intellectual developments are to be found recent debates on ethnic and black identity. I shall link these to Paul Gilroy's important critique of anti-racist politics and the notion of cultural purity. I will attempt to assess these recent contributions to left political debate in the light of recent, and perhaps future, developments in Europe.

CULTURAL CONSTRUCTIONS OF THE 'NEW EUROPE'

Attempts to define a 'new' European unity draw on a reservoir of ideas, myths and assumptions which date back to Christopher Columbus' sighting of the Americas in 1492 and to the beginnings of European conquest. As Jan Nederveen Pieterse reminds us, it is ironic that 1992 marked both an important development in the 'new Europe' and the 500th anniversary of what was Europe's first encounter with the old world (Pieterse,1991: 6). The year 1492 is one to be mourned by the indigenous peoples in the Americas as much as it is to be celebrated by the descendants of the first white settlers. How 1992, the year of the single European market, will be remembered in 500 years' time, and by whom, remains to be seen.

The presence of cultural processes working both for and against greater European unity has demonstrated the adaptability of racist discourses. Historically, racism has been a part of, or subordinate to, the various nationalisms of Europe from their peak towards the end of the nineteenth century to their revival, notably in Britain, in the 1980s. Yet it has always contained elements which have transcended those nationalisms, for instance the idea of a global hierarchy of races with Europe as a whole (not Britain, Germany or France independently) on top. In this sense, racism has the capacity to feed into both Eurocentric and nationalist thought, providing evidence for and against greater European unity. This paradox should become clearer in what follows.

In the course of 1992 there were several indications that the process of European unity was beginning to falter on the nationalisms of its member states, for example the referenda in Denmark and France on the Maastricht Treaty, and British and Italian withdrawal from the European Monetary

System. The nation state continues to have its advocates, who have harnessed it to a series of highly defensive and exclusivist political projects, of which Thatcherism is just one (Hall, 1991a: 25). At the same time, there is evidence that national identity is being eroded in a world increasingly dominated by transnational organisations and treaties, including the European Community; multinational companies; systems of global communication; a growing sense of ecological interdependence; and international migration, which is literally bringing those on the margins into the centre (ibid.).

In their efforts to capitalise on as well as transcend European nationalism, the advocates of the new European unity have appealed to a Eurocentric tradition to which nation states have contributed. The following is how a Dutch ambassador described the 'new Europe'. It is worth noting how the history and culture of the continent are reduced to a few key ideas, traditions and catch-phrases. The ambassador asks,

> What determines and characterises European culture?... Europe is formed by the... community of nations which are largely characterised by the inherited civilisation whose most important sources are: the Judaeo-Christian religion, the Greek-Hellenistic ideas in the fields of government, philosophy, arts and science, and finally the Roman views concerning law.

> (cited in Pieterse, 1991: 3)

In fact, this 'new' brand of 'EC-centrism', which has already inspired one composer to write a new Euro-anthem,[1] has a powerful legacy of European racist thought on which to draw. According to George Mosse (1978), eighteenth-century Europe was the 'cradle of modern racism' and throughout that century and the one that followed race increasingly became seen as the key to understanding history. The assumption was made by scholars across Europe that the world could be divided up into biologically defined races with the 'white' race allegedly superior to its 'black' and 'yellow' counterparts. In other words, whilst racism was harnessed to individual nationalist projects, the 'superior race' transcended nation states and, if anything, belonged to a wider European stock. Different terms came to be associated with white European, including Caucasian, Anglo-Saxon and Aryan. Friedrich Blumenbach, a German anthropologist, introduced the term Caucasian in 1795 to describe white Europeans whom he described as the most beautiful, whilst Negroes and Mongolians were deemed the least so. The term 'Aryan' was taken from Sanskrit legends (Barzun, 1965: ch. 6) and became the object of intense controversy in the nineteenth century, with Europe's nations claiming to be the resting place of these blond, blue-eyed conquerors of India. The term came to be the natural antithesis of Jew (and later socialist and gypsy as well) in the twentieth century.

In an interesting reference to anti-Semitism, Balibar argues that, as a tradition, it developed across Europe but became harnessed to individual nationalist projects. He writes, 'Anti-Semitism functioned on a European scale: each nationalism saw in the Jew. . . its own specific enemy and the representative of all "hereditary enemies"' (Balibar, 1991: 62). The myths of anti-Semitism – the ritual murders, the wandering Jew and the protocols of Zion – were widely propagated throughout Europe during the nineteenth century. In fact, the idea that Christian babies were slaughtered as part of a sacrificial offering at Passover remained alive into the twentieth century, especially in remote rural parts of Eastern Europe (Mosse, 1978: 114). The alleged Protocols of the Elders of Zion suggested a conspiracy of Jewish leaders to bring about world domination through alliances between Jewish banks and socialists (amongst others), were forged during the Dreyfus affair in France with the help of the Russian secret police.[2] The French wanted to discredit Dreyfus and the Russians wanted to justify Csarist anti-Semitism, which was invoked more widely to rally people otherwise divided by class or religion. In a similar fashion, Houston Stewart Chamberlain saw the struggle between Aryan and Semite as the struggle for civilisation: the Jews were portrayed as the devil and the Germans as the chosen saviours and heirs of the Greeks and Romans (ibid.: 106).

In France, De Gobineau also portrayed the history of civilisation as a global racial struggle, in his late nineteenth-century writings. His prognosis, however, in the short term at least, was less optimistic than Chamberlain's. He argued that the white race had been weakened through mixing with subordinate and inferior classes and races. He described Latin nations, notably those of southern Europe as a decadent, slavish and worthless stock having been semitised and melanised (Barzun, 1965: 78–9). In the immediate future, he foresaw a period in which those inferior groups (for example 'blacks', whom he described as a 'mob on the loose' and the 'yellow race', which he dubbed 'materialistic') would dominate. In the longer term, however, these groups would inevitably be defeated by the white race modelling itself on 'Renaissance heroes' (Mosse, 1978: 55).

Britain made its own important contribution to European racist thought. The eugenics movement, pioneered by Francis Galton, sought to increase the numbers of those deemed to be the most able amongst the population. Hence, it was argued, the birth rate of the 'unfit' should be checked and the 'fit' encouraged to reproduce through early marriage (ibid.: 74). His survey of men in leadership positions (judges, politicians etc.) showed that such positions were held by family members over successive generations, thus confirming, in his view, that genius was hereditary!! On the other hand the moral character of 'inferior' races ('mongolians, Jews, Negroes, Gypsies and American Indians') was wild and untamable, and they had an arrested intellect (Galton, 1979: 59ff.). James Hunt, in his inaugural address to the Anthropological Association in 1863, reminded the audience that whatever anthropology's findings, no evidence could deny the superiority of the races of Europe and the inferiority of those from Africa (cited in Gabriel, 1976: 51). The superiority of the Anglo-Saxon was drawn in a literary context as well, in the novels of Daniel Defoe, Walter Scott, Charles Kingsley, Rudyard Kipling and others. Literature and the arts, as I have suggested before, complemented these so-called 'scientific' findings (Barzun, 1965; Dabydeen, 1986).

An important point about these ideas was the extent to which, together, they helped to construct a European racist tradition. As Mosse says, 'these ideas were widely dispersed throughout Europe': the German-speaking lands, the French and the English were all 'crucial laboratories of racial thought' (Mosse, 1978: 66). In the case of the eugenics movement the work of both Francis Galton and Karl Pearson was studied in Germany so that 'there was a great deal of cross-fertilisation between the two nations' (ibid.: 75ff; see also Barzun, 1965). But it was not just a matter of communication between individuals or the exchanges of ideas, but the substance of the ideas themselves that brought Europeans together. Racism bound nation states in a common ancestry. It joined the peoples of Europe of all classes to a common stock and served to explain European global dominance at the height of its empire.

Needless to say, in drawing so selectively on past European traditions, 'from Plato to Nato', the Dutch ambassador's remarks, cited above, are significant as much for what they omit as what they include. Working-class traditions and struggles, social inequalities around gender, sexuality as well as 'race' and ethnicity are conveniently left out of this perspective. Numerous conflicts across the centuries of European history are also eclipsed in this view, as the idea of a European consensus is constructed. The ambassador ignores religious divisions between Protestant, Catholic and Muslim and the fact that parts of Europe were Islamic in the twelfth and thirteenth centuries. Furthermore, he assumes that democracy was conceived in classical Greece and has been with us ever since, when in reality Europe has also been the birthplace of colonialism and slavery, Fascism and the Gulag, each fostering, in both colonial and neo-colonial contexts, a succession of despotic regimes.

The view of the ambassador appeals to a unitary history of Europe which not only conceals a large part of its own history from itself but bears no resemblance to the histories of many peoples now settled in Europe. For example, the histories of African, Caribbean and Asian peoples, now settled in Britain, of north Africans, now settled in France, of Turks now living in Germany, all challenge the view of empire defined in terms of a European historiographical tradition. Their interpretations of their own histories offer new and radically conflicting versions of hitherto well-accepted historical truths. (For example, the Indians who rebelled against British colonialism in 1877 might have been 'mutineers' in English history but were heroes in the history of the struggle for Indian independence.)

One significant irony in debates around Europe as it approached 1992 was the way in which both those seeking greater European unity *and* those defending national chauvinisms, did so using a common racist discourse. Thatcherism offered one of the best examples of a nationalist project 'driven by a very aggressive form of racism' (Hall, 1991a: 26), but there also existed, on the other side, a Eurocentric racism, which appealed, very effectively, to cultural traditions which date back to the zenith of European imperialism. As I have suggested, there was a readily available repertoire of ideas, myths and distortions which were available to work on receptive audiences across Europe and which were already emerging in the intellectual as well as political rationalisations of the new Europe. The continuities and contradictions here have been well captured by Balibar, who has observed the way both Europe as a whole and its respective nation states have harnessed racism to successive conflicts from the fifteenth century onwards:

> the state transforms antagonisms and persecutions that have quite other origins into racism in the modern sense (and ascribes verbal markers of ethnicity to them). This runs from the way in which, since the times of the Reconquista in Spain, theological anti-Judaism was transposed into genealogical exclusion based on 'purity of blood' at the same time as the raza [race] was launching itself on the New World, down to the way in which modern Europe, the new 'dangerous classes' of the international proletariat tend to be subsumed under the category of 'immigration', which becomes the name given to race within the crisis-torn nations of the post-colonial era.
>
> (Balibar, 1991: 52)

INSTITUTIONALISING EURO-RACISM

The European Community seems to have found it easier to agree about immigration than about agricultural or monetary policy: perhaps because the former potentially unites Europe against the common threat of outsiders whilst the latter puts one member state at an advantage over another. In this section I shall look at various institutional initiatives which are helping to forge a common European perspective on race, under, according to Balibar, the category of immigrant and, it might be added, those of migrant and refugee. Despite the significant popular pressure to preserve national identities within Europe, structures were undoubtedly in place, in 1992, above and outside national boundaries; structures which will crucially determine national policies on immigration. It is surprising, given the strength of nationalist resistance to greater European unity, that such an important plank of nationalism, that is the right to say who does and does not belong to the nation, has already, to some degree, been taken out of the hands of member states. Perhaps such developments might have provoked greater resistance had their existence been more widely known.

Since 1975, proposals regarding immigration have been discussed by the Trevi group. This group, which has been made up of EC Ministers of Justice and the Interior and civil servants was, in origin, an intergovernmental forum to combat terrorism. In fact, Trevi is an acronym which stands for terrorism, radicalism, extremism and violence. Hence, what started out as an anti-terrorist forum and liaison network extended its brief over the years to include drug trafficking and more recently the immigration and internal movement of illegal immigrants and undesirables. So, the group has effectively forged policy links between terrorists, drug runners, refugees and migrant workers from outside Europe. The short mental leap from would-be immigrants and refugees to those black and other minority peoples settled inside Europe has previously been made in the UK, and there is already evidence of problems encountered by black citizens of EC countries seeking to cross EC national boundaries. Liaison between member states on these matters operates through police and security networks; in Britain's case, through a European section of the Special Branch under MI5.

Amongst the Trevi group's concrete initiatives was a common visa policy to act as a mechanism for selective immigration control. It was, and is, selective in the sense that not all visitors are required to apply for visas prior to entering the EC. Those countries that are, and they numbered 59 in 1992, included countries from southern Africa, central and southern America and South East Asia. In contrast, Canada, Australia and Japan are exempt. In other words, Third World status has played a major part in determining which peoples will be subject to additional entry controls.

Another body, the Ad Hoc Group on Immigration, made up of Interior Ministers, has also been concerned with the development of a common visa policy. At the insistence of the British Government, the group has agreed that, as far as 'third country' (see below, p. 164) nationals are concerned,

> they would not have the 'right of entry', even if they satisfy all the conditions of entry. . . . So, even if a person seeking to enter the EC had the correct entry visa, all the necessary documents setting out the purpose and conditions of the proposed visit, could prove that they had sufficient means of support themselves throughout the period of their visit, and could show that they had the resources for their return journey, they would still have no right of entry to the EC.
>
> (Read and Simpson, 1991: 38)

The need to police European borders in the light of the kind of thinking that has gone into the above discussions and proposals, has been expressed in the Schengen Treaty, which was ratified in 1990. The purpose of the treaty was to increase external border controls and to tighten up on entry into those countries that are signatories to the treaty, whilst at the same time work towards ending internal controls. It is likely that the treaty, which was signed by France, Germany and the countries of Benelux and Italy, with Spain and Portugal having observer status in the group, will be used as a model for all EC in the 1990s (ibid.: 39). At the moment, internal border controls do not operate for Schengen group members but do for the other EC member states. The task of administering the removal of remaining internal barriers and co-ordinating the work of groups like Trevi has fallen to the Rhodes Group of Coordinators. This group was responsible for the Palma Convention, which timetabled the implementation of various agreements, including the common visa policy, the deadline for which was the end of 1992 (ibid.: 41).

The co-ordination of immigration and refugee policy has been made easier because, for the past thirty years or so, EC member countries' policies on both immigration and refugees have been converging. They have, without exception, become tighter and tougher. On the specific issue of refugees, the EC had plans in the early 1990s to 'harmonise' its policy through the issuing of a community-wide directive. Even Sweden had tightened up its stance on refugees, so much so that only 25 per cent of those who were granted refugee status in 1988 would have qualified for entry in 1991 (Allen and Macie, 1990: 382). The National Association of Citizens Advice Bureaux (1990) summarised the situation in the following way:

> There seem to be some underlying trends on the policy-making efforts around refugee policy; firstly they originate from a policing and security angle rather than out of a concern for human rights. . . secondly that none of the intergovernmental groups (Schengen etc.) are accountable to any of the European institutions. . . thirdly. . . these policies are taking shape without any of the proposals or considerations being made public.
>
> (para 3.1)

One of the features of the development of European policy on immigration, refugees and visas has been its clandestine nature. All of the above groups, with the exception of the Rhodes group, which was set up under European law and hence is answerable to the European Parliament, have been evolving polices (with profound social implications) outside the context of democratically elected structures.

In contrast, attempts to develop anti-discrimination policies and to strengthen the Social Charter to include the rights of minorities have foundered on the principle of subsidiarity. In practice this has meant that, when pressure has been put on the European Commission to tackle racial discrimination, the Commission has responded by urging member states to respond individually. In defending the absence of any reference to racial discrimination in the action programme relating to the Social Charter, the Commission wrote:

> While the Commission is not making any proposal in respect of discrimination on grounds of race, colour or religion, it nevertheless stresses the need for such practices to be eradicated. . . through appropriate action by Member States and the two sides of industry.
>
> (cited in Read and Simpson, 1991: 25)

In many ways developments in Europe mirror the history of immigration and race relations legislation in Great Britain. In the case of immigration this comprises tough immigration legislation, with heavy sanctions for those who breach it; immigration rules, imposed on Parliament without the option to reject; and the bureaucratically controlled, clandestine web of procedures and practices within which both laws and rules are administered. On the other side there is the 1976 Race Relations Act, admittedly the only one of its kind in Europe, outlawing racial discrimination. However, unlike immigration laws and rules, the powers of this law are widely regarded as extremely limited,[3] and it relies as much on exhortation and encouragement as it does on legal enforcement. This strategy, of using a carrot rather than a stick on discrimination, coincides with the view taken by other member states and by the EC itself.

As a result of the convergence of its immigration policies, there are emerging three classes of people in Europe: citizens, nominally with full rights; demizens with full rights but with 'third country' nationality; and migrants who have no rights whatsoever. The latter make up about 7.5 million, and in some countries, like Germany, there are more migrants than demizens. In fact, in the early 1990s only 15 per cent of 'third country' nationals had been born in Germany. The UK has been moving increasingly towards the German model since the 1971 Immigration Act, and particularly since the 1981 Nationality Act, although there still remain limited opportunities for children in the UK to acquire citizenship after ten years (Labour Research, 1990: 16). Linked to this, and relating to Commonwealth connections, there is also a much greater black and ethnic minority population, settled and with full citizenship rights (at least in principle) in the UK. Nevertheless, the above three categories broadly coincide with divisions in the UK, between whites with full citizenship rights; black people, with the same legal but not *de facto* rights and, finally, a group of temporary migrants, asylum seekers and some illegally settled with few, if any, rights, whatsoever. Cutting across these categories is a further set of gendered divisions. Complex articulations of racism, ethnicity and patriarchy have created distinctive work patterns (e.g. self-employment, domestic-related labour) for migrant women as well as providing the basis for a variety of forms of resistance (Morokvasic, 1991: 81).

A further parallel between Britain and the rest of Europe has been the use of the debates on immigration to conceal racist motives. Hence, Britain has apparently been concerned with the overall number of immigrants, when in fact the real demand has been to control black immigration. It can be shown how UK immigration and nationality laws have actually safeguarded white immigration and nationality while at the same time restricting black immigration and citizenship. Another example of a double standard running through British nationality and immigration legislation has been policies on Hong Kong. Whilst the Gibraltarians and the residents of the Falkland Islands/Malvinas were given legal entitlement to become British citizens, no such right was extended to the people of Hong Kong. Events in Tiananmen Square in 1989 provoked a further discussion of the rights of the people of the island, after 1997, when it formally loses its crown colonial status and becomes part of the People's Republic of China. In practice, the response to the prospect of an influx of people of Chinese origin has been tempered by political arguments (opposition to immigration from left-wing political regimes, in this case China, has always been more muted), and economic considerations (in this case expressed in a welcome to those immigrants with capital and 'expertise'). Nevertheless, it is by no means clear how 'measured' this response will remain as 1997 approaches.

Elsewhere, Europe's response to developments in Eastern Europe, and Germany's in particular, also illustrate the contradictory, and hence racist, character of European policies on immigration. A particular irony has been West Germany's open door policy to East Germany, which has coincided with its denial of basic citizenship rights to its own migrant population, not to mention its relationship with Third World peoples in general. Günter Grass has noted this double standard:

> the scope for practical hatred between rich and poor Germans. . . is relatively slight (augmented as they are by a deep-rooted nationalism) compared with the complex multifariousness of the opportunities for hatred which presently exist between the industrial nations and the peoples of the Third World.
>
> (cited in Read and Simpson, 1991: 58)

The assumption pervading post-war debate in Britain, that the 'race' problem is that of black immigration, also found its way into European deliberations in the build-up to 1992, often thanks to English contributions to the debate. In a Royal Institute of International Affairs discussion paper, Alan Butt Philip writes:

> If internal borders are to go, then viable and robust alternatives where needed must be operational. Nothing could damage the purpose of replacing border controls more comprehensively than for the worst imaginable outcomes (a flood of illegal immigration, illicit drugs, international crime and terrorism) actually to occur.
>
> (Philip, 1989: 25)

Philip's proposed solution is the intensifying of 'inter-agency cooperation' which means, in practice, rights of surveillance, hot pursuit and the use of new technologies (ibid.). Philip counts social costs, as opposed to the economic benefits, of 1992, in terms of controlling illegal immigrants, who are lumped together with criminals, drug dealers and terrorists. The problem of guaranteeing the social, political and economic rights of minority groups after 1992 is thus eschewed. In fact, the common-sense linkage made by Philip helps to create a climate in which those rights are harder to secure.

In exploring some of these common themes, Glyn Ford, in his committee's report for the European Parliament, makes some interesting observations on the European press (European Paliament, 1990). In Denmark, a study confirmed that three-quarters of the material on immigration dealt with crime and racism. In France, migrants appear disproportionately in social disorder stories, and Le Pen's fourfold obsession – immigration, insecurity, delinquency and unemployment – has entered into popular media mythology. In Italy, the stereotype of the Arab as a sexually perverse and oppressive Muslim is an important feature of media reporting. Research in Germany, too, shows how the press focus on negative and particularly criminal characteristics of the Turkish community. However, differences are noted:

> Even the worst papers in West Germany would not dare to print headlines like 'Arab pig sneaks back in' (*The Sun*, 23 January 1986) or 'Get out you Syrian swine' (*The Sun*, 25 October 1986) or to call a member of an ethnic minority a 'scum product' (*The Sun*, 27 February 1989). Secondly there are more violent images: 'black youth' is characterised as 'rioters'/'black mob' (*The Daily Express*, 30 September 1985). Cartoons present black people in Britain as primitive cannibals in 'tribal' or 'jungle' settings. Thirdly, there is a major battle taking place in some of the British press against anti-racism. Anti-racists are labelled as 'race spies' controlling people's thoughts, imposing censorship, being 'loony leftists', etc.
>
> (European Parliament, 1990: 140)

Ford attempts to explain these differences partly in terms of the pressure on the German press to express its racism covertly because of its recent history. Interestingly, in Germany, what has replaced the cruder versions to be found in the English press is the taken-for-granted idea of the superiority of German culture and the inevitability of conflict between different cultures resulting from the innate preferences of human beings for their 'own kind' (ibid.).[3] The emphasis on cultural difference and innate antagonism, however, hides an important dimension of German migrant relations. It is not just a question of cultural difference but of economic, political and social exploitation. In his graphic account of life disguised as a Turkish migrant worker, Günter Wallraff (1988) describes working conditions in employment usually reserved for migrant labour: in a McDonald's in Hamburg, where 'the only thing they don't do is put us on the grill'; on a building site in Düsseldorf where he was instructed to climb up onto a burnt-out roof to clear up immediately after a fire, with rubber soles on his shoes (ibid.: 31); inhaling concentrated coke dust for three hours underground (ibid.: 71); testing drugs, whose possible side effects were suffocating attacks and disturbance to blood circulation (ibid.: 125); and, finally, working at the oldest nuclear power plant at Wurgassen, where workers doctored their dosimeters (which read levels of radioactivity) so that they could clock up sufficient working hours (ibid.: 171).

There are many complex processes involved in institutionalising racism in Europe. At one level this has happened *organisationally* through groups like Trevi and the Ad Hoc Group on Immigration. At another level, these groups have added legitimacy to a variety of cultural assumptions underpinning their work, notably that it is not immigration *per se* into Europe that is the problem but black immigration in particular. They have accomplished this in a number of ways, for example through their visa policies and the selective granting of citizenship rights. More than this, however, the remits and policies of these groups have sought to associate black immigration with crime, more specifically with drug trafficking, terrorism or just plain illegal entry. The twin processes of *racialisation* and *criminalisation* of would-be migrants from the 'Third World' have thus formed part of an emerging EC-wide agenda on immigration, an agenda which many elements of the European press, in Britain above all, have been at the forefront in setting.

In some respects EC developments, as I have suggested, represent an integration and co-ordination of what is already happening in individual member countries. In other ways European initiatives provide an opportunity to rework old imperial themes of the last century and to reconstruct the old divisions between Europe and Europe's former colonial territories. These political and cultural processes have a *material* aspect too, as Günter Wallraff's vivid autobiographical account testifies. Immigrants, migrants, refugees and illegal entrants continue to play an integral role in Europe's economy: both in declining industries and in the service sector characterised by low pay, poor working conditions and non-unionisation. Their vulnerability to right-wing extremism has exacerbated their formal political *disenfranchisement* (in many cases), which stands in marked contrast to the growth in political representation of far right political parties across Europe. Nevertheless, even with political rights, it is by no means clear how redress against groups like Trevi, non-accountable and clandestine as they are, could be achieved.

THE FAR RIGHT: SNAPSHOTS ACROSS EUROPE

In the context of debates surrounding European unity, racism has been a supplement both to discourses aimed at maintaining national identities, as well as to those seeking to transcend them. It is also to be found in the political themes of the far right, which enjoyed a revival, in many parts of Europe, in the 1980s. It is possible that the erosion of national identity, of which Stuart Hall talks, has precipitated a crisis, out of which the far right has grown. The combination of the emergence of new and threatening global, supranational powers, on the one hand, and the significant presence of the colonial 'other' inside Europe on the other, may well have provoked a political reaction which has sought to reassert and defend national identities in racist terms. Attempts to promote greater European unity is one example of a threat to national sovereignty and, as such, might be considered a more specific factor in the revival of the far right in Europe.

On the other side of Europe, the break-up of the Eastern bloc, associated with crises of political legitimation and national sovereignty, unleashed an upsurge in ethnic nationalism and anti-Semitism. In both cases, cultural or alleged racial differences have been exploited in order to justify practices including attacks on 'foreigners', the desecration of Jewish graves and 'ethnic cleansing'. In both Western and Eastern Europe the crisis of the nation state may have proved critical in the emergence of extreme forms of nationalist response. What is also ironically the case, however, is that the organisations of the far right have actually benefited from stronger European links, whilst some of them have invoked racist discourses which go beyond their own nation states to justify their nationalist claims. The relationship between nationalist discourses of the far right and those of mainstream political parties in Europe is uncomfortably close at times, as some snapshot examples of recent and current practices in Europe will indicate.

In Germany, in 1989 the neo-Nazi (Republican) Party won eleven seats on the West Berlin city parliament and subsequently seats in many German cities. The party has links with neo-Nazi skinheads who have been responsible for widespread violence against outsiders (*Newsweek*, 27 April 1992). Apart from predictable policies on trade unions, censorship, and the withholding of social security and political rights from foreigners, the party has also advocated compulsory training of girls for the roles of wife and mother, that HIV virus carriers should have their genitals tattooed, and that an abandoned nuclear power plant should be transformed into a labour camp for political opponents (European Parliament, 1990: 18). Over 2.5 million Germans voted for Fascist parties in the European elections, with the Republikaners winning six seats. Since unification, there has been an upsurge in racial attacks on Jewish cemeteries and on Vietnamese and Mozambiquan workers (Read and Simpson, 1991: 57–8). More recently, far right wing organisations, notably the Republican Party, made gains in the April 1992 regional elections, particularly amongst voters under twenty-five, where the vote for the far right was as high as 15–20 per cent. The number of racial attacks has also risen dramatically, reportedly up fourfold in the first three months of 1992 (*Guardian*, 7 April 1992, 8 April 1992).[4]

The ideas and proposals of the far right in Germany have a well-established tradition in German politics, stretching back beyond the Third Reich's theories of race and its policies on Jews to the nineteenth century and the emergence of German nationalism and national socialism. The culture of 'race' was reflected in nineteenth-century romanticism and the music of Richard Wagner, whose Ring Cycle 'embodied the quintessence of Gobineau's principles of German race-superiority' (Barzun, 1965: 89; see also Allen and Macie, 1990: 386). The distinction between Germans, on the one hand, and Slavs, Semites and now foreigners on the other, has been part of a strong racist cultural tradition which seeks to define the *Volk* in terms of outsiders and of the need for *Lebensraum*, or living space. This cultural tradition, exploited by the Nazis in the 1930s, remains a key plank of attacks on outsiders and the threat they allegedly pose to the German nation. Some of the views of the far right have been endorsed in a number of national measures taken by the German Government. Repatriation was legalised in 1982 and, in the early 1990s, the status of foreigners is such that they have no security of residence, no right to vote and no rights of family reunion. Being born in Germany does not automatically confer citizenship (ibid.: 383).

In Belgium, the legal status of foreigners is arguably weaker than in many other parts of Europe, including the United Kingdom. In Brussels a number of boroughs were legally entitled to refuse rights of entry to foreigners. What is more, the justification for this kind of practice was to 'protect health and morality and to prevent crime'. These common-sense racist assumptions, which have a familiar ring to British ears, were encapsulated by the Belgian Interior Minister in 1987, when, on behalf of his government, he declared that he dare not gamble on society in 2020. He warned:

> We risk suffering the same fate as the Roman Empire when it was engulfed by the Barbarians. These are the Moroccans, the Turks, the Yugoslavs, the Muslims. . . They have nothing in common with our civilisation.
>
> (cited in Merckx and Fekete, 1991: 76)

The specific backlash against Muslims has been felt in Belgium since the Iranian revolution of 1979. In 1986, 100 armed police, using water cannons and armoured police vehicles, were involved in closing down an Iranian cultural centre in Brussels. The closure was justified on the grounds of fears of an expansion of Islamic fundamentalism among the Muslim population. Such official responses have not prevented, however, the far right from making significant electoral gains. The Fascist party, Vlaams Blok, has representation both in the European and national Belgian Parliaments and, in November 1991, it won 25 per cent of the seats on Antwerp's city council. As a footnote and, indeed as an antidote to those expecting some kind of collective response to such practices from within an emerging Eurosocialist movement, it is worth mentioning that the socialist party in Belgium, in an apparent gesture of support for the indigenous working class, argued that foreigners should not have the vote in local or national elections (ibid.).

In France, racism has been associated with the growth in fortunes of Jean Marie Le Pen's Front Nationale (FN), which boasts a membership of 100,000 and received over 2 million votes in the European elections including the election of Le Pen as an MEP. In local elections the FN won up to 60 per cent of the vote in Dreux and 47 per cent in Marseilles (Read and Simpson, 1991: 46). In 1992, the party gained 13 per cent of the vote in regional elections. Its platform has been anti-Arab and anti-Semitic, with its calls for repatriation and an end to the Islamification of France. Beyond these more overt forms of racism, Le Pen preaches a more subtle thesis on outsiders which has helped build his support. He asserts:

> I prefer my daughters to my nieces, my nieces to my cousins, my cousins to my neighbours, my neighbours to my fellow citizens, my fellow citizens to foreigners. What's wrong with that?
>
> (Le Pen cited in *Newsweek*, 27 April 1992)

According to the European Parliament Inquiry Report, the FN has not only been strong in the south but in the industrial north and east too, where it has challenged the declining influence of the French Communist Party for the working-class vote (1990: 23). In common with many far right wing parties in Europe, the FN subscribes to a historically revisionist interpretation of World War II, which denies the existence of the Holocaust and the deaths of approximately 6 million Jews and seeks to confine anti-Semitism to a brief historical period in the 1930s and 1940s.

Racism in France, however, is not confined to the activities of the FN, nor to the political right. In one city, Vitry, the communist mayor gave orders to bulldoze a hostel where immigrant workers were living (Lloyd and Waters, 1991: 62). The Socialist Government, too, was divided in its response to the notorious affair of the scarf in 1989, in which Muslim schoolgirls were not allowed to wear headscarves to school, in accordance with their custom, because, it was alleged, this would be a breach of the principle of secular education. Eventually the government capitulated to the girls' demands and they were allowed to return to school with their scarves (ibid.). In fact, many of France's mainstream political leaders have acknowledged the relevance of, and deferred to, Le Pen's views. Valéry Giscard d'Estaing objected to the invasion of 'foreigners' and called for the citizenship laws to be changed to prevent children of 'foreign' parents born in France from having citizenship rights (*Newsweek*, 27 April 1992). Meanwhile, restrictions on immigrants have been increased. A payment of 1,000 francs to unemployed immigrants to go home has been authorised (Allen and Macie, 1990: 383). France also requires some one million of its foreign workers to carry a document including 40 items of information, 'unprecedented in France since the register of Jews during the Nazi occupation' (ibid.).

Even Sweden, with its progressive reputation on social issues, has been tightening up its policies on immigration and refugees. In a climate which has been described as increasingly restrictionist and oppressive, there has been a growing incidence of attacks on refugees, particularly Chileans and Turks (ibid.: 385). The far right have been quick to capitalise on this unrest and a group calling themselves the New Democrats has been advancing, both in numerical strength and political respectability. By way of response, the Social Democratic Government introduced new regulations restricting the rights of entry and settlement of immigrants and refugees. In the 1991 elections, the New Democrats gained 21 seats on a platform which was explicitly racist. (It also included proposals to reduce the price of wine in restaurants and abolish traffic wardens.) As a result of their success, they held the balance of power in a centre-right coalition in the wake of the defeat of the Social Democrats, who had been in power for 53 of the previous 59 years.

Italy, which has provided Switzerland with a cheap pool of migrant labour in the past, has now, itself, turned to immigrants (particularly illegal immigrants from north Africa) to provide cheap labour for the tomato picking and fishing industries. The advantage of illegal labour is not only that it is cheap, but that it lacks the rights, including bargaining conditions, available to indigenous labour. There is also a strong skinhead movement in Italy, which has organised marches and rallies (chanting Duce and anti-immigrant slogans) as well as carrying out attacks on north African migrants. In an incident in Rome, an Ethiopian woman was thrown off a bus by someone claiming that she was sitting on a white-only seat (Read and Simpson, 1991: 57). This kind of incident is becoming increasingly the norm in a country in which almost 2 million of the electorate voted for the neo-Fascist MSI party (ibid.). Although the overall vote for the MSI was comparatively small in the 1992 general election, it was sufficient to secure a seat for Alessandra Mussolini (Benito's granddaughter) in the new parliament. Meanwhile, the Italian Labour Minister has called on Italians to produce more babies to keep away the armadas of immigrants from the southern shores of the Mediterranean (Kazim, 1991: 88). The implicit ('natural') fear of immigration and outsiders, to which this call appeals, was given further weight by none other than Umberto Eco, doyen of postmodernism, who stated:

We are not facing an immigration phenomenon. We are facing a migratory phenomenon. And like all great migrations its final result will be the inexorable change in habits, an unstoppable interbreeding that changes the colour of skin, hair and eyes.

(ibid.: 88)[5]

These kinds of incidents and wider political developments are not confined to the old Western Europe. Since the events of 1989, the former Eastern bloc countries have experienced an escalation of racial incidents. I have already mentioned East Germany, but anti-Semitism and attacks on black workers and visitors have also revived in Poland and Hungary. Skinhead groups have formed in Hungary and Czechoslovakia and German Republican links have been promoted with sympathisers in these countries. In Poland this growth has been partly legitimised by the actions of the Catholic Church, both in its defence of a Carmelite nunnery at Auschwitz, and by explicitly racist statements made, without sanction, by some of its leaders. Anti-Semitism was also an undercurrent running through the Polish elections, including Lech Walesa's own personal campaign. Although he denied that this was an issue, he did find it necessary to publicly confirm that he was 100 per cent Polish.[6]

WHAT'S LEFT OF THE LEFT? THE 'NEW TIMES' DEBATE AND ITS IMPLICATIONS FOR EURO-RACISM IN THE 1990s

The left's 'New Times' debate emerged in the late 1980s partly in response to political conditions in Western and Eastern Europe and partly out of perceived global shifts which were thought to have implications for socialist politics in the West. The political success of Thatcherism in Britain, the failure of the left to develop a mass political movement, nationally or internationally, the abuses of Soviet power (and the collapse of the Eastern bloc when it came) and developments towards greater European unity, all provided added impetus to a fundamental reassessment of conditions and political strategy. In this section, I shall briefly sketch the themes of 'New Times' analysis, with particular reference to the way in which the discussions have developed around social identity, notably the shift from class to more fragmented forms. I shall link these to current debates surrounding the relative usefulness of the terms 'black' and 'ethnic' as forms of contemporary social identity. Paul Gilroy's critique of anti-racist politics is of relevance here, and I will link it to these debates. The dangers of the 'New Times' programme will be drawn out with reference to some trenchant critiques of its politics, by A. Sivanandan and others. Whilst 'New Times' marks an important and opportune reflection on left politics and related discussions of race, ethnicity and anti-racism, there remains more than a lingering doubt about its sense of politics, which the critiques of both 'New Times' and relatedly, postmodernism, have succinctly and entertainingly captured.[7]

The 'New Times' debate originated in the British Communist Party, and took historical developments in Eastern Europe as one of its key reference points. More specifically, the background to the debate was an on-going struggle in the party between the pro-Soviet and Eurocommunist factions. The now defunct journal *Marxism Today*, very much associated with the Eurocommunist tendency in the party, had been publishing articles analysing the phenomenon of Thatcherism throughout the 1980s. The *Manifesto for New Times*, published in 1989, sought to turn the deconstructions of the 1980s into a reconstructed programme for the 1990s and, in so doing, update the party's previous major political statement, *The British Road to Socialism*.

As I have suggested, the 'New Times' intervention was not just significant in party political terms. Its importance also lies in its relevance to discussions of identity, in particular in recent attempts to reassess the concepts of ethnicity and race and the status of anti-racist politics. To illustrate these debates I have chosen to look at the important and highly influential work of Stuart Hall. I have deliberately chosen this chapter to undertake such an assessment, since I have argued, throughout this book, the need to undertake such discussions with reference to historical circumstance and political context. The 'new' Europe provides one such context. The following discussion necessarily takes a circuitous route back to an issue of more immediate concern in this chapter: the significance of 'New Times' as a potential political response to European developments, post-1992.

So, to what does the 'new' in 'New Times' refer? The following represents a brief sketch of some of the changes referred to in 'New Times' discussions: a rapid expansion of information technologies; specialised, flexible and decentralised forms of production replacing old Fordist forms of assembly line mass production; new social divisions particularly around consumption; a break-up of old class boundaries; the ascendancy of popular culture over art, and the increasing significance of subjectivities organised around complex and fragmented identities. According to Stuart Hall, Thatcherism as a political project successfully harnessed itself to these changes. In this sense 'New Times' represented a political response by one section of the British left, which not only acknowledged these changes, but sought to construct new forms of politics around them.

Amongst the more detailed discussions contained in the 'New Times' documents, as well as conference presentations, are some references to black identity, ethnicity and anti-racism, which are indicative of a radical intellectual and political departure from conventional left wisdom on the politics of race. Through a close examination of these 'New Times' documents and conference discussions and the recent writings of Stuart Hall, it is possible to chart a progressive shift away from a politics concerned exclusively with class to one in which the politics of anti-racism is displaced by new and fragmented forms of ethnic identities.

The first appears in a document, *Facing up to the Future*, which recognises the narrowness of a class-based political agenda: 'exploitation through work is not the only determinant of how power and resources are distributed. Other forms of oppression and domination systematically structure inequalities.' It goes on:

> Women and Black people thus have a potential point of common interest which cannot be reduced to class and goes well beyond the work-place. Sexism and racism affect their sense of self, their identification with other people, throughout social life.
>
> (*7 Days*, 3 September 1989: 4)

However, the links between race and class are not altogether severed, as the following extract from the 1989 *Manifesto for New Times* indicates: 'Black people will be disproportionately represented in the peripheral labour force of the new times contract cleaners, late night security guards, petrol pump attendants and fast-food face workers' (1989: 14). The manifesto does go on, nevertheless, to acknowledge that racism takes specific forms which cannot be reduced to class. Racial harassment and immigration controls cannot be understood in terms of traditional notions of class, as the following confirms: 'a commitment to overcome a web of institutionalised racism must be a central plank to a modernised class politics and a wider progressive politics of equal life chances' (ibid.).

Although written prior to both the above-cited documents, two of the articles I want to consider now actually represent an important development of the position illustrated above. Both are written by Stuart Hall, a major contributor to the 'New Times' debate (1987, 1988). What Hall develops here is an argument for the further erosion of identity, not into black and around race as the above extracts advocate, but around new forms of ethnicity and

173

ethnic identity. The argument is based on the principle of fragmentation and difference which, it should be remembered, is a key condition of 'New Times'. I shall link Stuart Hall's argument to two further contributions from recent debates which are relevant to these developments.

Hall admits that the term ethnicity has been used, in the past, to accentuate cultural differences at the expense of the common black experience of racism, to the point of actually concealing the latter. However, political conditions have moved on and his argument here is based on a shift, already noted in the previous chapter, away from black cultural politics, the aim of which is to challenge *relations of representation*. The latter has entailed challenging racial stereotypes as well as the denial of black access, for example, to education, employment and housing. Now the focus is on the *politics of representation* where subjectivities are actively constituted. In this latter phase, ethnicity is potentially more useful since it provides and creates space for delineating new and complex forms of identity. On this point Hall writes: 'what brings ethnicity into play is the recognition of the immense diversity and differentiation of the historical and cultural experience of black subjects' (1987: 20).

This point is developed in a subsequent article when he talks about the silencing of the very specific experiences of Asian people through the use of the term 'black':

> Although Asian people could identify, politically, in the struggle against racism, when they came to using their own culture as the resources of resistance. . . when they wanted to create, they created with the histories of the languages, the cultural tradition, the positions of people who came from a variety of different historical backgrounds.
>
> (1991b: 56)

On the one hand, then, Hall's argument for a re-vamped concept of ethnicity is broadly compatible with the new forms of identity and social fragmentation that are said to characterise 'New Times'. On the other, Hall's arguments surrounding ethnicity would seem to go beyond the extracts taken from the 'New Times' documents themselves, with their emphasis on black identities and forms of racism. (In Hall's terms, this politics would be rooted in the 'relations of representation'.) Although the logic of Hall's analysis takes us in the direction of new ethnic identities, he has also acknowledged the need to retain the term 'black' under certain circumstances. At one point he refers to the situation in Dewsbury as an example of its continuing relevance; so long, in other words, as racism continues to persist and flourish (see Chapter 4).

Hall's argument was taken one stage further in a somewhat different context, at a 'New Times' weekend in October 1989, in a discussion entitled 'Post-modernism: The Crisis of the Grand Narrative'. The 'grand narrative' (associated in postmodernist thought with such ideas as universal progress, scientific reason and global political projects like socialism) was applied, in this instance, to anti-racist politics. Specifically, the postmodernist critique of the grand narrative was illustrated with reference to the controversy surrounding the publication of Salman Rushdie's *Satanic Verses*. The affair, according to one of the panellists, Barnor Hesse, was not about racism, as the grand narrative of anti-racism implies, or concerned with 'black' people. What the Rushdie affair was about was British Muslim ethnicity.

To these critiques may be added Paul Gilroy's important essay 'The End of Anti-Racism' (1990) which was discussed briefly in Chapter 1 and which echoes some, though by no means all, of Hall's conclusions. Gilroy's objections to anti-racism are threefold. First, he argues that the politics of anti-racism makes black people appear as victims, always being done to, negatively, rather than acting positively for themselves. Second, he maintains that the field of anti-racist politics has become bureaucratised and institutionalised, with black professionals defending 'black' issues in order to reconcile their own contradictory position, that is, as both black and professional (see Chapter 3). Third, and linked to this last point, is the argument that anti-racist politics has never caught the popular political imagination. In fact, attacks from the right have insulated it still further. Finally, the thrust of anti-racist politics is to sectionalise a wider struggle based on class and gender. The failure to grasp the interrelationship of these struggles has further undermined the impact of anti-racism and at the same time drained the potential impact of black community politics.

Gilroy is clearly talking about particular forms of anti-racism, notably those which have become institutionalised within town halls. He is not, it would seem, calling for an end to, or even a displacement of anti-racist politics in general, nor of black politics either. Where he comes closest to Hall is in his critique of the passive roles assigned to black people by anti-racist discourse. What he shares with Hall, therefore, is a common demand to give space to autonomous, positive, alternative and possibly new forms of cultural expression above and beyond those implied by the seemingly fixed, static and essential category 'black'.

Overall, there is much to be said in defence of these recent contributions to our understanding of race, ethnicity and anti-racist politics. They capture the historically specific sources of identity, which provide space, not only for 'Asian' ethnicities to be captured more precisely,[8] as Hall suggests, but new complex, hybrid identities, particularly amongst the young, that have been alluded to at various points in this book. Institutionalised, bureaucratised anti-racism has precluded more positive, active assertions of cultural strength. It has also partially succeeded in removing terms like 'racism' and 'black' from the community contexts in which they first had relevance and meaning. Beyond these more specific arguments, it is hard to deny the 'New Times' critiques of class politics, the need to acknowledge other forms of oppression and other sources of identity and, out of these, the need to develop alternative political strategies.

The usefulness of 'New Times' arguments, including the specific contributions on race, ethnicity and anti-racism, can now be assessed more fully in the light of developments considered in the first part of this chapter. This assessment will inevitably make wider reference to poststructuralism and postmodernism, elements of which can be said to have underpinned many of the ideas so far considered in this section. I shall ask some questions which raise a number of difficulties, for me, with the 'New Times' critique.

The most obvious question, perhaps, relates to what Stuart Hall has called one of the great social identities of the modern world: race (1991b: 44–5). How are we to express those collective experiences described in the first part of this chapter? The danger exists in the 'New Times' arguments of precluding, obscuring or marginalising those shared political experiences of racism. Furthermore, it could be argued from this chapter that such experiences have got worse, not better, in the 'New Times' world in which we now live. The growing importance of a new class of migrants, illegal immigrants, refugees, asylum seekers is, as I have suggested, one aspect of these developments.

Certainly the focus on the politics of representation, at the expense of the relations of representation, would seem premature given the restricted access of would-be immigrants, migrants and refugees to Europe; the rights of black European residents within Europe; the escalation of racial attacks on different minority groups of migrants, immigrants, refugees and Jews; the wider context in which these events have been unfolding, including nationalism and the revival of Eurocentricity; the common-sense conflation of the immigrant/refugee with illegality, drug running, terrorism and crime; and the perceived common threat of migrants, immigrants and black European citizens to a pan-European or national identity, or both.

The second question is concerned with the role of anti-racist forces in Europe. Far from constituting a political relic, evidence suggests a growth in anti-racist politics throughout Europe. In 1989, groups from Denmark, France, Holland, Germany and the UK formed the Communities of Resistance Campaign across Europe. Meanwhile, other organisations are seeking to ensure that decisions taken on immigration are made by democratically elected bodies like the European Parliament, and not by clandestine, non-accountable groups like Trevi and the Ad Hoc Group on Immigration. The revival and growth of the far right across Europe suggests a need to build anti-racist alliances. How will the assumptions and categories of 'New Times' assist here? Will they not suppress such interventions under the nuance of ethnic, or worse, individual difference?

The need for some kind of collective political response has been witnessed in Britain in the re-emergence of the Anti-Nazi League and the formation of the Anti-Racist Alliance. No one who has worked in such organisations could deny their limited support, factionalism or the narrowness of their popular appeal, but the question remains for the advocates of 'New Times': how to respond to the European-wide growth in support for the far right. Moreover, what role will the collective actions of black/anti-racist communities be assigned in this politics, if any? In a strong polemic aimed at 'New Times' arguments, Sivanandan makes reference to these struggles:

These are movements, collectivities, that issue from the grassroots of economic, social and political life, from the bare bones of existence, from people who have nothing to lose but their chains, nothing to choose but survival, and are therefore dynamic, open, organic. They are not inward looking, navel gazing exercises like identity politics or narrow self-defining particularities like single issue politics. They do not issue from the self but from the community, not from choice but from need and are organic in the sense of sharing a common life.

(1990a: 28)

Sivanandan may be accused of failing to acknowledge the significance of identity politics, which can be seen in part as a response to the limitations of other forms of politics, including class-based and institutionalised anti-racist politics. On the other hand, his polemic seems well targeted when it is aimed at those intellectual and political positions which fail to locate themselves in the collective forms of struggle he describes and, in choosing their starting point elsewhere, effectively serve to eclipse and devalue those forms of struggle.

My third question, addressed to the arguments of 'New Times', concerns the relationship between migrants in Western Europe and peoples of colour in the 'Third World'. The chemical workers of Bhopal; the coffee pickers, farm labourers and cotton pickers of Central and South America, and the women workers of the microelectronic industries in the Far East, share certain conditions in common, thanks to the role of western governments, neo-liberalism, multinational corporations and international financial institutions. Their struggles surrounding pay and working conditions, their attempts to reclaim their land, resources, political autonomy and culture, have helped create new classes/communities of resistance. In what ways does the politics of 'New Times' accommodate these struggles? So far 'New Times' writers, with the exception of Stuart Hall himself, have been largely silent on Third World issues. On the general failure of postmodernism to address Third World issues, Jan Nederveen Pieterse writes, 'since third worldism is out of fashion they look down on, if they look at all, on the poor in the third world. . . . The discourse of post modernism, busy critiquing modernity, turns its back on the pre-modern [sic] world' (1991: 6). The omission of the pre-modern and postmodern distinction and the exclusive association of the Third World with 'the poor' would have strengthened Pieterse's central point. Postmodernism has emerged from a particular vantage point (defined geographically, politically or in terms of class?) and, by its very concerns, has insulated itself from the experiences and demands, for example, of those groups of Third World workers cited above.

The danger with Stuart Hall's critique is that the basis for social categories is constantly undermined by the pressure to reduce the social to ever-fragmenting and fragmented identities. The result is a seeming arbitrariness in

the points of closure around the social/individual. Stuart Hall has acknowledged this himself in his critique of Derrida (1991b: 50). In preceding chapters
I have argued, on the contrary, that the points of closure at which boundaries
are drawn around race, class, gender, ethnicity, sexuality or something else,
are far from arbitrary. They may be calculated or assessed, from inside or
outside the boundaries of closure. Strategies play a vital role here including
an acknowledgement of historical circumstance. What is more, any points of
closure will have political effects, some profound, others less so, whether these
effects are intended or not.

Amongst contributors to debates on identity there is little agreement. On
the one hand, Linda Hutcheon (1989) celebrates postmodernist fiction, precisely because it does not stop at an analysis of class but accommodates race
as well as gender and nationality. Likewise the 'New Times' manifesto refers
to gender and race as evidence of the need to modernise class definitions. Hall
and Hesse, on the other hand, have moved beyond these categories to the
next stage of fragmentation: they wish to replace the terms 'black' and 'racial'
with the more 'finely' tuned concept of ethnicity.

Where all this might lead is not altogether a mystery. Although Jean
Baudrillard has little time for any social categorisation, he does, in *Fatal
Strategies,* make reference to one remaining social division, between hostages
and terrorists. This division, he argues, has 'replaced that other (circuit) of
masters and slaves, the dominating and the dominated, the exploiters and the
exploited. Gone is the constellation of the slave and the proletarian' (1990:
40). He goes on, 'we are all hostages and all terrorists. . . all hostages to our
own identity' and cites oil as a hostage 'for the producing countries against the
West' (ibid.: 42). The idea that social divisions of the kind described in this
chapter have no relevance; that the new subordinate class is that of hostage,
which includes pretty well all of us; and that the West is victim of the Gulf
states' terrorism, are views which have much in common with those of western
conservative governments. It is certainly hard to imagine how this discussion
might provide the basis for a future left political agenda, however that is
defined.[9]

'New Times' has helped to break down the grand theories based on class,
and, having done so, has found space for divisions based on race and other
social identities. However, in the process it has embarked on a trajectory of
fragmentation which appears to have no end. Consequently, those concepts
and categories referred to earlier in the discussion of Europe, which were
found to be of increased, not declining significance, have apparently been
abandoned, or at least eclipsed, in the politics of 'New Times'.

In its extreme forms, postmodernism, on which 'New Times' has drawn,
flattens inequalities and real differences beneath an attachment to superficial
differences and heterogeneity. Lyotard describes the contemporary condition
thus: 'Eclecticism is the degree zero for contemporary general culture: one
listens to reggae, watches a western, eats McDonald's food for lunch and local

cuisine for dinner, wears Paris perfume in Tokyo and "retro" clothes in Hong Kong' (cited in Callinicos, 1989: 76). As Callinicos pointedly observes, 'It all depends on who "one" is' (ibid.). In answer to his own question, he argues that the politics of postmodernism is linked to the social position of its producers. Postmodernism, in other words, is the means by which a socially mobile intelligentsia 'has sought to articulate its political disillusionment and its aspiration to a consumption-oriented life style' (1989: 177).

Sivanandan makes a similar point in an irresistible quote:

> The self that new timers make so much play about is a small selfish inward looking self that finds pride in lifestyle, exuberance in consumption and commitment in pleasure – and then elevates them all into a politics of this and that. . . stretching from hobbies and pleasure to services. . . . A sort of bazaar socialism, bizarre socialism, a hedonist socialism, an eat, drink and be merry socialism. . . a socialism for disillusioned Marxists who had waited around too long for the revolution – a socialism that holds up everything that is ephemeral and evanescent and passing as vital and worthwhile, everything that melts into air as solid, and proclaims that every shard of the self is a social movement.
>
> (1990a: 23)

Of course such hardened political campaigners as Callinicos and Sivanandan know that the best form of political defence is a good polemic. What their highly engaging and pertinent critiques do, however, is not only to reduce their opponents' writing to its crudest versions. In caricaturing it thus, they also avoid some uncomfortable political truths about the left in Britain and elsewhere in Europe, which those working within the 'New Times' agenda have at least attempted to address: its (the left's) lack of popular support, its over-reliance on certain class positions at the expense of other key divisions, and its failure to grasp the complex ways individuals make sense of their worlds and act politically, without necessarily engaging in institutionalised politics, attending meetings and protest rallies or going on strike.

But the differences between the conditions described in the first part of the chapter and the politics of 'New Times' may not be as great as they appear. First is the argument that ethnicity has displaced black identity. Instead of seeing the debate in either/or terms, the evidence from Europe suggests that both are equally relevant. In other words, there may be situations when the issue is one of access, stereotyping or institutionalised discrimination in which those affected might seek a shared identity. Yet there may be instances when this is inappropriate, for example where groups are seeking to constitute themselves in culturally specific ways. The choice depends on the context and issue at stake. Neither black nor ethnic is a fixed or essential category, nor is there a need to make a stark choice between them. Rather they should be seen as fluid and contingent, the appropriateness of their use depending on circumstance.

There is a further sense in which the two terms, ethnicity and racism, might be seen as complementary. The idea that ethnicity represents a positive, autonomous form of cultural expression, whilst racism is all about the negative labelling and the imposition of dominant white culture on passive blacks, misses an important interconnection. This may be illustrated by thinking about the ways in which institutions – record companies, film studios, schools, local authorities – fail to respond to the demands of different ethnic groups. Their failure to do so, thereby inhibiting the positive expressions of culture, is itself a form of *racism*. In the Rushdie affair, the failure to meet Muslim demands, including the demand to provide separate schools, created a struggle over both the relations and the politics of representation. It was about ethnicity but it was also about racism. This is not to say that institutions are solely responsible for all forms of cultural expression, but to acknowledge that most, if not all, of the material aspects of our lives; where and how we live, for example, cannot be fully understood without reference to institutional sites.

Likewise, whilst many relevant points are raised in Paul Gilroy's critique of anti-racism (1990), the oppositions posed in his article may also be more apparent than real. The acknowledgement of institutionalised racism does not, as he suggests mean a denial of agency. Political actors always contest, assert and constitute themselves in a context only partly of their own making. Anti-racist politics is an attempt to make sense of that context. It does not have to construct victims. On the contrary, its object is to facilitate the exercise of agency on a more equal basis. Nor does racism or anti-racism have to exhaust cultural practices. There are many ways to write about black, Jewish, Irish, etc.. culture without making reference to racism. But there are also ways of writing about racism and culture in the same context.

At the risk of labouring a point made throughout this book, a stronger argument regarding the usefulness of strategies, built around political categories, is to assess them in terms of particular historical and political circumstances. Avtar Brah raises some important problems with all categories, including black and Asian, which seek to impose fixed and universal definitions. What is more important, she argues, is to examine specific racisms and how these place different groups in relationship to each other. She extends this in her discussion of patriarchy and class: 'The search for grand general theories specifying the interconnections between racism, gender and class has been less than productive. I would suggest that they are best construed as historically contingent and context specific relationships' (1992: 19–20).

The relationship between struggles around race, class and gender cannot be resolved abstractly, but only in context. The prioritisation of anti-racism in some political contexts in the 1980s was a conscious attempt to resist institutional attempts to introduce gender and class and a myriad of other ethnicities in order to blunt and dilute anti-racist demands. In other contexts, it has been strategic to link the different levels of struggle or change the order of priority, depending on a calculation of the weakest link. Modood's proposal (1988) that we should not refer to Asians as black is only partly addressing the problem. 'Asian' may well be the most appropriate category in some contexts, but not in all. Religious, gender-based and national differences may also be appropriate depending on the situation. Black, too, may be contextually and strategically relevant, and the efforts to abandon this term could weaken our understanding of the common experience and processes at work in western societies. The need to see these categories as dynamic and historically contingent is underlined by Paul Gilroy in his discussion of classes in formation in *There Ain't No Black in the Union Jack*. One important point he makes there is the need to see social categories as fluid and dynamic, not fixed in some abstract formulation which can be used to assess the correctness, or otherwise, of any political strategy.

CONCLUSIONS

Europe is steeped in racist traditions, some of which are overtly nationalistic in focus while others embrace a wider European tradition. The dominance of particular racisms depends on the historical and political circumstances. In Europe, the build-up to 1992 has reawakened a Eurocentric racism which cuts across national boundaries and appeals to cultural traditions which Europe, as a whole, shares. This white Eurocentricity has been strengthened by contributions of Blumenbach and Herder from Germany, Knox and Hunt from Britain and De Gobineau from France. There is an important on-going struggle between those seeking to defend their national identities and forces seeking to transcend these in the construction of a European identity. Ironically, both sides are drawing on a common stock of racist knowledges.

The reconstruction of a European identity has been built around the exclusion of non-white peoples from the Third World. Policies on immigration and refugees have been linked to keeping other groups of 'undesirables' out of the new Europe. Whilst the generic term black will certainly be used as a basis for exclusion, particular European countries have their own dominant outsiders: in France, Muslim north Africans; in Germany, Turks; and in Britain peoples of African-Caribbean and south Asian descent. In Britain, however, the crisis in Hong Kong, with the killings in Tiananmen Square and the transfer of sovereignty to China in 1997, has rekindled a racism with its own history and tradition in the West.

These racisms have been compounded by the re-emergence of anti-Semitism, ever present, but on the increase, in terms of physical attacks, across Europe. Of particular importance here have been the liberalising reforms and revolutions in Eastern Europe, which have, in their wake, unleashed anti-Semitism both in Poland (where it has been given added legitimacy by political and Catholic Church leaders), and in the former Soviet Union. In Britain, too, there has been an upsurge of racist attacks on Jewish people as well as the desecration of Jewish cemeteries. So the revival of another racism, with its own distinctively European tradition, has coincided with political and historical events in mainland Europe. This is not to suggest that the lines of continuity, which date back to the Middle Ages, have ever been altogether broken, but just to acknowledge that there have been periods when forms of anti-Semitism were more hidden, marginal, less politicised and the subject of fewer media amplifications, than at others.

To the proliferation of racisms within and across Europe must be added the wave of ethnic nationalisms which has swept Eastern Europe in the wake of the break-up of the Soviet Union and the Eastern bloc. These complex processes call for terms which cannot be reduced to the single category black or to a single strategy, that of anti-racism. To this extent Stuart Hall is right to want to acknowledge the fragmentary processes at work in western societies. So, too, is Paul Gilroy in his concern that anti-racist politics has dominated the political agenda on race, often to the exclusion of other possible strategies and forms of mobilisation. However, as Avtar Brah points out in the context of the Organisation of Women of African and Asian Descent (OWAAD), there were good historical reasons for these kinds of alliance, and there may well be in the future. The weakness of 'New Times' and postmodernism, from which it draws much of its language, has been its failure to specify the circumstances in which different strategies call for different mobilising terms.

The terms black, Asian, African-Caribbean, South East Asian, not to mention gendered and class sub-divisions of these, are all potentially appropriate, depending on the circumstances. Neither the substitution of one absolute, for instance Indian or Asian, for another, black, nor the break-up of identities into an infinity of strands, is an adequate response to changing political conditions in the 1990s. Avtar Brah offers a much firmer basis for assessing different forms of racial and racially gendered as well as class structured practices, when she advocates an analysis which is historically contingent and, it might be added, institutionally specific.

Whilst 'New Times' and its intellectual precursors emphasise the minutiae of difference at the expense of structured divisions and political strategies, their critics, notably Sivanandan, offer the alternative grand narrative with class as its focus. For all the attractiveness of its critique of 'New Times', and its broad contextualising, in global terms, these arguments not only stretch the significance of class, but also oversimplify the complexity of political and economic developments and overestimate the success of class-based strategies. These reservations, when they are juxtaposed, suggest the need for an analysis which offers the potential specificity of the 'New Times' concept of ethnicity with the political focus of the old times critique. An analysis is required which is much more historically and institutionally specific and which includes an assessment of how different racialised structures of representation and their material forms are experienced, lived out and contested. In so doing, many struggles may take place outside of conventional forms of political struggle. To acknowledge these alternatives is one important contribution that recent developments on the intellectual and political left have made to our understanding. Their political implications could do much to contest (and not just on the continent of Europe) the seemingly 'rational' excesses of the single European market, which, like other market-places explored in this book, serves both to conceal racism and to uncouple it from any potential framework of regulation and control.

CONCLUDING REMARKS

My intention here is to not give a detailed summary of each chapter but to pull together some connecting conceptual threads. In some respects the focus and arguments in this book coincide with a number of poststructuralism's concerns: its emphasis on context; its opening up of texts to historical assessment; its critique of essentialism, and the shift from the structured text to the engagement of the reading subject. This focus has partly resulted from my engagement with the preoccupations and priorities of cultural studies from the late 1980s onwards. It has also arisen out of my interest in institutions, political processes and questions of strategy which, in many respects, are compatible, in my view, with some of the critiques of structuralism. These latter interests have certainly tempered my enthusiasm for any preoccupation with text at the expense of institutional context, with the politics of pleasure at the expense of an acknowledgement of more traditional political issues, notably inequalities and injustice, and any retreat into the realm of infinitesimally fragmented identities at the expense of highlighting and exploring the formation of social identities. These latter concerns were most evident in Chapter 7.

One of my broad aims has been to illustrate and explore a variety of 'racial' representations in terms of their institutional settings and wider political culture. Manchester's 'Fear and Fantasy' exhibition was used to illustrate the ways in which different meanings can be attached to the same paintings, depending on how, when and by whom we are invited to look at them. The importance of *context* has been a recurring theme of the book and, in particular, the need to move beyond the level of representations onto the sites, both local and global, on which they have been inscribed, negotiated and contested.

Foucault's work (1977, 1980) can be seen as important in making sense of these connections. Above all, his writing has acknowledged the importance of looking at discourses in terms of their institutional forms of expression and the tactics of power contained within them. In this book I have explored how racist discourses have changed over time, not just in content but in the institutional means by which they have been expressed and the discursive strategies employed to secure their effective control over material aspects of our culture. Foucault has included in his analysis of such strategies the regulation of discourse through omission; the definition and redefinition of what are acceptable and non-acceptable boundaries of discourse, and the way institutions/discourses can be used to control/police, for example the 'panoptic mechanism', which allows a few to observe and control the many without them even knowing. These processes have been illustrated here with reference to contemporary social and political issues, for example the Rushdie affair and the Gulf War; key institutional sites, notably the family, education and work; and global discourses and discursive strategies, for example Bhopal, which have been used to construct a common-sense understanding of the world (and hence 'us') and relatedly, forms of control (and hence 'them').

This raises a number of important questions, the first of which has to with *power*. The concept of power has been used in this book not so much to refer to individual action or to its possession or attachment to a particular position. Rather, it has been used to designate discursive power, expressed institutionally as well as materially in lived culture. In fact, the book has been much more concerned with the effects of power and the conditions under which it is produced than with identifying the interests on behalf of which power is exercised. On the contrary, it has been assumed that interests, like identities, are not fixed any more than power is intrinsically attached to a position. Both are mediated through discourse and around arenas of struggle.

In this context what becomes relevant is how, and under what conditions, different forms of mobilisation are possible and what means or strategies are open to particular sets of political forces. Conditions in any one arena of struggle necessarily depend on conditions in other arenas, so the focus of analysis must always be a wider set of political and cultural conditions, which brings us back to an analysis of context (Hindess, 1982). In this sense it is useful to think about power as everywhere, in the way Foucault suggests; not only in terms of how dominant systems of representations inscribe positions but how subordinate, marginal or peripheral cultures can too, in ways which subvert, rework and contest imposed positions. Power sheds light on how subjectivities are constructed through discourse, but also on how they are contested through struggle.

The discussion of power begs a further consideration of *strategies*. This is a complex term, since it not only refers to rational calculation, but to subconscious motives. In the case of the former, strategies can either seek to relate means to objectives or they can identify the ways in which discourses secure their effects via a variety of tactical mechanisms, including power. Strategies are at the heart of a number of discussions throughout this book, including the assessment of organisational responses to domestic violence, demands both for and against separate Islamic schools, different language uses by young people and fast food consumer protests. The point about all these strategies is that they are interventions in highly particularised contexts. To make sense of them it is necessary to locate discourses (about domestic violence and so on) in an understanding of those institutionalised contexts out of, and through, which they emerge. The purpose, here, has not been to judge or prescribe the objectives to which these strategies are tied, but to acknowledge the importance of context in assessing different forms of intervention.

The merits of different policies and practices on fostering and adoption were shown to depend, above all, on the circumstances which prevailed. For example, it could be argued that racial matching might be the most appropriate strategy in local authorities where black and ethnic minority parents are not being actively recruited and/or where black children are disproportionately taken into care and/or where assimilation has underpinned a policy of transracial adoption. Of course, this strategic response is by no means straightforward, not least around questions of identity and the dangers of imposing a single black identity on young people whose sense of themselves may be much more hybrid and complex. Under such conditions, it is all the more important to defend the policy in strategic terms, to retain flexibility in its implementation, and certainly not to seek to support it unequivocally, and in every case, on the basis of some primordial notion of black identity.

The question of strategy is not one that can be confined to the realm of the conscious. Drawing on developments in psychoanalysis and feminism, the work of Fanon, Bhabha, Hall and others has explored the importance of strategic mechanisms within the realm of the unconscious. The ambivalent character of control, on the one hand, and desire on the other, has entailed a variety of strategic mechanisms including, according to Bhabha, that of mimicry. Elsewhere, the playful preoccupation with cultural difference in terms of food, artifacts and exotica can also be understood in terms of psychic motives; in Hall's words teasing with the transgressive other. Multiculturalism in this sense becomes a strategy for the satisfaction of hidden psychic desires.

The question of strategy at both the conscious and the unconscious level leads directly into a discussion of *identity* and the terms people use to describe, define and make sense of themselves. The examples used in this book suggest an extremely complex, contextual and contingent use of self and collective cultural definitions. Identities have been formed on the basis of affiliations to race, ethnicity, gender and sexuality, as well as to class. Beyond these categories, however, the discussion of language suggests that even these sources of identity do not exhaust the hybrid forms emerging amongst young people. Here, traditional boundaries have merged and combined in highly particularistic ways, throwing up new forms of attachment, sometimes rooted in neighbourhood, at other times in some global sub-cultural style and, elsewhere, in neither.

Once again, these examples have confirmed the importance of understanding identity in terms of processes which can only be understood through a detailed analysis of context. In this sense, the sources of identity (racial, ethnic, gender, etc.) are not as important, in and of themselves, as who uses them and for what purpose. They are not fixed in concrete, but are amenable and adaptable to, and usable in, a variety of situations. The onus is on the cultural analyst not to prescribe one source of identity over another on the grounds of conceptual coherence or intrinsic qualities, but rather to assess the significance of identity through an understanding of context and strategy. Identities can thus be explored in terms both of their mobilising, as well as potentially demobilising, roles.

It follows that the above examples can be used both as an argument against any notion of essential, intrinsic or primordial identities and as an illustration of the continuing significance of black identities (the specific object of recent critiques of essentialism) in particular settings. On the one hand, then, the argument against any one primary attachment was illustrated with reference to the variety of responses of women to domestic violence. In some instances, according to Mama, their ethnicity has been stressed; at other times their gender. But Mama's analysis could also be used to demonstrate the continuing significance of black gendered identities in the struggles around state institutional responses to domestic violence. Similarly, the role played by Woman Against Fundamentalism in the Rushdie affair and on the issue of separate Islamic schools shows the way in which black and ethnic identities were subordinated to those constructed around gender. The latter was thus used to mobilise in struggles against patriarchal forms within the Muslim community. In other instances, however, bell hooks has acknowledged the dangers here of focusing on internal conflicts within the black community (between men and women) and thus lending weight to racist arguments. In the Rushdie affair this danger was well illustrated by Robert Kilroy Silk's critique of patriarchal forms within Islam, which he went on to compare to the favourable position of women in the West.

However, processes of identification, like strategies, are not always conscious. Laura Mulvey's analysis of identification (Mulvey, 1992), in which she relates it to subconscious processes of voyeurism and ego construction, is relevant here. Moreover, such processes have been shown to be as important for the construction of 'white' ethnicities as they have been for constructions of 'otherness'. In fact, both psychoanalysis and feminism may be grafted onto Edward Said's cultural analysis, to demonstrate the interdependence of identities of 'self' and 'other'.

The term black has been used both as a source of self-identification and as a label to define 'otherness'. First invoked as a source of empowerment for African-American and British blacks in the 1960s and 1970s, it has, more recently, been used in British institutional contexts as part of an equal opportunity/anti-racist discourse. Paul Gilroy's critique of anti-racism in these contexts has been particularly challenging. He refers to the failure of the discourse to connect with popular experience and the ways in which organisational cultures appropriate and incorporate such terms as black and anti-racism. Hence the discourse of the latter can lose its original meaning and gain a new, potentially constraining, significance as it becomes increasingly removed from the very people whose rights it is suppose to secure. Add to this the continuing evidence of inequalities, the retrenchment of many local authorities on equal opportunity initiatives in the wake of the abolition of the GLC and ILEA and the fourth successive Conservative victory in the 1992 general election, and it is not surprising to find that anti-racist politics, which contained seeds of some promise in the early 1980s, has become a source of disillusion and despair in the early 1990s.

This radical critique of anti-racist politics has coincided with attempts on the other side of the political spectrum to dismantle the welfare state and promote new consumer identities built around an enormous variety of cultural and social practices, locally and globally, in both the public and private spheres. Both Gilroy's critique and neo-liberalism have converged in their opposition to institutionalised anti-racist politics and have thus served to legitimise the arguments for market solutions to questions of race and ethnicity. In fact, the case studies confirmed the significance of markets as sites for constructing, commodifying, expressing and resisting 'race'. In particular, the political attachment to markets in the 1980s has had profound implications for cultural constructions of race and social practices defined in racial terms. One of the clearest examples of this has been the organisation of educational policy around markets based on parental choice. Global markets also affect movements of peoples and capital as well as the products of labour and capital: from McDonald's fast food to tourism in the Third World to the export of African-American film and music and its 'consumption' by young people in Britain.

At the same time, defenders of markets have attacked any idea or principle which appears to threaten the alleged free (market) flow of producers and consumers. Objections to positive discrimination or affirmative action, and its weaker versions reflected in equal opportunities policies and practices, have been grounded in a defence of the market. Even some recent socialist forums, under the influence of the 'New Times' political debate in Britain in the late 1980s, present themselves as a market-place of ideas. One important conclusion to emerge out of these case studies is the need to examine markets in their institutional context. The pretence that markets are somehow institutionally 'clean' has helped to ensure that they have remained extremely limited mechanisms for contesting inequalities and providing alternative forms of cultural expression. On the contrary, they have largely worked, as I shall argue, in the opposite direction.

So whilst the case studies reflected new forms of marketing 'race', they also served to illustrate the limitations of the market as a mechanism for contesting racist cultural forms, experiences and inequalities. Markets are also limited in their scope to provide the means for genuinely radical and alternative forms of cultural expression. Overall, markets fail because of their inability to address external conditions which help to shape production and consumption processes. In education, for example, the market inevitably privileges some parents over others, not only on the basis of their ability to pay but also on their willingness to defend the dominant mono-cultural orthodoxy. A weakness of both the 'New Times' political debate and, relatedly, the more radical forms of postmodernism, is their implied or unaddressed assumption that everyone has an equal opportunity to participate in the market-place of intellectual debate. Moreover, what has seemed to me an over-zealous and acontextual preoccupation with the politics of market-place identities has, in effect, ensured that some experiences are confirmed and celebrated to the exclusion and omission of others.

Likewise, individual merit and ability are used to defend the allocation of rewards via the market over principles like positive discrimination, which, it is alleged, prevents individuals from receiving their just deserts. However, the argument that ability and merit should determine outcome itself assumes that merit and ability are fairly ascribed and not culturally laden. In fact, neither merit nor ability is given by God or nature to individuals, but culturally bestowed in ways which are inevitably and deeply value-laden. Hence, to defend market allocations on the basis of these criteria must beg some important questions regarding how we come to be positioned as more or less 'able' to participate in producing and consuming market products, be they material or intellectual.

The argument that the market ensures a rational allocation of rewards and services, unfettered by allegedly irrational discriminatory practices, was found at the heart of the success of McDonald's hamburger enterprise, at least according to McDonald's executives. In defending the virtues of the market, they have been supported by some black economists and commentators and sections of the liberal race relations academy. In reality, as the chapter on McDonald's argued, the corporation depends on a cheap, flexible, highly vulnerable work-force, made up of the labour market's most exploitable sections, including young blacks, illegal immigrants and refugees, as well as women and older workers with fewer opportunities to find a secure alternative. The market does not protect black workers from experiencing discrimination on the shop floor or from failing to reach senior positions in the corporation. A whole set of market considerations, for example location of restaurants, advertising, packaging, food purchasing, franchising and so on, is culturally loaded, with profound implications for black workers and consumers in both the West and the Third World.

The idea of a global market was central to fast food conglomerates like McDonald's. It is also central to western perceptions of the 'Third World', through the unequal exchange of goods and services, including tourism. The West's constructions of the 'Third World', through, for example, the packaging of African wildlife and Thai sex life, help to define not only western constructions of 'otherness' but, more profoundly, the experiences and realities of indigenous peoples. The destruction of habitats and ways of life, in addition

189

to the commodification of ethnicity through the promotion of crafts, clothes, costumes, festivals and ceremonies for the tourist and export markets, has been widely understood in terms of the West's 'civilising' role in the 'under-developed' parts of the world.

Such has been the success of market-based philosophies that the market has also become an important terrain of oppositional struggle, as well as a means for developing alternative forms of cultural expression. The strategic use of the market in this way may well be partly due to growing disaffection with institutional anti-racist politics in Britain, spurred on by attacks on anti-racist policies by the mainstream media and Conservative politicians. Likewise in the US, there is a view that although civil rights politics has benefited a few, the major social divisions remain intact. As in Britain, this view has been supported by the radical right, and left.

In the United States, as in Britain, disillusionment with formal political institutions has led to a greater emphasis on the use of overtly cultural forms and industries as a means of political expression. Music has always played an important oppositional role and now, with the emergence of Spike Lee's films in the late 1980s, black film has become of increasing significance. In 1991, nineteen films were released by black directors in the US. Important though these mainstream cultural forms are, their impact is continually challenged by a number of countervailing cultural processes: their appropriation by white artists and white-dominated cultural industries; their subordination to white genres; and the creation of a class of black artists under pressure to speak for, or represent, non-white communities. Whilst the cult of the individual black artist and the substitution of black enterprise culture for white provides an important means for cultural expression (as well as undermining the domin-ance of white cultural forms), these reversals, by themselves, cannot be expected to address questions of distribution, opportunity structures and the even thornier question of accountability.

This is not to deny the significance of cultural strategies which have brought new and powerful forms of cultural expression to global audiences. However, there are limits even here, which cultural practitioners like Spike Lee have been quick to acknowledge. These limits are not just to do with processes of co-option or appropriation, of which the commercialisation of rap (in adver-tising, mainstream television and in the emergence of white rappers) is one clear example. Nor are these limits confined to cultural processes and institu-tional practices which continue to exclude the vast majority of black men and women from participating in mainstream cultural production. Despite the importance of cultural work in addressing popular consciousness and in providing the conditions for further advance, as Cornel West (1989) suggests, it does not, and cannot, in itself, translate automatically into other practices and onto other sites. Nor do those cultural practices in themselves acknow-ledge the influence that institutional changes elsewhere may have on opportunities for extending and resourcing forms of cultural expression.

It is at this moment, when institutional conditions provide greater or fewer opportunities for cultural expression, that the concept of cultural identity articulates with the concept of racism. The example of the 500 Years of Resistance campaign can be used to illustrate how indigenous peoples from Alaska to southern Chile proclaimed and reclaimed their history, celebrated their cultural roots and linked their sense of past and present with a continental-wide political project in the future. In so doing, almost in the same breath, they sought to acknowledge their continuing experience of racism, from slavery to contemporary forms of torture and genocide as well as the denial of rights to land, work, education, religion and language. Moreover, in this political context, it was the term 'indigenous' which brought diverse ethnicities together, whilst black was used to refer specifically to African-Americans whose origins in the Americas go back to the post-Columbus slave trade.

It is precisely because of the need to relate questions of cultural identity to questions of racism that the choice between popular cultural and institutional strategies is, for me, a false one. Since the two influence each other, strategies around both are equally valid. What is more, there is a pressing need to explore the connections between racism and cultural identity. In this respect, all sites offer different kinds of opportunities for intervention and struggle. This brings me back to questions of power, location, context and to the contingency of the labels we organise and mobilise around in those settings. It may be that identities around class, gender and race are currently being be flattened in the sudden rush from all quarters to get to the market, but as long as the conditions which gave rise to those forms of politics in the first place remain intact, there will always be the potential for their revival. In the long run the market will prove as illusory in addressing these social conditions as a trip in virtual reality.

Roland Barthes uses the idea of myth to refer to the way in which we come to see our lives and the events that shape them as 'natural'. In *Mythologies* he argues that the discourse of nature has played a profound role in suppressing historical processes (Barthes, 1973). The case studies in the present book have provided further evidence of the power of such naturalising mechanisms in discourse. These include the West's acceptance of the inevitability of Third World disasters, of famine, flood and war. Even disasters like the chemical leak at Bhopal in 1984 came to be regarded as somehow inevitable or natural. In this case, the 'inevitability' of the disaster was linked to the so-called 'natural' or innate characteristics associated with Third World peoples.

The idea of 'natural' difference was at the heart of what Martin Barker has called the 'New Racism': the assumption that people have a genetic predisposition to be attracted to their 'own kind' defined in racial terms (Barker, 1981). Even national identity was defined increasingly in racial terms in the 1980s (see Gilroy, 1987: ch. 2). The idea that differences are natural and conflict inevitable has been a key element in this naturalising process. In October 1991 the *Daily Mail* ran a series of investigations into people the paper varyingly described as a 'tide' and 'an underclass' from 'out of Africa'. The paper was referring to what it claimed were illegal refugees seeking to enter Europe on the pretence of fleeing from political persecution. Apart from their impact on jobs, education and national identity, the paper also predicted that neo-Nazi organised violence against 'foreigners' of the sort then occurring in Germany would result from the entry of refugees (*Daily Mail*, 8, 9, 10 and 11 October 1991). The *Mail* thus presented its readers with a choice between immigration control and the prospect of a Nazi revival. The argument used to legitimise the paper's proposal was based on the idea that human conflict was the inevitable and natural result of cultural difference.

The idea that such differences are intrinsic has been around for a long time. In Elizabethan drama, the prospect of a sexual relationship between Othello and Desdemona is condemned by a good cross-section of the characters, who perceive it as an offence against nature. Brabantio, Desdemona's father, on hearing of the relationship, is convinced his daughter must have been drugged and/or corrupted, 'for nature so preposterously to err' (Act I, scene iii). This obsession with mixed relationships has been taken up in Philip Cohen's dense and illuminating essay on the history of racist thought (1988). Cohen argues that hostility to mixed relationships and the need to maintain racial, class or cultural purity have been key cultural mechanisms in the maintenance of class and racial superiority.

In his film *Jungle Fever* (1991) Spike Lee tackles the issue of mixed relationships in a rather different way. The relationship between a black man and a white woman is rooted in mutual fascination: on the one hand with stereotypical versions of black machismo and on the other with mythical forms of white femininity. The relationship is doomed, precisely because Lee contains it within the trappings of these cultural assumptions. By constructing the relationship in this way Lee leaves the audience with more than an inkling that all such mixed relationships are fated and that the intrinsic cultural differences between African-American and white (in this case Italian-American) communities are to blame.

The idea of difference has been taken up in recent writing on ethnicity and cultural identity. Stuart Hall's work has been very influential in this respect, particularly his attempt to retrieve and recognise ethnicities swallowed up in the process of constructing black identities. There are many reasons why it is important to incorporate questions of identity into the politics of race, not the least of which is because it seeks to establish the basis on which peoples define themselves and make sense of their lives rather than merely subscribing to externally imposed categories and labels. This is part of an important recent critique of the label 'black' when the term is used to exhaust all forms of cultural expression and when it is imposed as part of an externally defined institutional discourse.

Defining what is natural, of course, helps to define what is unnatural, as the above examples suggest. The collapse of Eastern Europe and the Soviet Union in the late 1980s and the defeat of Iraq in the Gulf War not only served to confirm the US's global political dominance, but also underlined the apparent 'unnaturalness' of any alternative to western-style capitalism. In this dominant version of world events it was only a matter of time before the Eastern bloc capitulated to the seemingly inevitable or inherent logic of market rationality. The resultant 'new world order', as it has been called, was based on a consensus imbued with values of the free market. The collapse of eastern economies was widely interpreted as proof of the effectiveness of the state's main economic rival, the market. The market has been defined in numerous contexts but in this instance it has been seen increasingly in global terms, that is in its capacity to provide the most efficient mechanism for the distribution of capital, commodities and people, albeit, in the latter case, with the assistance of state immigration controls. Here, then, two major themes of the book converge. Now it is the market's turn to appear natural, inevitable and permanent, in contrast to its ephemeral and now apparently deceased political and economic rival: socialism.

The dominance of the market has helped to make other ideas seem unnatural. Any attempts to introduce positive action or discrimination in the market (as if markets were not subject to countless other interventions) fall prey to the 'unnatural' interference argument. How certain ideas have become culturally marginalised is an important theme of this book. Not only ideas, but social practices too. In the new world of service work, typified by McDonald's role in the global economy, collective action through trade unionism is considered by management to be irrelevant and antiquated, belonging to a bygone era. Non-unionised work-forces are seen, somehow, as a natural progression, part of the transition to the new post-conflict era of the 1990s.

The variety of racisms explored in this book may be understood in Balibar's words, as 'ever active formations, part conscious, part unconscious, which contribute to structuring behaviour and movements out of present conditions' (1991: 40). The association of racism with both institutionalised discourses and the tendency to essentialise black identities should not lead us to abandon these terms *per se* but to find space for them in new discourses, built around distinct forms of representation, institutional conditions and processes, experiences and strategies, some of which have been discussed in this book. To take one further example, whilst nationalist discourses have proved receptive repositories for racism, both European and ethnic discourses are also potentially amenable to the incorporation of racist themes. Recent experience in both Western and Eastern Europe has provided evidence of new articulations of racism within all three discourses.

More widely, the relationship between the local and the global has been a particular point of reference in the latter part of the book. In Hall's view, the relationship is a dialectical one with both the local and the global shaping conditions in which the other operates (1991b). The examples in this book suggest an even more complex relationship. The references to the United

States illustrated the multiplicity of influences and incorporations of the US into British cultural politics. In some cases these 'imports' have been incorporated, albeit on a selective basis, into subversive forms of youth culture while in other cases they have been accommodated within, and used to reinforce, dominant racist cultures. Examples from the popular press, fiction and film exemplified some of these forms. Evidence here challenged notions of a unitary, homogeneous culture imposed on passive global subjects. At the same time, evidence from elsewhere does underline the significance of global processes, including the role of multinationals, western governments and influential pressure groups in undermining the economies, working conditions, health, political stability and autonomy of peoples in the Third World. Against these formidable forces, localised struggles, from resistance movements through anti-racist campaigns to a whole range of forms of cultural practices and forms of expression, have sought to assert themselves. Their impact cannot only be assessed in terms of their own specific impact on the global, as Hall suggests, but also in terms of their potential connections with other localised struggles. Hall may be premature in dismissing the possibilities of global politics emerging out of local alliances and struggles. It is too early to predict what configurations may emerge from the threats posed to nation states from below, as well as above.

The examples I have used have been selected, primarily, with undergraduate students in cultural studies and the social sciences in mind. Numerous other examples could have been used and it is hoped that those used in this book will not pre-empt the identification and investigation of others along the lines of examples explored here. In general, the purpose of these case studies has been or could be in future to critique those processes which have obscured social divisions based on 'race', subsuming 'race' at worst to individuals and market-places, and at best to fragmented ethnicities. The book has aimed not only to use examples to critique those processes but to acknowledge counter-processes and struggles. Despite current efforts to write socialism off the political agenda and to rally instead around the slogans of 'New Times' and postmodernity, the conditions of inequality which historically underpinned socialism's emergence remain intact.

NOTES

1 INTRODUCTION

1 Whilst there is a strong argument for increasing the rates of participation in higher education, increased numbers do not, by themselves, guarantee a wider mix of students, nor do they necessarily address the resource implications of increased access.
2 A number of contributions to Grossberg *et al.*'s collection (1992) make similar points, including a further contribution by bell hooks herself.

2 HISTORY AS PRESENT: PRESENT AS HISTORY

1 'Fear and Fantasy: Images of Africa and Asia through the Eyes of the Colonisers', an Exhibition at Manchester City Art Galleries 21 April–3 June 1990, researched by Anandi Ramamurthy and Sarah Holdsworth. My thanks to Laura Denning for providing details of the exhibition.
2 At my own university in Birmingham the Barber Institute gallery has a number of such paintings, including Cuyp's *Huntsman Halted (Starting the Chase)* and Murillo's *The Marriage Feast at Cana*. No critical comment accompanies the paintings. On the contrary, the latter painting is described, in the Institute's guide, as one of 'the chief glories of the collection'.
3 In his more recent work Said extends this analysis to look at the role of western fiction in development of empire. 'In British culture, for instance, one may discover a consistency of concern in Spenser, Shakespeare, Defoe, and Austin that fixes socially desirable, empowered space in metropolitan England or Europe and connects it by design, motive, and development to distant or peripheral worlds (Ireland, Venice, Africa, Jamaica), conceived of as desirable but subordinate. And with these meticulously maintained references come attitudes – about rule, control, profit and enhancement and suitability [and these]. . . are bound up with the development of Britain's cultural identity' (1993: 61).
4 These protests began prior to the publication of the novel when Muslim scholars advised Penguin not to publish, both because of its blasphemous content and the damage it would cause to inter-community relations.
5 It should be noted that there was a detectable shift on the government's part in its support for Rushdie. It moved from a position of unqualified support for the author in which it took full advantage of the opportunity to attack fundamentalism, the black community and so-called liberal freedoms. Rushdie was almost 'white' during this initial period of the affair. Then, in a marked turn, its support seemed

to wane, as if at last some Whitehall bureaucrat had briefed the Foreign Secretary on the contents of the book, and informed him that Rushdie's target was not confined to Islam but extended to racism in Britain. (The book actually compared Britain to Hitler's Germany.) For the first time, the government expressed sympathy with Muslims who had been offended by the book.

6 The myth of sexuality is not one to which Angela Barry makes reference, unless she sees it as part of the myth of the entertainer.

7 Linked to this is the important question of how and to what extent North American TV in particular is viewed globally and how this relates to questions of race and identity. The debates around cultural imperialism could provide an important framework for developing these ideas (see Tomlinson, 1991).

8 David Duke, who subsequently ran for Governor in Louisiana as a Republican in 1991. He lost, capturing a respectable 37 per cent of the votes and then pledged to run for President in the US elections in 1992.

3 'THERE'S NO PLACE LIKE HOMEPLACE': RACISM, ETHNICITY AND THE FAMILY

1 This issue centred around the campaign waged by Victoria Gillick, parent and 'Powellight' (anti-immigrant) supporter (See David, 1986).

2 This allegation was subsequently found to be false. Emma Mae Martin was not on welfare at the time of Thomas' speech in the late 1980s (Marable, 1992).

3 A number of the contributions to Toni Morrison's collection of essays on the Thomas/Hill hearings make reference to the revival of interest in the Moynihan Report: 'recently the Moynihan report is itself back in the news' (Lubiano, 1992: 333).

4 In a critique of the black matriarchy thesis, Herbert Hyman and John Shelton Reed found that when the white families were surveyed in exactly the same way that black families had been in previous research, they were found to be equally matriarchal (Hyman and Reed, 1969: 346–54).

5 It has been argued, very convincingly, that customs associated with Islam, for example polygamy and the chador (or veil) were pre-Islamic (and in the case of the chador Christian in origin).These traditions were subsequently appropriated by conservative forces within Islam. For a fuller discussion of the impact of the Iranian revolution on women see Afshar, 1987. The Koran, on the other hand, is open to a much more egalitarian interpretation, according to these arguments (Rana Kabbani, 'The Gender Jihad', *Guardian*, 22 January 1992).

4 CONSUMING EDUCATION

1 Part of the research for this chapter was carried out for an Open University module, 'Working with Parents', which formed part of a professional development course for teachers entitled 'Race, Management and the Curriculum'.

2 A series of publications from the political right which began to challenge the principles of equality of opportunity, comprehensivisation and the end of selection.

3 See Ken Jones (1989: 47ff.) for a fuller discussion of the Black Papers' attack on the alleged 'state monopoly of education' and its 'army of bureaucrats'.

4 It is interesting to see how the *Sun* newspaper supported the actions of white parents by quoting an Asian mother who was reported to have stated a preference for her daughter to be taught with white youngsters. 'Bright Lady' was the *Sun's* editorial comment the following day (17 September 1987) (Searle, 1989: 63). The ploy of finding someone black or from an ethnic minority serves to legitimise the

paper's stance and seemingly escape the charge of racism. See also above, p.63.

5 Interestingly, in Bradford in 1993 the 'free choice' principle was challenged by parents of mainly Bangladeshi and Pakistani origin when they found their children were being consistently denied the chance to go on to one of the city's high achievement schools and instead were being sent to under-subscribed schools with low academic standards. The local authority had drawn the catchment areas in such a way that other areas of the city included catchment areas with at least two high achievement schools. The one area with predominantly working-class Asians, Manningham, had no catchment area, hence the indirectly discriminatory allocation policy. It is worth comparing the proportions of white and Asian children who were given no choice in their secondary school. The figures were 5 per cent for white children, 12 per cent for Asians in the city as a whole and 30 per cent for Asians in Manningham. One of the campaigners, Abu Bashir, of a local Bangladeshi community organisation said: 'We are saying enough is enough. We want the same chances as other parents' (*Guardian*, 26 July 1993).

6 See also Gordon and Rosenberg, 1989.

7 This is not the same as saying that anti-racism killed Ahmed Ullah, which was the line taken by several of the tabloids, including the *Sun*, which attributed the murder to a legitimate backlash against anti-racist policies (28–9 April 1988) cited in Searle, 1989: 68.

8 In contrast, Birmingham LEA had been at the centre of a controversy over the appointment of a white home–school liaison teacher in a school, most of whose parents' first language was not English.

9 See also Jordan, 1989:29ff. for a further discussion of black English.

10 It is important to note that, in line with recent research evidence, I am treating Creole or Patois (the former is the term used by linguists, the latter by language users) as languages in their own right, not just deformations of standard English (Edwards, 1979: 16ff.).

5 'UNDERNEATH THE ARCHES': McDONALD'S, MARKETS AND EQUALITY

1 In *The Black Bag* (Channel 4, 5 November 1991), a group of six Bangladeshi Muslim school-leavers, with one GCSE between them, talked half jokingly about their most promising job opportunities in terms of working at McDonald's.

2 In the 1970s it was reported that the dean of Hamburger University had golden arches on his shirt and very few books in his office, one of which was a copy of *I'm OK, You're OK*, a seminal self-help manual of the 1970s (Boas and Chan, 1976: 68).

3 John Edwards rejects the idea of positive discrimination but does favour a weaker form of positive action. I am more concerned here with his general critique which, arguably, applies to all forms of intervention, including that which he appears to support.

4 This point was made in a different context in Chapter 3; see p. 65.

5 Ironically, Wilson observed, the power of the city was declining at a time when blacks were gaining political influence in large urban areas (1987: 139).

6 Out of a total of 80 restaurant staff throughout Birmingham 19 were black and of those, 8 were women. Of the 19, only two were of south Asian background, one of whom was in a senior position.

7 The representation of black staff nationally is more complex. In 1986 there was one black member of staff in the top 14 position in the country, but 50 per cent of supervisors were black, according to information passed on to the Commission for Racial Equality by the company's personnel officer.

8 1989 figures.
9 For all its merits the agreement did not survive long. The company subsequently withdrew its investment in Nicaragua.
10 This common-sense reduction of US culture to McDonald's (and Madonna?) has been picked up by John Tomlinson when he notes that McDonald's has come to represent US culture to the world in a way that 'no New York clam house, pizza parlour, Jewish deli or chop suey restaurant' ever can (1991: 75).

6 GLOBAL JOURNEYS

1 The lyrics are based on an article by John Cavanagh, 'The Journey of a Blouse: A Global Assembly'. Lyrics and music by Bernice Johnson Reagon, Songtalk Publishing Co., 1985.
2 The front page of the *Guardian* newspaper on 3 May 1991 provides a very good example of Third World reporting. Under a banner headline 'Twin Disasters hit Third World', there were two reports of the cyclone killing upwards of 100,000 in Bangladesh and the famine in the horn of Africa threatening a million lives within two weeks. Between the two was an article on aid, comparing the £62 million spent on the crisis of Kurdish refugees on the Turkish and Iranian borders with Iraq with the £2.5 million proposed by the government as aid to the Bangladesh flood victims. It also pointed out the massive cutback in aid under the Conservative Government, and said that Britain's aid bill was one of the lowest in northern Europe as a percentage of GNP.
3 This argument has been confirmed by David Weir (1987: 119–20), who documented examples of spills at pesticide plants in the US including a gas leak at Union Carbide's US plant in West Virginia in 1985, *after* the installation of a new computerised leak detection system.
4 The various recent 'green' discourses should not be confused with the ideas implicit in the first green revolution, although a number of them overlap in terms of their racist assumptions and language. The continuities between the ideas of natural selection, eugenics and environmental organisations like Earth First and publications like *Resurgence* have been made by Lola Young (1993).
5 The work of Susan George has been extremely significant in drawing our attention to these processes (see George, 1976b; George and Paige, 1982; and George and Bennett, 1987).
6 It is also worth pointing out that what Band Aid sent to Africa was returned, within hours, in debt repayments. Moreover, the disruptive effects of food aid on local agriculture and, more widely, on the recipient economies, have been argued by Lobstein (*c.* 1986).
7 Although it could be said that some of the more recent aid activities and programmes (including follow-ups to the 1980s initiatives) have made some attempt to explore underlying causes of famine as well as expose the limitations of projects which distort local economies and inhibit long-term improvements.
8 These issues were explored in BBC 2's *Framing the Famine* (1990).
9 Tunisian Tourist Board.
10 Gordon's reputation was built on his success in suppressing anti-colonial revolts in China and the Middle East in the latter half of the nineteenth century. He eventually died in one such attempt at Khartoum.
11 BBC2's *Fragile Earth* series included a programme *On Safari* (9 June 1991) which also took up some of these issues.
12 See also *New Internationalist*, January 1987 and July 1988 and Enloe (1989).

7 EUROPE: 1992 AND BEYOND

1 The anthem, 'Ring of Stars', was composed by Steve McCauly, who wrote hit songs for the Hollies and David Soul in the 1960s and 1970s (Radio 4, *Today* programme, 4 April 1992).

2 Alfred Dreyfus was a French Jewish soldier who was accused of selling military secrets to the Germans in 1894. In an effort to convict him the High Command used the forged Protocols, whipping up popular opinion against Dreyfus. He was pardoned after twelve years in prison on Devil's Island.

3 It should not be forgotten that the 1976 Act exempts the government from its terms and sanctions.

4 Researchers predict an even higher poll for the far right in eastern Germany when regional elections are held there in 1994 (*Guardian*, 8 April 1992).

5 Perhaps the author has been reading too many Ian Fleming novels. In an essay on the narrative structure of Fleming's novels, Eco's description of the typical Bond villain echoes his description of the new migrants in Italy (Eco, 1982)!

6 One lesser documented development since 1989 has been the growing trade in women from Poland and Hungary to Germany for the purposes of arranged marriages and prostitution. Cheaper costs, including transport, have encouraged agencies in the old Western Europe to look closer to home than Bangkok and Manila to recruit their prospective work-force (Morokvasic, 1991: 69).

7 Intellectually, 'New Times' can be situated within elements of the broad, disparate, and often conflicting, strands of postmodernist thought. Politically, 'New Times' intellectuals have become attached to more recently formed alliances including Demos and the Democratic Left.

8 This could be broken down still further in numerous ways, of course, including, given the significance of Hong Kong discussed above, the distinction between south and south-eastern Asian.

9 Not that this would bother Baudrillard unduly.

BIBLIOGRAPHY

Afshar, H. (1987) 'Women, Marriage and the State in Iran', in Afshar, H. (ed.) *Women, State and Ideology: Studies from Africa and Asia*, London: Macmillan.

Allen, S. and Macie, M. (1990) 'Race and Ethnicity in the European Context', *Sociology*, 41(3): 375–93.

Anthias, F. (1990) 'Race and Class Revisited – Conceptualising Race and Racisms', *Sociological Review*, 38 (1): 19–42.

Anthias, F. and Yuval-Davis, N. (1992) *Racialized Boundaries: Race, Nation, Gender, Colour and Class and the Anti-Racist Struggle*, London: Routledge.

Appignanesi, L. and Maitland, S. (eds) (1989) *The Rushdie File*, London: ICA/Fourth Estate.

Arhens, G., Ahmed, F. and Patel, S. (1988) 'Irrespective of Race, Sex, Sexuality', in Cant, R. and Hemmings, S. (eds) *Radical Records: Thirty Years of Lesbian and Gay History*, London: Routledge.

Arnold, E. and James, M. (1989) 'Finding Black Families for Black Children in Care: a Case Study', *New Community*, 15(3), April: 417–25.

Ascher, F. (1985) *Tourism, Transnational Corporations and Cultural Industry*, Paris: UNESCO.

Bagley, C. and Young, L. (1981) 'Policy Dilemmas and the Adoption of Black Children', in Cheetham, J. (ed.) *Social Work and Ethnicity*, London: Allen and Unwin.

Balibar, E. (1991) 'Racism and Nationalism', in Balibar, E. and Wallerstein, I. *Race, Nation, Class: Ambiguous Ethnicities*, London: Verso.

Ball, S. (1990) *Markets, Morality and Equality in Education*, Hillcole Group Paper, 5, London: Tufnell Press.

Banton, M. (1967) *Race Relations*, London: Tavistock.

Banton, M. (1977) *The Idea of Race*, London: Tavistock.

Banton, M. (1987) *Racial Theories*, Cambridge: Cambridge University Press.

Barker, M. (1981) *The New Racism: Conservatives and the Ideology of the Tribe*, London: Junction Books.

Barrett, M. and McIntosh, M. (1982) *The Anti-Social Family*, London: Verso.

Barry, A. (1988) 'Black Mythologies: The Representation of Black People in British Television', in Twitchin, J. (ed.) *The Black and White Media Book: Handbook for the Study of Racism and Television*, Stoke-on-Trent: Trentham.

Barthes, R. (1973) *Mythologies*, St Albans: Paladin.

Barzun, J. (1965) *Race: A Study in Superstition*, New York: Harper.

Baudrillard, J. (1988) *America*, London: Verso.

Baudrillard, J. (1990) *Fatal Strategies*, London: Pluto.

Beattie, N. (1985) *Professional Parents*, London: Falmer.

Bernal, M. (1987) *Black Athena: the Afroasiatic Roots of Classical Civilisation, vol. 1, The Fabrication of Ancient Greece 1785–1985*, London: Free Association Books.

Bernal, M. (1991) 'Black Athena': Talk given at the Institute of Contemporary Arts, 19 December.

Bhabha, H. (1986a) 'Introduction', in Fanon, F., *Black Skin, White Masks*, London: Pluto.

Bhabha, H. (1986b) 'Of Mimicry and Man: The Ambivalence of Colonial Discourse', in Donald, J. and Hall, S. (eds) *Politics and Ideology*, Milton Keynes: Open University Press.

Bhabha, H. (1990) 'The Other Question: Difference, Discrimination and the Discourse of Colonialism', in Ferguson, R., Gever, M., Minh-ha, T. and West, C., *Out There: Marginalization and Contemporary Cultures*, New York: New Museum of Contemporary Art.

Bhabha, H. and Parekh, B. (1989) 'Identities on Parade', *Marxism Today*, June: 24–9.

Bhat, A., Carr-Hill, R. and Ohri, S. (1988) 'The Radical Studies Race Group', in *Britain's Black Population, a New Perspective*, Aldershot: Gower.

Black Markets: 'Images of Black People in Advertising and Packaging in Britain (1880–1990)' (touring exhibition), Wolverhampton Art Gallery, 10 March–20 April 1990.

Boas, M. and Chan, S. (1976) *Big Mac: the Unauthorised Story*, New York: Dutton.

Bolt, C. (1971) *Victorian Attitudes to Race*, London: Routledge and Kegan Paul.

Brah, A. (1992) 'Difference, Diversity and Differentiation', in Donald, J. and Rattansi, A. (eds) *'Race', Culture and Difference*, London: Sage, for the Open University.

Brendon, P. (1992) *Thomas Cook: 150 Years of Popular Tourism*, London: Secker and Warburg.

Brown, P. (1990) 'The "Third Wave": Education and the Ideology of Parentocracy', *British Journal of Sociology of Education*, 11(1): 65–85.

Bryan, B., Dadzie, S. and Scafe, S. (1985) *The Heart of the Race*, London: Virago.

Callinicos, A. (1989) *Against Postmodernism*, Cambridge: Polity.

Cannon, G. (1987) *The Politics of Food*, London: Century.

Carby, H. (1982) 'Schooling in Babylon', in *The Empire Strikes Back*, London: Hutchinson/Centre for Contemporary Cultural Studies.

Carmen, Gail, Neena and Tamara (1987) 'Becoming Visible: Black Lesbian Discussions', in *Feminist Review Reader*, London: Virago.

Carty, B. (1991) 'Guatemala's Killing Fields', *New Internationalist*, December: 12–13.

Cashmore, E. and Troyna, B. (1983) *Introduction to Race Relations*, London: Routledge.

CCCS [Centre for Contemporary Cultural Studies] (1981) *Unpopular Education: Schooling and Social Democracy in England since 1944*, London: Hutchinson.

Centre for Contemporary Cultural Studies (1982) *The Empire Strikes Back: Race and Racism in 70s Britain*, London: Hutchinson.

Chattopadhyay, K. (1985) *Handcrafts of India*, New Delhi: Indian Council for Cultural Relations.

Coard, B. (1971) *How the West Indian is Being Made: ESN in the British School System*, London: New Beacon for the Caribbean Education and Community Workers' Association.

Cohen, P. (1988) 'The Perversions of Inheritance: Studies in the Making of Multi-Racist Britain', in Cohen, P. and Bains, H. (eds) *Multi Racist Britain*, London: Macmillan.

Collins, P. Hill (1990) *Black Feminist Thought*, London: HarperCollins.

Commission for Racial Equality (1988) *Learning in Terror*, London: CRE.

Commission for Racial Equality (1990) *Schools of Faith: Religious Schools in a Multicultural Society*, London: CRE.

Communist Party (1988) *Facing Up to the Future,* 7 *Days* supplement, London: Communist Party.

Connolly, C. (1991) 'Washing Out Our Linen: One Year of Women Against Fundamentalism', *Feminist Review,* 37, Spring: 68–77.

Dabydeen, D. (ed.) (1986) *The Black Presence in English Literature,* Manchester: Manchester University Press.

Dabydeen, D. (1987) *Hogarth's Blacks,* Athens: University of Georgia Press.

Dale, R. (1989) *The State and Educational Policy,* Milton Keynes: Open University Press.

Daniels, T. (1993) Talk given at the Ninth Birmingham International Film and Television Festival, 15 October.

Daniels, T. and Gerson, J. (1989) *The Colour Black: Black Images in British Television,* London: British Film Institute.

David, M. (1980) *The State, the Family and Education,* London: Routledge.

David, M. (1986) 'Moral and Maternal: the Family in the Right', in Levitas, R. (ed.) *The Ideology of the New Right,* Cambridge: Polity.

David, M. (1993) *Parents, Gender and Education Reform,* Cambridge: Polity.

Davis, A. (1981) *Women, Race and Class,* London: The Women's Press.

De Grazia, A. (1985) *A Cloud over Bhopal: Causes, Consequences and Constructive Solutions,* Bombay and New York: Irales Foundation for the India America Committee for the Bhopal Victims.

Dennis, F. (1989) 'Called By Africa', *The Listener,* 13 April.

Department of Labor (1988) *Workforce 2000,* Indiannapolis, Ind.: Hudson Institute.

DES (1985) *Better Schools* (Cmnd 9469), London: HMSO.

Dinham, B. (1987) 'Mass Death at Bhopal: Whose Responsibility?', in Gill, D. and Levidow, L. (eds) *Anti-Racist Science Teaching,* London: Free Association Books.

Docking, J. (1990) *Primary Schools and Parents,* London: Hodder and Stoughton.

Dominelli, L. (1988) *Anti-Racist Social Work,* London: Macmillan.

Duncan, C. (1989) 'Home, School and Community in a Multi-Racial Context', in Wolfendale, S. (ed.) *Parental Involvement,* London: Cassell.

Eco, U. (1982) 'The Narrative Structure in Fleming', in Waites, B., Bennett, T. and Martin, G. (eds) *Popular Culture: Past and Present,* London: Croom Helm.

Edwards, J. (1987) *Positive Discrimination, Social Justice and Social Policy,* London: Tavistock.

Edwards, V. K. (1979) *The West Indian Language Issue in British Schools: Challenges and Responses,* London: Routledge and Kegan Paul.

Edwards, V. K. (1986) *Language in a Black Community,* Avon: Multilingual Matters.

Enloe, C. (1989) *Bananas, Beaches and Bases: Making Feminist Sense of International Politics,* London: Pandora.

Erlich, P. (1968) *Population Bomb,* New York: Ballantine Books.

European Parliament (1985) *Committee of Enquiry into the Rise of Fascism and Racism in Europe.*

European Parliament (1990) *Committee of Enquiry into Racism and Xenophobia,* Series A, Document A3–195/90.

Everest, L. (1985) *Behind the Poison Cloud,* Chicago: Banner Press.

Fairclough, N. (1989) *Language and Power,* London: Longman.

Fanon, F. (1986) *Black Skin, White Masks,* London: Pluto.

Feminist Review (eds) (1987) *Sexuality: A Reader,* London: Virago.

Flew, A. (1987) *Power to the Parents,* London: Sherwood.

Foucault, M. (1977) *Discipline and Punish: The Birth of the Prison,* Harmondsworth: Allen Lane/Penguin.

Foucault, M. (1980) *Power/Knowledge,* Brighton: Harvester Press.

Frank, A. G. (1978) *Dependent Accumulation and Underdevelopment*, London: Macmillan.

Friedman, J. (1988) 'Cultural Logics of the Global System', *Theory, Culture and Society*, 5 (2–3).

Fryer, P. (1984) *Staying Power: The History of Black People in Britain*, London: Pluto.

Fryer, P. (1988) *Black People in the British Empire*, London: Pluto.

Gabriel, J. (1976) 'The Concepts of Race and Racism: an Analysis of Classical and Contemporary Theories of Race', PhD thesis, University of Liverpool.

Gabriel, J. (1989a) 'Racism in Historical Models', *Science as Culture*, 6: 124–30.

Gabriel, J. (1989b) 'Developing Anti-Racist Strategies', in Alcock, P., Gamble, A., Gough, I., Lee, P. and Walker, A., *The Social Economy and the Democratic State: A New Policy Agenda*, London: Lawrence and Wishart.

Gabriel, J. and Ben-Tovim, G. (1978) 'Marxism and the Concept of Racism', *Economy and Society*, 7 (2): 118–54.

Galton, F. (1979) 'Hereditary Talent and Character', in Bidiss, M. *Images of Race*, Leicester: University of Leicester Press.

Gamble, A. (1981) *Britain in Decline: Economic Policy, Political Strategy and the British State*, London: Macmillan.

George, S. (1976a) *How the Other Half Dies: The Real Reasons for World Hunger*, London: Penguin.

George, S. (1976b) *Feeding the Few: Corporate Control of Food*, Washington, DC: Institute of Policy Studies.

George, S. (1985) *Ill Fares the Land*, London: Writer and Readers Cooperative.

George, S. and Bennett, J. (1987) *The Hunger Machine: the Politics of Food*, Cambridge: Cambridge University Press.

George, S. and Paige, N. (1982) *Food for Beginners*, London: Writers and Readers Cooperative.

Gilder, G. (1982) *Wealth and Poverty*, London: Buchan and Enright.

Gill, O. and Jackson, B. (1983) *Adoption and Race: Black, Asian and Mixed Race Children in White Families*, London: Batsford.

Gill, D. and Levidow, L. (eds) (1987) *Anti-Racist Science Teaching*, London: Free Association Books.

Gilman, Sander L. (1992) 'Black Bodies, White Bodies: towards an Inconography of Female Sexuality in Late Nineteenth-century Art, Medicine and Literature', in Donald, J. and Rattansi, A. (eds) *'Race', Culture and Difference*, London: Sage.

Gilroy, P. (1987) *There Ain't No Black in the Union Jack*, London: Hutchinson.

Gilroy, P. (1990) 'The End of Anti-Racism', in Ball, W. and Solomos, J. (eds) *Race and Local Politics*, London: Macmillan.

GLC [Greater London Council] (1984) *Anti-Arab Racism*, A Palestinian Solidarity Campaign pamphlet, London: GLC.

Gobineau (1979) 'On Human Character', in Bidiss, M. *Images of Race*, Leicester: University of Leicester.

Goldman, A. (1979) *Justice and Reverse Discrimination*, Princeton: Princeton University Press.

Goonatilake, S. (1984) *Aborted Discovery: Science and Creativity in the Third World*, London: Zed Press.

Gordon, P. (1986) 'Racism and Social Security', *Critical Social Policy*, 17: 23–40.

Gordon, P. (1990) 'A Dirty War: The New Right and Local Authority Anti-Racism', in Ball, W. and Solomos, J. (eds) *Race and Local Politics*, London: Macmillan.

Gordon, P. and Klug, F. (1986) *New Right, New Racism*, London: Searchlight.

Gordon, P. and Rosenberg, D. (1989) *Daily Racism, the Press and Black People in Britain*, London: The Runnymede Trust.

Gossett, T. (1963) *Race: the History of an Idea in America*, Dallas: Southern Methodist University Press.

Goulbourne, H. (1991) 'Varieties of Puralism: the Notion of a Pluralist, Post-imperial Britain', *New Community*, 17(2): 211–27.

Grossberg, L., Nelson, C. and Treichler, P. A. (1992) *Cultural Studies*, London: Routledge.

Hall, S. (1981a) 'In the Whites of Their Eyes: Racist Ideologies and the Media', in Bridges, G. and Brunt, R. (eds) *Silver Linings*, London: Lawrence and Wishart.

Hall, S. (1981b) 'Teaching Race', in James, A. and Jeffcoate, R. *The School in a Multi-Cultural Society*, London: Harper and Row.

Hall, S. (1987) 'Minimal Selves', in *The Real Me: Post-modernism and the Question of Identity*, ICA documents 6, December, London: ICA.

Hall, S. (1988) 'New Ethnicities', in *Black Film: British Cinema*, ICA documents 7, London: ICA.

Hall, S. (1991a) 'The Local and the Global: Globalization and Ethnicity', in King, A. (ed.) *Culture, Globalization and the World System*, London: Macmillan.

Hall, S. (1991b) 'Old and New Identities: Old and New Ethnicities', in King, A. (ed.) *Culture, Globalization and the World System*, London: Macmillan.

Hall, S. and Jacques, M. (1989) *New Times: the Changing Face of Politics in the 1990s*, London: Lawrence and Wishart.

Hall, S., Critcher, C., Jefferson, T., Clarke, J. and Roberts, B. (1978) *Policing the Crisis: Mugging, the State and Law and Order*, London: Macmillan.

Hardy, J. and Vielar-Porter, C. (1992) 'Race, Schooling and the 1988 Education Reform Act', in Gill, D., Mayor, B. and Blair, M. *Racism and Education*, London: Sage, for the Open University.

Hart, A. (1989) 'Images of the Third World', in Reeves, M. and Hammond, J. (eds) *Looking beyond the Frame: Racism, Representation and Resistance*, London: Links Publications.

Hartmann, P. and Husband, C. (1974) *Racism and the Mass Media*, London: Davies Poynter.

Hatcher, R. and Troyna, B. (1990) *British Schools for British Citizens*, paper presented to the conference, 'New Issues in Black British Politics, 1989/90', Radcliffe House, University of Warwick, 14–16 May.

Hebdige, D. (1988) *Hiding in the Light: on Images and Things*, London: Routledge.

Hewitt, R. (1986) *White Talk Black Talk: Inter-social Friendship and Communication amongst Adolescents*, Cambridge: Cambridge University Press.

Hindess, B. (1982) 'Power, Interests and the Outcomes of Struggles', *Sociology*, 16(4): 493–511.

Hirst, P. and Zeitlin, J. (1991) 'Flexible Specialisation versus Post Fordism; Theory, Evidence and Policy Implications', *Economy and Society*, 20(1): 1–56.

hooks, b. (1991) *Yearning: Race, Gender and Cultural Politics*, London: Turnaround.

Hutcheon, L. (1989) *The Politics of Post-modernism*, London: Routledge.

Hyman, H. and Reed, J. S. (1969) 'Black Matriarchy Reconsidered: Evidence from Secondary Analysis of Sample Surveys', *Public Opinion Quarterly*, 33: 346–54.

Index on Censorship (1989), 18 (5).

Inner London Education Authority (1984) Committee on the Curriculum and Organisation of Secondary Schools, chaired by Hargreaves, D.: *Improving Secondary Schools*, London: ILEA.

Jenkins, R. (1987) 'Equal Opportunity in the Private Sector: the Limits of Voluntarism', in Jenkins, R. and Solomos, J. (eds) *Racism and Equal Opportunity Policies in the 1980s*, Cambridge: Cambridge University Press.

Jensen, A. (1969) 'How Much Can We Boost IQ and Scholastic Achievement?', *Harvard Educational Review*, 39(1): 1–123.

John, G. (n.d.) *The Black Working Class Movement in Education and the 1985–86 Teachers' Dispute*, pamphlet.

Johnson, R. (1989) 'Thatcherism and English Education: Breaking the Mould or Confirming the Pattern?', *History of Education*, 18(2): 91–121.

Johnson, R. (1991) 'My New Right Education', in Cultural Studies, Birmingham (ed.) *Education Limited*, London: Unwin Hyman.

Jones, K. (1989) *Right Turn: the Conservative Revolution in Education*, London: Radius.

Jones, S. (1988) *Black Culture, White Youths*, London: Macmillan.

Jones, T. (1987) 'Bhopal: Backward or Advanced?', in Gill, D. and Levidow, L. *Anti-Racist Science Teaching*, London: Free Association Books.

Jordan, J. (1987) 'Black on Black', *New Socialist*, 48, April: 32–7.

Jordan, J. (1989) *Moving Towards Home*, London: Virago.

Kazim, P. (1991) 'Racism Is No Paradise', *Race and Class*, 32(3), January/March: 84–9.

Khan, S. (1992) 'Re-Assessing Ethnicity, Questioning Boundaries: Searching for a Greek Cypriot Community in North London', B.Soc.Sci. dissertation, Dept of Cultural Studies, University of Birmingham.

Labour Research (1990) *1992 and Immigration*, 79 (4): 15–17.

Levidow, L. (1987) 'Racism in Scientific Innovation', in Gill, D. and Levidow, L. *Anti-Racist Science Teaching*, London: Free Association Books.

Lewis, G. (1985) 'From Deepest Kilburn', in Heron, L. (ed.) *Truth, Dare or Promise?: Girls Growing up in the Fifties*, London: Virago.

Lewis, R. (1988) *Anti-Racism: A Mania Exposed*, London: Quartet.

Little, R. and Smith, M. (eds) (1991) *Perspectives on World Politics*, London: Routledge.

Lloyd, C. and Waters, H. (1991) 'France: One Culture, One People?', *Race and Class*, 32(3), January–March: 49–65.

Lobstein, T. (*c.* 1986) 'Band Aid or Real Aid?', *Science for People*, 60: 12–15.

Lubiano, W. (1992) 'Black Ladies, Welfare Queens, and State Minstrels: Ideological War by Narrative Means,' in Morrison, T. (ed.) *Race-ing, Justice, En-gendering Power. Essays on Anita Hill, Clarence Thomas, and the Construction of Social Reality*, New York: Pantheon.

Macbeth, A. (1989) *Involving Parents*, London: Heinemann.

MacCannell, D. (1976) *The Tourist: A New Theory of the Leisure Class*, London: Macmillan.

Macdonald, I., Bhavani, T., Khan, L. and John, G. (1989) *Murder in the Playground: the Report of the Macdonald Inquiry into Racism and Racial Violence in Manchester Schools*, London: Longsight Press.

Mama, A. (1989a) 'Violence against Black Women: Gender, Race and State Responses', *Feminist Review*, 32: 1–48.

Mama, A. (1989b) *The Hidden Struggle*, London: Race and Housing Research Unit.

Manning, M. (1990) 'The Kids Are Lippy', *New Statesman and Society*, 16 February: 12–13.

Marable, M. (1992) 'Clarence Thomas and the Crisis of Black Political Culture,' in Morrison, T. (ed.) *Race-ing, Justice, En-gendering Power. Essays on Anita Hill, Clarence Thomas, and the Construction of Social Reality*, New York: Pantheon.

Martin, R. and Rowthorn, B. (1986) 'Thatcherism and Britain's Industrial Landscape', in Martin, R. and Rowthorn, B. (eds) *The Geography of De-Industrialisation*, London: Macmillan.

Marxism Today (1989) *The Manifesto for 'New Times'*, London.

Mason, D. (1990) 'Competing Conceptions of "Fairness" and the Formulation and Implementation of Equal Opportunity Policies', in Ball, W. and Solomos, J. (eds) *Race and Local Politics*, London: Macmillan.

Massey, D. (1986) 'The Legacy Lingers On: the Impact of Britain's International Role on its Internal Geography', in Martin, R. and Rowthorn, B. (eds) *The Geography of De-industrialisation*, London: Macmillan.

Masterman, L. (1980) *Teaching about Television*, London: Macmillan.

Mathieson, A. and Wall, G. (1982) *Tourism: Economic, Physical and Social Impacts*, London: Longman.

Meadows, Donella H. *et al.* (1974) *The Limits to Growth: A Report for the Club of Rome's Project on the Predicament of Mankind*, London: Pan Books.

Merch, A. (1974) *The Idea of China*, London: David and Charles.

Merckx, F. and Fekete, L. (1991) 'Belgium: the Racist Cocktail', *Race and Class*, 323, January–March: 67–78.

Miles, R. (1989) *Racism*, London: Routledge.

Miles, R. (1993) *Racism after Race Relations*, London: Routledge.

Modood, T. (1988) '"Black", Racial Identity and Asian Identity', *New Community*, 14 (3), Spring: 397–404.

Morokvasic, M. (1991) 'Fortress Europe and Migrant Women', *Feminist Review*, 39: 69–84.

Morrison, T. (ed.) (1992) *Race-ing, Justice, En-gendering Power. Essays on Anita Hill, Clarence Thomas, and the Construction of Social Reality*, New York: Pantheon.

Mortimore, J. and Blackstone, T. (1982) *Disadvantage and Education*, London: Heinemann.

Moser, P. (1988) 'The McDonald's Mystique', *Fortune*, 4 July: 100–4.

Mosse, G. (1978) *Toward the Final Solution*, London: Dent.

Mount, F. (1982) *The Subversive Family: An Alternative History of Love and Marriage*, London: Jonathan Cape.

Mulvey, L. (1992) 'Visual Pleasure and Narrative Cinema', reproduced in Easthope, A. and McGowan, K. (eds) *A Critical and Cultural Theory Reader*, Milton Keynes: Open University Press.

Nain, G.T. (1991) 'Black Women, Sexism and Racism: Black or Anti-Racist Feminism?', *Feminist Review*, 37, Spring: 1–22.

National Association of Citizens Advice Bureaux (1990) 'An Overview of Working with Refugees', Research and Development Briefing Paper, London: NACAB.

Naybour, S. (1989) 'Parents, Partners or Customers', in Sayer, J. (ed.) *Schools and External Relations*, London: Cassell.

Nixon, J. (1985) *A Teachers' Guide to Multicultural Education*, Oxford: Blackwell.

Offe, C. (1984) *Contradictions of the Welfare State*, London: Hutchinson.

O'Shaughnessy, H. (1989) 'Decline and Fall of Paradise Island', *Observer*, 29 January.

Osler, A. (1989) *Black Girls Speaking Out*, London: Virago.

Ouseley, H. (1988), 'Reforming Education: Equal Opportunities Lost', *Local Government Studies*, 14 (1).

Pajaczkowska, C. and Young, L. (1992) 'Racism, Representation and Psychoanalysis', in Donald, J. and Rattansi, A. (eds) *'Race', Culture and Difference*, London: Sage, for the Open University.

Parmar, P. (1982) 'Gender, Race and Class: Asian Women in Resistance', in CCCS *The Empire Strikes Back*, London: Hutchinson.

Parmar, P. (1989) 'Other Kinds of Dreams', *Feminist Review*, 31, Spring: 55–65.

Parmar, P. with Minh-ha, Trinh T. (1990) 'Women, Native, Other', *Feminist Review*, 32, Autumn: 65–74.

Phoenix, A. (1988) 'The Afro-Caribbean Myth', *New Society*, 83: 10–13.

Philip, A. (1989) 'European Border Controls: Who Needs Them?', Royal Institute of International Affairs, discussion paper 19.

Pieterse, J. N. (1991) 'Fictions of Europe', *Race and Class*, 32(3): 3–10.

Pieterse, J. N. (1992) *White on Black: Images of Africa and Blacks in Popular Culture*, London: Yale University Press.

Pines, J. (ed.) (1992) *Black and White in Colour: Black People in British Television since 1936*, London: British Film Institute.

Qureshi, S. and Khan, J. (1989) *The Politics of the Satanic Verses*, Leicester: Muslim Studies Institute.

Ramdin, R. (1987) *The Making of the Black Working Class in Britain*, Aldershot: Gower.

Rampton, B. (1989) 'Some Unofficial Perspectives on Bilingualism and Education for All', *Language Issues*, 3(2): 27–32.

Ranson, S. (1988) 'From 1944 to 1988: Education, Citizenship and Democracy', *Local Government Studies*, 14(1): 1–19.

Read, M. and Simpson, A. (1991) *Against the Tide*, Nottingham: Spokesman.

Rex, J. and Mason, D. (eds) (1986) *Theories of Race and Ethnic Relations*, Cambridge: Cambridge University Press.

Rich, P. (1986) *Race and Empire in British Politics*, Cambridge: Cambridge University Press.

Ritzer, G. (1993) *The McDonaldization of Society*, London: Pine Forge.

Rodney, W. (1988) *How Europe Undeveloped Africa*, London: Bogle L'Ouverture.

Rushdie, S. (1988) *The Satanic Verses*, London: Viking.

Rutter, M., Maughan, B., Mortimore, P. and Ouston, J. (1979) *Fifteen Thousand Hours: Secondary Schools and their Effects on Children*, London: Open Books.

Sahgal, G. and Yuval-Davis, N. (1990) 'Refusing Holy Orders', *Marxism Today*, March: 30–5.

Said, E. W. (1978) *Orientalism*, London: Penguin.

Said, E. W. (1993) *Culture and Imperialism*, London: Chatto and Windus.

Searle, C. (1989) *Your Daily Dose: Racism and the Sun*, London: Campaign for Press and Broadcasting Freedom.

Shan, S. J. and Bailey, P. (1991) *Multiple Factors: Classroom Mathematics for Equality and Justice*, Stoke-on-Trent: Trentham.

Shipman, M. (1990) *In Search of Learning*, Oxford: Blackwell.

Singh, A. (1986) 'A Commentary on the IMF and World Bank Policy Programme', in Lawrence P. (ed.) *World Recession and the Food Crisis in Africa*, London: James Currey.

Sivanandan, A. (1988) 'The New Racism', *New Statesman and Society*, 4 November: 8–9.

Sivanandan, A. (1989) 'New Circuits of Imperialism', *Race and Class*, 30(4), April–June: 1–19.

Sivanandan, A. (1990a) 'All That Melts into Air is Solid: the Hokum of New Times', *Race and Class*, 31(3): 1–30.

Sivanandan, A. (1990b) 'The Common Hurt of the Underclass', *New Statesman and Society*, 16 February: 28–30.

Solomos, J. (1986) 'Varieties of Marxist Conceptions of "Race", Class and the State: a Critical Analysis', in Rex, J. and Mason, D. (eds) *Theories of Race and Ethnic Relations*, Cambridge: Cambridge University Press.

Sowell, T. (1981) *Markets and Minorities*, Oxford: Blackwell for the International Center for Economic Policy Studies.

Sowell, T. (1987) *Compassion versus Guilt, and Other Essays*, New York: West Morrow.

Steele, S. (1990) *The Content of Our Character*, New York: St Martin's Press.

Stone, M. (1981) *The Education of the Black Child in Britain*, London: Fontana.

Sutcliffe, B. (1986) 'Africa and the World Economic Crisis', in Lawrence, P. (ed.) *World Recession and the Food Crisis in Africa*, London: James Currey.

Tang Nain, G. (1991) 'Black Women, Sexism and Racism: Black or anti-racist Feminism', *Feminist Review*, 37.

Teitelbaum, K. and Reese, W. (1983) 'American Socialist Pedagogy and Experimentation in the Progressive Era: the Socialist Saturday School', *History of Education Quarterly*, 23(4): 429–54.

Tizard, B. and Hughes, M. (1984) *Young Children Learning*, London: Fontana.

Tizard, B. and Phoenix, A. (1989) 'Black Identity and Transracial Adoption', *New Community*, 15(3), April: 427–37.

Tizard, B and Phoenix, A. (1993) *Black, White or Mixed Race? Race and Racism in the Lives of Young People of Mixed Parentage*, London: Routledge.

Tomlinson, J. (1991) *Cultural Imperialism*, London: Pinter.

Tomlinson, S. (1984) *Home and School in Multi-Cultural Britain*, London: Batsford.

Transnational Information Centre (1987) *Working for Big Mac*, London: Transnational Information Centre.

Troyna, B. (ed.) (1987) *Racial Inequality in Education*, London: Tavistock.

Troyna, B. (1990) 'Reform or Deform? The 1988 Education Reform Act and Racial Equality in Britain', *New Community* 16(3), April: 403–16.

Troyna, B. and Hatcher, R. (1992) 'Racist Incidents in Schools', in Gill D., Mayor, B. and Blair, M. *Racism and Education*, London: Sage, for the Open University.

Turner, L. and Ash, J. (1975) *Golden Heroes*, London: Constable.

Wallace, M. (1979) *Black Macho and the Myth of the Superwoman*, London: John Calder.

Wallerstein, I. (1974) *The Modern World System: Capitalist Agriculture and the Origins of the European World Economy in the Sixteenth Century*, New York: Academic Press.

Wallerstein, I. and Hopkins, T. (1982) *World Systems Analysis*, Beverly Hills and London: Sage.

Wallraff, G. (1988) *The Lowest of the Low*, London: Methuen.

Warnock, J. (1987) *The Politics of Hunger in the Global Food System*, London: Methuen.

Webster, D. (1988) *Looka Yonder: The Imaginary America of Populist Culture*, London: Routledge.

Weir, D. (1987) *The Bhopal Syndrome*, London: Earthscan.

West, C. (1989) 'Black Culture and Postmodernism', in Krueger, B. and Marioni, P. (eds) *Remaking History*, Port Townsend, WA: Bay Press.

Wetherell, M. and Potter, J. (1992) *Mapping the Language of Racism: Discourse and the Legitimation of Exploitation*, Hemel Hempstead: Harvester.

Williams, F. (1989) *Social Policy: A Critical Introduction*, Cambridge: Polity.

Williams, R. (1961) *The Long Revolution*, Harmondsworth: Penguin.

Williamson, J. (1978) *Decoding Advertisements*, London: Boyars.

Wilson, A. (1987) *Mixed Race Children: A Study of Identity*, London: Allen and Unwin.

Wilson, W. J. (1980) *The Declining Significance of Race: Blacks and Changing American Institutions*, London and Chicago: University of Chicago Press.

Worsley, P. (ed.) (1987) *The New Introducing Sociology*, 3rd edn, Harmondsworth: Penguin.

Wright, C. (1987) 'Black Students – White Teachers', in Troyna, B. (ed.) *Racial Inequality in Education*, London: Tavistock.

Young, L. (1993) 'Natural Selection? Ideology, Ecology, "Race"', Raymond Williams memorial lecture, 12 October.

INDEX